Marine Corps Warrior

THE LIFE OF
JOHN P. "PAT" FLYNN, JR.

CHIEF

Marine Corps Warrior

THE LIFE OF
JOHN P. "PAT" FLYNN, JR.

by
Sean J. Flynn

1531 Yuma • P.O. Box 1009 • Manhattan, Kansas 66505-1009 USA

© 2003 Sean J. Flynn
Printed in the United States of America on acid-free paper.

ISBN 0-89745-267-4

Sunflower University Press is a wholly-owned subsidiary
of the non-profit 501(c)3 Journal of the West, Inc.

Go tell the Spartans, thou who passest by,
That here, obedient to their laws, we lie.

> Simonides of Ceos, epitaph for
> the fallen Spartan soldiers of the
> Battle of Thermopylae, *ca.* 480 B.C.

For his grandchildren:

Michael, Erin, Megan, Kevin, Sean,
William, Cathleen, David, and Phillip

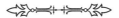

In Memoriam

Bob Ashley, Richard Bell, Byron H. Beswick,
Alfred Hutchison, Curtis Kaupp, John Francis McAvoy,
Dennis McPherson, Irving Shaknov, Lance P. Sijan,
Arthur Wagner, and Duke Williams, Jr.

Contents

Acknowledgments		xi
Preface		xiii
Chapter 1	Grandfather and Grandmother	1
Chapter 2	Okinawa *Gunto*	22
Chapter 3	Flying Nightmares	48
Chapter 4	Captive	71
Chapter 5	Chief of the Annex	91
Chapter 6	God and Country	113
Chapter 7	Cold Warrior	128
Chapter 8	Always a Marine	155
Chapter 9	Always Faithful	180
Notes		186
Bibliography		205
Index		212

Acknowledgments

OF COURSE, no one knew my father better than my mother, Frances Flynn. Over the past two years, during all hours of the day and night, she answered hundreds of my questions during dozens of phone and face-to-face conversations. On countless occasions, she located just the right letter, telegram, photograph, or newspaper clipping. I fed off her energy, picked at her memory, and marveled at her insights. In many ways, this biography is our biography.

My wife Deborah acted as partner, critic, cheerleader, and patient listener. Her editorial recommendations improved the flow and tone of this text, and her enthusiastic reactions whenever I "got it right" were satisfying beyond words.

A generous grant from the Marine Corps Heritage Foundation made possible a research trip to Washington, D.C., where the staffs of the Marine Corps Historical Center, the Marine Corps University Library, the Naval Historical Center, the National Archives (College Park Branch), and the Library of Congress proved courteous and helpful. The staff of Haskell Indian Nations University, Lawrence, Kansas, provided important documents, and Jodie Barker and Judy Lehi, librarians at Dakota Wesleyan University, Mitchell, South Dakota, met all of my inter-library loan and acquisition requests. Dakota Wesleyan student Robin Ridgway offered her computer skills and endured my frustrations during the early stages of the project.

John Warner challenged me to write this book and provided valuable feedback on several chapters. His support was critical, as were the contributions of Peter Perla, Harlo E. "Ed" Sterrett, Duane Thorin, and the staff of the Office of the Judge Advocate General, Department of the Navy. I am also grateful to Amie Goins of Sunflower University Press for her thoughtful editing of this manuscript.

I pray that the spirit of my brothers and sisters — Mark, Colleen, Teresa, and Tim — lives in these pages. If it were not for their children's need to know their grandfather, this book would have been dedicated to them.

Preface

IN 1978, three months before his death, my father, Lieutenant Colonel John P. "Pat" Flynn, Jr., traveled with my mother and my youngest brother to southern California to spend Christmas with my family. I was then a young Private First Class, assigned to the Marine Corps Air Station in El Toro, California, where my father had served as an aviator in the 1950s and 1960s. He enjoyed his tour around the airbase, where he re-experienced the sights and sounds of jets like the A-4 Skyhawk, a plane he had flown extensively for five years. A few days after his tour, he nodded approvingly as my brother Tim and I loaded my car to go spear fishing, a sport Dad had excelled at in the years following World War II.

Upon our return from the beaches around Dana Point, we found Dad in my sister's driveway, holding a lively conversation with an old Marine Corps friend and former Korea POW, Jerry Fink. As I got out of the car, Dad, a smile stretched across his face, handed me a small cardboard box containing a personal gift from Mr. Fink. To this day, I do not know what was in that box, for my father was less excited about its contents than the message scribbled across the top: "To Chief Flynn — The Only One Who Ever Deserved It." I believe that my father took as much pride in those words as he did in the address to him by the Secretary of the Navy during a Pentagon awards ceremony in January of 1954.

In hindsight, I recognize that in sharing Mr. Fink's boxtop note, my father was asking me to understand and appreciate how much his Marine peers valued his contributions to the Corps.

Lieutenant Colonel John P. Flynn's 24-year military career spanned World War II, the Korean War, and the early years of the Vietnam War. There is nothing particularly remarkable about that achievement. Tens of thousands of officers served during that era, and many of them rose above the rank of Lieutenant Colonel. But several aspects of Flynn's career deserve serious consideration, and much of this book is devoted to that task.

First and foremost, Flynn's conduct during his POW captivity in North Korea was nothing short of heroic. During 16 months of captivity, he suffered brutal psychological torture and long stretches of solitary confinement as Chinese Communist interrogators worked to extract a false germ-warfare confession from him. They failed. For over a decade after the war, the Marine Corps and the Air Force regarded Flynn as an embodiment of the "Code of Conduct for Members of the Armed Forces of the United States," the Executive Order that established behavioral expectations for captured American servicemen. As one of the military's most popular Code of Conduct spokesmen, Flynn impacted thousands of officers while enhancing the Marine Corps' reputation for intensive individual training and *esprit de corps*. And as a devout Roman Catholic, Pat Flynn rated faith as the most formidable weapon against Communist propaganda. He ensured that his audiences grasped the significance of religion for bolstering the individual POW's resistance to interrogation and indoctrination.

Many of Flynn's contemporaries emphasized the colorful nature of his career. Flynn was a spellbinding public speaker and an extraordinary trumpet player; had World War II not intervened, he would have become a professional musician. He won honors as an All-Navy football player. He mastered salt-water fishing and scuba diving, designed his own aqualung, spear guns, and radio-controlled airplane models, and in retirement produced inspirational artwork for South Dakota churches. On Okinawa during World War II, and in Korea, he joined Marine infantrymen in the field.

He bailed out of a burning F4U Corsair over the Pacific in 1945, and in a three-week period in 1952 survived a fiery takeoff crash and the destruction of his F7F Tigercat by Chinese antiaircraft artillery. He participated in two military aviation records. He endured a savage street fight in Japan in 1962, and three years later survived a helicopter crash in the high peaks of the Sierra Nevada range. Time and again, the men I interviewed described Flynn as one of the most talented, fascinating Marines they had encountered.

And there was no mistaking Pat Flynn's Native American lineage, of which he took enormous pride. Early on, his features and skin color had earned him the call sign "Chief." Though a loyal Marine, Flynn likewise viewed himself as a faithful Lakota warrior. A direct descendant of Chief Spotted Tail, the uncle of the great Crazy Horse, the young Pat Flynn had been raised on stories of Plains Indian warfare and the battlefield exploits of Sioux horsemen. When he joined the military, he believed that in judging him, his superiors and fellow officers would judge Native Americans in general, and, thus, he pushed himself harder, competed more fiercely, and took more risks.

Upon his retirement from the Marine Corps, those who knew Flynn or knew of him agreed that the name Chief signified more than his Indian heritage. The dozens of veterans interviewed for this book were nearly unanimous in their opinion that Pat Flynn was one of the best natural leaders they had served with. In addition to this reputation as one of South Dakota's military heroes, he should be remembered as one of the state's great Native Americans.

Sean J. Flynn
Mitchell, South Dakota

Chapter 1

Grandfather and Grandmother

> The Lakota was brave. Over and over again father said to son, "You must be brave," or . . . "A coward is to be despised and my son must be honored for his bravery." Such teachings as these were drilled into . . . their consciousness.
>
> Luther Standing Bear,
> *Land of the Spotted Eagle*[1]

FIFTEEN MILES SOUTH of Winner, hidden amid the sandy hills and cottonwood groves of south-central South Dakota, lies Dog Ear Lake. How the 400-acre, spring-fed lake acquired its name remains a mystery, though it may honor the memory of a Lakota Sioux headman whose band frequented the area in the early 19th century.[2] The lake may also take its name from a nearby landmark, Dog Ears Buttes — so named, according to local legend, by Lakota who hunted near the buttes and observed that the formation resembled the ears of a dog. White settlers agreed and retained the landmark's name, though they revised it to the singular Dog Ear Buttes.[3]

Pat Flynn described the pre-history of the Dog Ear Lake area in his untitled 1979 family history. The account was obtained from Flynn's conversations with his half-Lakota grandfather, Joseph "Joe" Gordon (1875-1958), and his Lakota grandmother, Rosalie Boucher Gordon (1875-1941). Lakota oral tradition teaches that the Dog Ear Buttes carried great spiritual significance, their summits serving as altars for prayer, fasting, meditation, and thanksgiving for the abundance of bison, deer, and elk that once roamed the area. To acknowledge their religious importance, tribal elders referred to the northern butte as "Grandmother" and the southern butte as "Grandfather." Storytellers said that the poplar or "cottonwood" trees growing beneath the buttes spread from a single sapling brought to Dog Ear country on the back of a shaggy buffalo bull.

Dog Ear Lake was a rest area for Sioux bands, and in the mid- to late-1800s served as a landmark for white hunters, trappers, and settlers. During much of the 20th century, locals considered the lake an attractive entertainment and recreational spot, though in recent years, Dog Ear's appeal has diminished, and its shores are now only frequented by duck hunters and the occasional fisherman in pursuit of bullhead catfish, yellow perch, or northern pike. But in the years between the two world wars, there were few tranquil moments at the Dog Ear settlement of John (Sr.) and Lucille Flynn, a bustling commercial and entertainment center for the residents of south-central South Dakota and north-central Nebraska.

The story of the Flynns and Dog Ear Lake begins in 1881, when John Flynn's father, James, left Tralee in County Kerry, Ireland, for a new life in America. James arrived in Boston but worked his way westward, eventually securing employment as a baker in Elgin, Illinois. There he met and married Erminnie Grace Ingalls of Allison, Iowa, a union that produced fifteen children, eight of whom survived childhood. James and "Minnie" lived in Elgin until 1898, when they relocated to the Mt. Greenwood area of Chicago to open a bakery, restaurant, and saloon. In 1904, James learned of the federal government's opening of the Rosebud Indian Reservation in Gregory County, South Dakota. Along with 105,000 other applicants, Flynn vied for homestead entry to Gregory County, and in the lottery drawing that followed won a 160-acre allotment on what would become the western edge of Gregory township. In the late summer of 1904, he loaded his wife, children, and six hunting dogs (parting presents from friends) on the train for the ride from Chicago to the end of the line at Bonesteel, South Dakota. The Flynns rode by stagecoach for the final 28 miles of their journey to Gregory.[4]

James Flynn devoted himself to building construction and farm work. In 1905, he opened "J. J. Flynn and Company," one of Gregory's first saloons and the site of Catholic religious services until the completion of St. Joseph Church in 1908. Acknowledging that his eight children gave him a vested interest in local education, citizens elected Flynn the first chairman of the Gregory School Board. In what must have been a departure for a long-time saloonkeeper, Flynn also served as one of Gregory's first law enforcement officers. He continued to purchase land for his sons, securing an allotment on the north side of Dog Ear Lake in Tripp County, immediately west of Gregory County, opened to white settlement in 1908.[5]

James and Minnie Flynn eventually returned to Chicago, where James died of a heart attack in 1915. Some of the children, including their third son John Patrick, stayed on at the Flynn Brothers Farm west of Gregory. In 1919, John began courting Lucille Gordon, the half-Lakota daughter of Joseph "Joe" and Rosalie Gordon, who lived on a farm south of Gregory. On April 14, 1920, John and Lucille were married at the Paxton Catholic Church, and in May 1921, the couple moved to the Flynn homestead on Dog Ear Lake. Within a year, John and Lucille had built a two-story home and established a small farm, raising beef and dairy cattle, a few hogs, and poultry. By the mid-1920s, the Flynns' interests extended beyond agriculture. They operated a general mercantile store, a creamery station, and a small automobile repair garage that boasted two fuel pumps. They constructed a large dance hall, cleared prairie land for a baseball diamond, rodeo grounds, and airstrip, and built a straw-insulated icehouse for storing blocks cut from Dog Ear Lake during the winter months.[6] In seven years of backbreaking work, John and Lucille Flynn had created a trading post and entertainment center that impacted a large area of southern South Dakota and northern Nebraska.

According to Pat Flynn's family history and advertising bills from the 1920s and 1930s, Dog Ear Lake and its dance pavilion were synonymous with fun and amusement. Guests at the Flynns' Community Picnics, held on Sundays in July and August, participated in horse races (often dominated by Joe Gordon's racehorse stock), foot races, wheelbarrow races, and such novelty competitions as tub races, potato races, and egg races. A more intense level of competition could be found at the horseshoe pits or on the baseball diamond, where teams representing the communities of

Rosalie Gordon (l) and Erminnie Flynn, Pat Flynn's grandmothers.

Dog Ear Lake, Millboro, Colome, Winner, Witten, and Keya Paha played for $25 and $50 purses. For a few dollars, adventurous merrymakers could take an airplane ride with L. W. Sylvester, Gene Warren, or "Slim" Halmgremson. Bareback bronc riders tested their skills on the rodeo grounds, and fishing and boating enthusiasts spent the day on the lake. Dog Ear nights were devoted to dancing. In a playful nod to his Chicago roots, John Flynn organized a Big Bowery Dance on the lake shore, music courtesy of Standiford's Melody Brothers or The Winner Band. An Old Time Dance took place in the dance pavilion, where pianist Lucille Flynn and her fiddle-playing father Joe Gordon serenaded the dancers to waltzes, polkas, and standards. John Flynn advertised his picnics as "A Big Time for All, Old and Young." Few who attended the parties, picnics, holiday celebrations, or high school reunions at Dog Ear accused him of exaggerating.

As Pat Flynn described in his family history, his parents, John and Lucille, formed an effective partnership. In addition to managing the mercantile store, John worked the farm and livestock and maintained Dog Ear's buildings, docks, roads, and grounds. He bought produce, ran the cream station, and, in his spare time, repaired customers' automobiles and farm equipment. John's clientele reflected the diverse ethnic makeup of rural South Dakota. Homesteaders of Czechoslovakian, German, Irish, Polish, and German-Russian descent traveled by automobile, on foot, horseback, or in horse-drawn buggies, wagons, or sleds to conduct business at Flynn's store and take in a Saturday-night dance.

Though operating Dog Ear demanded his full attention, John Flynn enjoyed his share of diversions. On at least one occasion, he helped smuggle whiskey into South Dakota. Some of John's family had profited in Chicago's illegal liquor trade, embodied in the person of Al Capone. The Chicago Flynns arranged liquor shipments to railroad yards in Gregory or Dallas, South Dakota, hiding the contraband on train cars, beneath loads of lumber marked "John Flynn, Dog Ear Lake." Under darkness, John and some trusted neighbors unloaded the shipment and transported it back to Dog Ear for local distribution and sales within the dance hall. John apparently earned the trust of Chicago's Irish mob, for on at least one occasion, they sent two gunmen to Dog Ear to lay low after a "hit." John's young son Pat, curious about the sharp-dressed, reclusive Chicago men sleeping in the creamery shed, surprised them one morning as they were stripping and cleaning their Thompson sub-machine guns. With a 25-cent gift and a pat on the head, the boy was told to leave the shed, respect the men's privacy, and tell absolutely no one what he had witnessed. Pat obeyed, especially after his father learned of the encounter and scolded him for his nosiness.

Like her husband, Lucille Flynn found ways of balancing work with pleasure. She raised five children: Rose Marie (b. 1921), John Patrick, Jr., or "Pat" (b. December 20, 1922), Dennis (b. 1924), Grace (b. 1928), and James or "Jim" (b. 1935). Chores, cooking, washing, sewing, and serving the needs of customers and travelers demanded her constant attention. But neighbors, friends, Catholic parishioners, and dance lovers in southern South Dakota and northern Nebraska remembered another Lucille, a musician who was, quite simply, the finest piano player around. Trained in her early years by the stern nuns of St. Francis Mission School and in her high school years at Pierre Indian School, Lucille was by age 16 performing with her father, a renowned Gregory County fiddler. Her technical skills and her immense repertoire of memorized pieces went unmatched by anyone in the region (if not the entire state), making her a favorite entertainer among locals.

Lucille's musicianship proved invaluable to the Dog Ear enterprise. She played piano during silent movie showings in the dance hall, selecting music to match the mood and tempo of the motion picture. In his 1979 Flynn family history, her son Pat, recalling some of his earliest memories of Dog Ear, described the excitement that the silent pictures and live piano generated among area farm kids:

> All my friends from the surrounding homesteads would be there. . . . We couldn't read the actors' lips or their spoken words at the bottom of the action and yet we always knew who to cheer for and who to throw peanuts at.

For Pat and his siblings, the movies were a welcome escape from milking cows, feeding cattle, horses, chickens, and geese, chopping and stacking wood, and cleaning the store, dance hall, and cream station. Pat stacked hay bales in the summer and cut and hauled ice in the winter, and when he was old enough to drive, went to Winner with his brother, Dennis, to pick up beer kegs for the dance hall. Of course, growing up in South Dakota had its advantages, and when not laboring, Pat found Dog Ear Lake a boy's paradise. He spent his free time hunting, fishing, horseback riding, catching frogs, turtles, and minnows, and wrestling and boxing with friends and relatives.

Boys like puppies, but Pat Flynn's first four-legged friend was most unusual. In December 1929, as Pat was recovering from a bout with pneumonia, a party of hunters rode onto the Dog Ear grounds to replenish their supplies. Their arrival was a raucous event, marked by an attack on the hunters' greyhound pack by Mutt, the Flynns' aggressive Airedale terrier. After John Flynn broke up the dogfight, the hunters called him and Pat to the back of their wagon to display the dead coyotes whose pelts would draw good prices on the fur market. Huddled beneath a blanket was a single, frightened coyote pup that had been spared the club. For a bottle of whiskey, John purchased the pup for his son. Coyote and Pat became fast friends and remained so, until the animal acquired a taste for fresh farm chickens. Coyote was eventually destroyed, and Pat turned his affection back to Mutt and to Popeye, the large, one-eyed bull snake who slithered about the Flynn yard searching for field mice while deterring rattlesnakes from burrowing under the house.

With the exception of his first- and fifth-grade years (when he attended, respectively, the St. Joseph Convent in Gregory and St. Ambrose Catholic School in Deadwood), Pat's elementary education took place in small country schools near Dog Ear Lake. His elementary report cards indicate an A and B student with satisfactory marks in citizenship and deportment. Pat became an avid reader and developed a lifelong passion for painting in oils and watercolors and drawing in charcoal.

But it was music that captured his interest. At about nine or ten years of age, Pat took up the cornet, and under his mother's tutelage, strengthened his lip and mastered scales. Maintaining a regimented practice schedule, he developed a technical maturity that belied his age; by the time he reached his senior year in high school, he was one of the finest trumpeters in the state. He won a superior rating at the 1941 state-regional band contest and attended a national music festival in St. Paul, Minnesota, in May 1941. According to undated clippings from the *Gregory Times-Advocate*, Flynn earned a third-place finish in St. Paul, where he made a 78-rpm recording of "Carnival of Venice," still recognized as a challenging piece by accomplished trumpeters.

Pat excelled in interscholastic contests, but his most gratifying musical moments came during live performances with his mother and grandfather. Lucille and Joe expected Pat to increase his stamina, memorize dozens of songs, and improvise solos. He rose to the challenge, thriving on the live performances and the joy they brought dancers. In the Dog Ear Pavilion and dance clubs throughout South Dakota and Nebraska, Flynn developed a love affair with music and a determination to pursue a career as a professional musician.

Dog Ear dance nights promoted good cheer, but they witnessed their share of violence as well, a reflection of the difficult economic times facing rural South Dakotans in the 1920s and 1930s. Completely dependent upon American farmers during World War I, the European continent recovered in the early 1920s, leaving Great Plains producers with large grain surpluses. The subsequent drop in crop and livestock prices in the early 1920s ushered in two decades of farm-belt depression, marked by rising debt, farm failures, and foreclosures. Declining property values, coupled with low farm income and delinquent loans, set off a string of South Dakota bank failures. The economic instability of the 1920s made

South Dakotans especially vulnerable to the Great Depression of the 1930s, when drought, dust storms, severe winter cold, and grasshopper infestations exacerbated economic problems, pushing rural folk to the limits of their endurance. In South Dakota, the south-central and western parts of the state, including Tripp and Gregory counties, were especially hard hit.[7] Within this tense, uncertain environment, some rural South Dakotans migrated west to Washington or California. Most farmers and ranchers stayed, however, hoping to earn non-agricultural income or to join federal work relief programs on a part-time basis.

John Flynn did his best to support neighbors by extending credit and loaning money to friends, produce sellers, and mercantile customers. In a 1963 letter to his mother, Pat Flynn recalled how his parents had "dipped into the cash register to help scared and frustrated people when the dark dust clouds enveloped the Dakotas."[8] The Flynns continued to host picnics, holiday gatherings, and Saturday-night dances, but the rural crisis often brought out the worst in good people. Fights at Dog Ear became more numerous — and violent. As a young girl in the 1930s, Pat's sister Grace witnessed a near-murder in the dance hall when, following a fistfight, one of the antagonists headed for his car to retrieve a pistol to shoot his opponent. The potential victim begged onlookers to cover him with a tablecloth and pronounce him dead of a heart attack. While the "deceased" was lying motionless beneath the cloth, the crowd displayed appropriate shock and grief. The ploy succeeded, for the potential murderer proved unwilling to put a .38 slug into a warm corpse. Other fights lacked gunplay and theatrics, but fistfights proliferated in the 1930s, much to Lucille Flynn's chagrin. "Someone would yell 'Fight! Fight!'" Grace remembers, "and everyone would go outside. But Mom would just keep playing the piano, right through the fight."[9]

Even Joe Gordon found himself in an altercation, challenged by young toughs determined to best the big half-breed with the massive hands. In his later years, Pat Flynn recalled for his children the night that two men coaxed Gordon, then in his late 50s, behind the Flynn house to settle a dispute sparked by excessive whiskey and a racial slur. With tears rolling down his cheeks, Pat yanked on his grandfather's coat and begged him to walk away. But Gordon went to meet the men, ordering his grandson to stay back and out of sight. After long, agonizing minutes punctuated by cursing, grunts, and body blows, Gordon emerged from behind the house, bleeding and limping. Behind him lay the bodies of his two adversaries,

Young Pat Flynn with his coyote pup at Dog Ear Lake, 1929 or 1930.

one groaning, the other unconscious. The courage exhibited by his grandfather left an enduring impression on Flynn and explains his tenacity during a legendary street brawl with a martial arts expert outside a Japanese bar in the fall of 1962.

By 1934, the year the "black blizzard" dust storms struck the Great Plains, economic conditions became so bad that the Flynns left the mercantile store in the hands of neighbors and relocated to Deadwood, South Dakota, home of Lucille's sister and her husband, an employee of the Homestake Gold Mine. The mine was one of the few South Dakota industries earning profits, a result of the sharp rise in gold prices during the Great Depression.[10] John hoped to find work in the mine but was never hired. Unable to make money in the Black Hills, the Flynns returned to Dog Ear Lake, where environmental and economic conditions remained poor. Drought dragged on through the hot summers of 1935 and 1936, when Dog Ear Lake shrank to the size of a small pond and grasshopper infestations on the northern Plains reached their peak.[11]

By 1937, the worst of the agricultural crisis having passed and economic conditions improving, requests for the music of Joe Gordon and Lucille Flynn became more numerous. Dog Ear celebrations returned, with dances, picnics, and baseball games drawing large crowds. At Fourth of July picnics, no entertainment proved more exciting than the airplane rides offered by Slim Halmgremson, whose Curtiss Robin two-seater drew long waiting lines. For three dollars of his hard-earned chore money, Pat Flynn took a ride with Halmgremson, a moment that Flynn later described in his family history as "a germinating event of my life's profession."

For Pat Flynn, the mid-1930s were significant for other reasons. As the oldest male heir of the family, he became the focal point for the teachings of his grandfather, Joe, and grandmother, Rosalie, who had lost their two sons to childhood illness in 1907. Joe Gordon made sure that his grandson could live off the land like his Indian ancestors. The two took long camping trips and spent countless hours walking across the prairie and around the lake examining wild roots, identifying mushrooms, tracking deer, trapping small mammals, running set-lines, reading the clouds and the stars, digging for freshwater clams, constructing lean-to's and snow houses, and building fires. In a 1965 interview, Flynn credited his grandfather for teaching him the art of survival, describing Gordon, the man who "reared him and helped forge the man that befuddled the Chinese" during the Korean War, as "quite a taskmaster. He was great for living off the land even if it was 30 below and [*if*] your hands and feet were frozen you had better not let out a peep." He could lovingly caress a fiddle, but Joe Gordon was, in the words of his grandson, a hard teacher not prone to "emotionalism."[12]

In addition to survival training, Gordon taught his grandson how to box. The boy followed his grandfather's instructions for warding off blows, absorbing body punches, moving his feet, and jabbing. Flynn developed a reputation as a scrappy fighter, proving to larger and older opponents that, with proper technique and lighting quickness, a skinny Irish-Indian kid could hold his own in fisticuffs.

Gordon's most important lessons, however, were on the history of the family's Native American heritage. Pat Flynn took great pride in his Irish roots and credited his self-discipline to an upbringing in an Irish-Catholic home where his parents instilled in their children a respect and reverence for Catholic doctrine. Yet it was Flynn's Indian heritage that would define his military career.

Among the Lakota and other Native peoples, grandparents are the primary teachers of children. Flynn's maternal grandparents shaped his values and beliefs, versed him on his Lakota heritage, and impressed upon him the expectations facing a young man destined to be a Lakota warrior. Flynn wrote in his family history that he was

> raised from birth under the complete influence of my Indian grandparents and was given the truth of their heritage as a part of my manhood ceremony at age 12. On that occasion I was given the name "Long Elk" by my grandfather and sworn to keep the secret from everyone including his oldest daughter, who was my mother. The burden was given to me simply because I was their eldest surviving male descendant. Their two boys died when very young.

The Gordons raised Flynn as the son they never had. "Pat," remembered his sister Grace Scott in an interview, "was the full-blood of the family."

From his grandparents, Pat learned of his great-great-grandfather Spotted Tail, the Sioux warrior-diplomat and uncle of Crazy Horse.

Spotted Tail's name does not fire the imagination like that of his nephew's, but as the last Indian recognized as a chief by the U.S. government, he deserves equal attention. Because his life spanned the history of the Euro-American conquest of the Great Plains, Spotted Tail experienced all the uncertainties faced by decentralized Plains tribes struggling to maintain the buffalo culture in the 1860s and 1870s. Once a feared warrior of great acclaim, by 1868 Spotted Tail had come to accept the unstoppable military superiority of the federal government. On April 29, with General William T. Sherman urging Plains Indians to accept a peace treaty or "be swept out of existence," Spotted Tail signed the Fort Laramie Treaty. The document placed the Brulé Sioux on a reservation near the Missouri River and ended their right to live as they chose.[13]

For Spotted Tail, 1868 was significant for another reason. In that year, his daughter and her husband of one year, a Quebec-born Métis (of mixed Indian and French-Canadian ancestry) trader named Francis Cashmere Xavier Boucher, moved to Spotted Tail's camp at Whetstone Indian Agency, Dakota Territory. A friendship developed between the chief and his Canadian son-in-law, himself of half-Sioux descent and well-traveled among the Plains tribes. Boucher's language skills (he spoke French, English, and Lakota) made him indispensable as an interpreter and advisor to Spotted Tail, especially during the tense decade of the 1870s, when government agents and Army Generals were threatening the still-nomadic "hostile" Sioux with massive retaliation unless they retired into reservation borders.[14]

Spotted Tail and Boucher secretly aided Sitting Bull, Crazy Horse, and other Sioux resistors by smuggling Winchester carbines and thousands of rounds of ammunition to their camps in the Powder River country of Wyoming and Montana. Following the Battle of the Little Bighorn in June 1876, the chief and his son-in-law found themselves the focus of an investigation by the Wyoming territorial delegation and Army officers at Fort Robinson, Nebraska, who accused the two of aiding and abetting the renegade Sioux.[15] Boucher redeemed himself in the minds of his accusers during the winter of 1877, when, at the request of General George Crook, he led an expedition to the camps of Crazy Horse and his followers and convinced them to turn themselves in at the Spotted Tail and Red Cloud agencies.[16]

Spotted Tail died in 1881, murdered by a jealous political rival.[17] Boucher lived to 1923, the last years of his life spent with his daughter

Rosalie Gordon and her husband in Gregory County. Upon Boucher's death, South Dakota Governor William H. McMaster expressed his sympathy to Rosalie in a letter dated April 12, 1923. "I have heard a great deal about your father," McMaster wrote, "he being one of the old pioneers of the State of South Dakota, and it is most assuredly a great honor to be the daughter of a man who left behind him such a splendid reputation."

Boucher passed on his memories of Spotted Tail and Crazy Horse to his daughter and son-in-law, who in turn lectured their oldest grandson, Pat Flynn, on the greatness of Lakota chiefs. The grandparents' message was clear and consistent: the grandson was heir to a great warrior tradition; when called upon, he must fight bravely; in peacetime, he must act honorably and unselfishly, in the best tradition of a Lakota warrior-protector. The message took root in the heart of the pupil, who would one day fight in lands far removed from the Great Plains battlefields that brought honor to his ancestors.

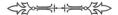

But at the moment, Pat Flynn's battles were limited to high school football fields and music halls. In 1937, Pat followed his sister Rose Marie to Colome High School, where he lived and slept in the bare-walled rooms of the boys' dormitory. The 53 Colome freshmen selected Flynn as their class president. He participated in band, athletic club, and football, a sport at which he excelled until age 27, when recurring shoulder and knee injuries permanently sidelined him. In his sophomore year at Colome, Flynn added yearbook class to his schedule, serving as art editor for the 1939 volume, "Cowboy."

Flynn's stellar performance as an end for the Colome Cowboy football team resulted in his transfer to Gregory High School. An uncle in Gregory and several other football fans (or, more accurately, sports gamblers) enticed Flynn to leave Colome and come to Gregory in the fall of 1939, where he boarded during the school week with the McKay family a block down the street from his junior classmate, Frances Gassen. However, determined to prevent Gregory from benefiting from their recruiting theft, Colome school officials withheld Flynn's transcript for several months, making him ineligible for the Gregory Gorillas football team for the 1939 season. A frustrated Flynn turned his energy toward art and music. Impressed by his drawing skills, the Gorilla yearbook staff named him art

The 1940-1941 Gregory High School football squad. Pat Flynn is in the back row, number 44.

editor for both the 1940 and 1941 editions. His broad smile and infectious personality made him popular with all students, but none more so than Frances Gassen. The couple attended movies and dances together and were, as Frances later wrote in her unpublished memoir, "considered a twosome."

By the end of the school year, Frances' parents were working to separate the couple. "As our junior year came to an end," recalls Frances in her memoir,

> it was becoming evident that Mom and Dad were not happy about this relationship between Pat and me. I was deeply hurt as I realized that it was because of his Native American heritage. My disappointment ran deep as I had never thought of my parents as being prejudiced. Among other things I wanted to tell them was that they had never given themselves a chance to know him, but I kept my mouth pretty well quiet and my thoughts to myself.

For his senior year, 1940-1941, Flynn returned to the football field, where the Gorillas went 4-1-1, including a satisfying 14-7 win over Colome. His obligations as the new student body president, coupled with his yearbook responsibilities, kept Flynn busy with extra-curricular activities. He devoted himself to his trumpet, preparing for solo and ensemble contests and school concerts. Flynn's development as a musician made him a valuable asset to his mother, who hired her son to play weekend gigs with her orchestra at area saloons and dance halls. In recalling Pat's senior year, Frances Flynn notes that there were many Monday mornings that he rushed from Dog Ear to Gregory to make his first class of the day. Lucille Flynn's performance schedule took its toll on the 18-year-old, whose grades, according to his report cards, hovered around the C range for most of his senior year.

But Flynn's academic performance did not lower his stature in the minds of the administrators, teachers, and students of Gregory High School. Prior to their graduation, Pat and Frances, who were for many the embodiment of the class motto, "Build for Character, Not for Fame," were selected as "Representative Seniors" of the Class of 1941. Pat's "sincerity and willingness," his "easy friendliness," and his organizational skills won him the respect of his classmates and the high school faculty.[18]

Two weeks before his graduation, Flynn applied to Haskell Institute (now Haskell Indian Nations University) in Lawrence, Kansas, an all-Indian commercial and trade college administered by the Bureau of Indian Affairs (BIA). Flynn's sister Rose Marie was attending Haskell, a school that provided Pat, a member of the Rosebud Sioux Tribe, with the financial assistance to pursue post-secondary education. Although Haskell's mission was to prepare students for leadership positions, the school maintained a curriculum devoted solely to vocational training. One objective of the Institute's commercial training program was to train office workers and secretaries for the BIA.[19] As historian Kenneth William Townsend notes, the purpose of Haskell and other Indian schools was "the introduction of practical education-teaching subjects that would permit students to assimilate into white society or return to reservations armed with skills and knowledge beneficial to their Indian communities."[20] Haskell Institute maintained a music department but did not grant music degrees. Flynn attended Haskell for financial reasons, and the fact that he was disinterested in commercial courses and longed to study music proved a constant source of frustration for him and the institute's administrators.

Flynn's Haskell application disclosed much about the 18-year-old's dreams and anxieties. Not surprisingly, Flynn listed "studying instrumental music and doing art work" as his favorite hobbies. When asked to indicate any problems he faced, Flynn expressed his concern with "the problem of going into military training," a dilemma that led him to seek the advice of his parents and high school teachers.[21] Eventually Flynn would have to fulfill his Selective Service registration requirement, a step that would almost certainly alter his plans. He discussed his military commitment with Frances, who remembers leaving *Gone With The Wind* in tears, fearful that the war in Europe would eventually lead to American involvement and ruin her future with Pat.

Flynn set aside his fears but continued to chafe at the limited degree options offered by Haskell Institute. The school asked Flynn to select one course of study from a total of 18 trade and vocations programs that included arts and crafts, baking, shoemaking, plumbing, and "poultry management." Undeterred, Flynn listed "music" and "art" as his first and second vocational choices, his third selection being the more conventional "business and commercial" program. In response to the question "What trade experience have you had?" Flynn replied that he had been "associated with Bands."[22]

Flynn searched for options that would allow him to pursue a music major, applying for a BIA loan to attend a four-year institution granting instrumental music degrees. His request was denied. In a harshly worded letter to the superintendent of the Rosebud Sioux Indian Reservation, the BIA education department concluded that "there is nothing in [*Flynn's*] record except the third place in the national music contest to show that he has outstanding ability in this field. Unfortunately, his high school record is not even good enough to be called mediocre." Flynn's time at Haskell, the BIA argued, would provide him a "good background" for four-year college courses. "Since his high school record in subjects of this nature is so poor, we must assume that he is not interested in academic work, or else he does not have the ability in this direction." BIA officials reminded Rosebud Sioux officials that "being a good musician is not enough to make . . . a good teacher of musical subjects."[23]

Stung by the comments, Flynn nevertheless accepted the Indian Office decision and enrolled in the commercial program at Haskell. But he refused to let the BIA's decision break his spirit or derail his dream of being a professional trumpeter.

While at Haskell, Flynn played intra-mural basketball and joined the Haskell boxing team, fighting in the middleweight class. Music absorbed much of his free time, and all on campus were impressed by his gifts. Jim Ward, Flynn's roommate in Keokuk Hall, in a March 21, 1979, letter to Frances Flynn, remembered his friend's many contributions to the Haskell student body, which, in the fall of 1941, was beginning to feel the effects of America's prewar military build-up:

> My clearest recollection of Pat was his musical talent and his boxing ability. On quiet evenings on the campus he'd open a window of our room, poke that corenet [*sic*] through it and play "Blue Berry Hill" in a manner that brought the entire school to a parade rest. Beautiful! And at lights out — "Taps" — played so as to lullaby a baby to sleep. And on stage — "Flight of the Bumble Bee." We marveled at the ease with which he handled the intricate notes of that piece.

In letters home, Flynn avoided references to grades but kept his parents abreast of musical and athletic events. "Received your letter, the overcoat, and the two bucks, which wer [*sic*] all very welcome," he wrote on

Pat Flynn (back row, second from r), trumpeter and part-time director of the Haskell Institute Orchestra, 1941-1942.

November 17, 1941, followed by an announcement of the Haskell Band's appearance in the Kansas University homecoming parade and their upcoming performance at the Kansas-Missouri football game that would decide the Big Six championship. "Be sure and tune in on this game," he wrote. "You might hear me play." Flynn added that he played a cornet solo for a Lawrence women's group and was preparing "The Carnival of Venice" for an upcoming chapel hour. "I haven't missed mass yet. I go to Communion quite often. . . . Therefore I am still 100 per cent loyal."

Flynn's letter was written three weeks before the Japanese attack on Pearl Harbor, and in Lawrence, Kansas, the sites and sounds of America's war machine were everywhere. Still intent on learning to fly, Flynn was particularly fascinated with the military aircraft. "The air is practically full of big four motored bombers and high-powered fighters," he continued in his November 17 letter. "When one of them goes over at around 400 miles per hour, the whole building vibrates."

As was the case with all Americans, the Pearl Harbor tragedy shocked Flynn. So he turned to music and athletics for distraction. On the first day of Christmas break, he hitchhiked to Dog Ear Lake to play a two-week engagement with his mother's orchestra. In February 1942, Flynn boxed as a middleweight in the Sixth Annual Topeka State Journal Golden Gloves State Championships. In an enthusiastic letter to his parents written February 3, 1942, he described his semi-final victory over a fighter from Topeka: "I batted him all over the ring the last round. I staggered him against the ropes and pounded his face with lefts and rights and was continuing in that manner when the bell rang. The crowd was on their feet the last round." Flynn's adversary for the championship fight, a soldier from nearby Fort Riley, worried him. The GI had knocked out his first-round opponent, a fellow who "was tough, so your son will have to fight like hell to be middle-weight champ of Kansas." Flynn's fear proved well grounded, for he was knocked out in the first round of what was his last organized boxing match.

Flynn had little time to heal his injuries or his pride, for a week and a half after the fight, he directed the Haskell Institute Orchestra in a tribute to Antonin Dvořák's. Mr. Cato, Haskell's music director, had fallen ill and Flynn was selected to fill in during Cato's five-week absence. At the February 15 performance, broadcast locally by the Haskell Radio Club, Flynn directed the orchestra in Dvořák's *Symphony No. 9* ("From the New

World") and played a solo in a rendition of "Humoreske." For his sacrifices during Cato's absence, Flynn earned the praise of Haskell's Superintendent, G. Warren Spaulding. "Your willingness to give so much of your effort and time really deserves a gold medal if I had one to give you," Spaulding wrote to Flynn in a letter dated March 4, 1942. Spaulding was struck by the young student-director's selflessness.

> Willingness of a student to serve, or for that matter anyone to serve, is the mark of a real person. I know you went into this special duty with but one thought in mind, and that was to offer help when help was really needed.

Despite his busy schedule, which included a part in the play *Headed for Eden*, Flynn maintained a C average and earned financial aid for the upcoming summer — 1942 — and for the 1942-1943 school year. But there was a catch. An evaluation of his loan request by Haskell's Registrar stipulated that Flynn would receive aid "only if he drops band."[24]

This was the last straw. His musical abilities and many contributions to the Haskell Band were appreciated by the administration but never taken as evidence of a special talent deserving of cultivation and professional guidance. The Bureau of Indian Affairs remained fixated on the value of "practical education," and music had no place within that educational paradigm. There seemed to be nothing Flynn could do to convince Indian Office administrators of the value of an Indian student pursuing a career as a musician.

In the end, Haskell's requirements meant little to Flynn, for in the spring of 1942, the 19-year-old enlisted in the Naval Air Corps Reserve. Flynn was not unlike other Native American males who saw in military service an opportunity for financial stability and a postwar career. But other factors had inspired Flynn and other Native Americans to enlist, not the least of which was the opportunity to bring honor to their family and tribe. "A warrior tradition certainly encouraged numerous Indians to enlist," writes historian Kenneth Townsend. By the time of World War II, many tribes faced the demise of traditional warrior societies and ceremonies. Combat duty, Townsend notes,

> permitted Indians who historically maintained and valued warrior societies the opportunity to revitalize tribal culture and in

the process gain personal prestige, respect, and honor in the manner of their ancestors.[25]

In May 1942, Flynn canceled his loan applications and secured short-term employment as a thresher operator for a pea cannery near Lawrence. In June, he asked Haskell Institute to forward his records to the Naval Aviation Selection Board in Mitchell, South Dakota. After a review of his physical examination and strong recommendations from several Haskell instructors, the board accepted Flynn for entry in the Naval Air Training Command, effective October 1942. He spent August and September in Chicago, where Irish-American relatives found him temporary work as a "water maintenance man" in the sewers of the Windy City.[26]

Following a short visit with his family in South Dakota, Aviation Cadet Flynn embarked for Kansas City, home to a United States Naval Reserve training center. He was getting his chance to fly. In time, he would learn to value all the more the walks with his grandfather around Dog Ear Lake.

Chapter 2

Okinawa *Gunto*

We have shared the incommunicable experience of war. We have felt, we still feel, the passion of life to its top. . . .

Oliver Wendell Holmes[1]

PAT FLYNN JOINED the Naval Aviation Cadet Training (NACT) Program at Kansas City Junior College in late October 1942. Over the next three months, NACT instructors determined if Flynn and other raw cadets possessed the stuff of naval aviators. Flight instructors looked for proficiency in the air, while ground instructors established classroom requirements that exceeded anything Flynn had faced at Haskell Institute. Courses in mathematics, physics, meteorology, navigation, civil regulations, general aircraft servicing, and military science were combined with physical training to prepare students for the more rigorous flight training that lay ahead.[2]

In a letter to his family on December 17, 1942, three days before his 20th birthday, Flynn recounted the strains of cadet flight school. "The subjects are getting rougher all the time," he wrote, noting that homework assignments made it impossible for him to "go to church in the evening." During a ground-school lecture, "one fellow dropped his pencil and missed out on six weeks work." But he sought no sympathy. "I have always wanted this so I think can take anything they can throw at me." Flynn expressed some frustration in his December 19 letter with the "city softies" struggling in physical training and shared his desire to get a "big tall wise guy" into the boxing ring. "We've been egging him on so I'll have a little fun out of it anyway," he wrote.

Above all, he rejoiced in the thrill of flying, despite the frigid winter weather that left the runway at Edwardsville, Kansas, "practically covered with ice," according to his Christmas letter of December 22. He described making practice spins and stalls in a Piper Cub J-3. "Going straight down from 3000 ft. with the earth spinning like a top sorta' upsets one's breakfast," he quipped. "But if we're going to make combat pilots we'll have to do a hell of a lot worse things than that." The war was never far from Flynn's thoughts, and he begged his mother to send him news from Europe, North Africa, and the Pacific, remarking that he lacked the time to read a paper or listen to the radio.

Flynn's comrades took note of his Indian heritage and teased him about it. After suffering an ankle sprain that kept him off his feet for several days, Flynn earned the nickname "Sitting Bull." He wrote to his parents in an undated letter that he passed on "practically the whole history of the Sioux tribe" to bunk mates who showed genuine interest in his family story. Of course, not everyone maintained prejudice-free views; Flynn informed his mother that he "had to get the respect of one individual . . . by threatening to beat knots on his head. He's alright now."

The young South Dakotan possessed natural flying abilities. At the end of his first dual instruction (instructor-assisted) flight, Flynn's teacher commented that his pupil was "at ease in the air" and displayed "a smooth control touch." Flynn grew comfortable working the plane through turns, glides, and climbs. He learned to maneuver in heavy traffic, an essential skill for cadets bound for bases where air space was clogged with trainers, fighters, bombers, and transports. On Christmas Eve, 1942, Flynn flew his first solo flight. By the time of his graduation from cadet training in February 1943, he had flown over 13 solo hours and wore the silver wings of the Civil Aeronautics Administration.[3]

Pat Flynn as an aviation cadet in Kansas City, early 1943.

His first training program behind him, Flynn transferred to the Navy Pre-Flight School at Del Monte, California, where he was assigned to the 4th Battalion, Company G, Platoon 1. Kansas City had provided Flynn with a taste of military life, but pre-flight school *was* military life. Cadets received regulation haircuts and uniforms. As writer Samuel Hynes notes, pre-flight cadets snapped to attention as instructors entered classrooms and "braced the bulkhead" when instructors walked down the halls.[4] The intensive 13-week program at Del Monte, once a popular resort, tested the cadets' physical and mental limits. A routine of close-order drill, platoon runs, push-ups, chin-ups, sit-ups, gymnastics, hand-to-hand combat tactics, and speed and agility drills was supplemented with boxing, wrestling, football, and obstacle-course races. According to an article in the *Monterey Peninsula Herald* on June 12, 1943, Flynn's battalion was the first Del Monte unit to qualify on the .22 caliber rifle range, where demanding Marine Corps marksmanship instructors exposed Flynn to the high standards of the country's elite fighting force.

Each pre-flight cadet "majored" in one or more physical activities and, not surprisingly, Flynn selected boxing and football. He won a reputation for his aggressiveness, but agonized over a serious injury he had inflicted on a "good friend" during a physical football game, as he described in his letter home on May 7, 1943. "A good clean block" on his classmate resulted in a leg "broken just about to the knee," an incident that earned Flynn the nickname "Killer." "I don't appreciate the fact that everyone calls me 'killer,'" Flynn wrote to his mother, "but the rougher a guy gets around here the better. They like it."

Cadets balanced physical training with classroom studies. Flynn received "big academic assignments," which he found "really tough," according to his letter home on March 27, 1943. At Del Monte, it was not uncommon for dozens of cadets to flunk out of a ground-school course that, if not promptly made up, resulted in their expulsion from the flight program. Flynn himself failed two courses and spent several weekends cramming for re-tests. "It's terrible how fast they're washing the cadets out of our Battalion," he wrote to his family on May 29. To maintain cadet morale, the Navy scheduled speakers with Pacific Theater combat experience to address the students. Flynn was particularly excited by a question-answer session with Marine Corps Captain Joe Foss, a native South Dakotan. As Flynn described in a letter home on June 3,

> [*Foss*] shot down 26 Jap planes to equal Eddie Rickenbacker's record. He is a swell guy. He answered our questions on different stuff. If all goes well I can be "out there" — Pacific — in another year.

All went well for Flynn, and at his Pre-Flight School graduation on June 12, 1943, his battalion was praised for their physical fitness scores, which were — as was noted in the *Monterey Peninsula Herald* that day — the highest of any battalion at Del Monte or any other Navy pre-flight training center. But Flynn had little time to enjoy the moment, for he was ordered directly to Primary Flight School, at the Naval Air Station (NAS) in Livermore, California.

Livermore instructors demanded precision in marching, carrying out work details, preparing for inspection, and, most importantly, in flying. "Precision," recalls former Navy aviator Matt Portz, ". . . was always demanded in flight training. A course of 090 degrees meant 090 degrees, not 089 or 091; an altitude of 1,500 feet was nothing less, nothing more; and a two-turn spin was not two and a quarter." Because all Livermore students "were considered potential carrier pilots," adds Portz, precision was "essential" for cadet trainees. S-turns, split-S's, slow rolls, loops, and Cuban-eight maneuvers — all conducted in open-cockpit, two-seat N2S biplanes — were graded on precision. At Livermore, and later at the Naval Air Training Center (NATC) in Corpus Christi, Texas, Flynn learned to take off and land in "the Navy way": getting into the air fast and landing in a full stall, in simulation of carrier takeoffs and landings.[5]

Flynn was amazed by the number of aircraft at Livermore. In a letter to his mother on June 25, 1943, he wrote that "[t]he sky is full of airplanes, all the time. . . . No wonder there are so many mid-air collisions." Several days earlier, he added, two student pilots had been killed in a mid-air flying accident. Flight instructors insured that cadets mastered a wide range of aerobatics, formation flying, and night flying. During formation flying, Flynn learned to "fly so close to the next guy you can read his instrument panel," as he wrote on July 24. He also suffered his first in-flight blackout, describing it, in a letter home on July 31, as "a funny feeling, because a guy don't lose consciousness and his eyes are wide open all the time, but the blood drains out of the head which makes everything go black." After the flight, Flynn learned that the instructor pilot had also blacked out "for about 3 seconds" as he put the plane through a power dive from an altitude of 6,000 feet.

Ground school at Livermore posed its own challenges. At Livermore (as opposed to Del Monte), the men could purchase beer, go to a movie, or attend a dance, "[b]ut a guy don't dare let down or he'll wash out in nothing flat," Flynn wrote in July 1943. Flynn struggled with his studies, flunking four subjects in the first month. He found the Aircraft Recognition course — which required cadets to identify over 85 American, British, German, Japanese, and Italian planes — particularly frustrating. In a dejected tone, Flynn described for his mother how cadets were "washing out and quitting right and left and it's no wonder. There aren't hardly anyone left in our platoon anymore."

Some men quit the Navy flight program to join with the Army Air Corps, a route that earned a quick commission and immediate orders to a combat zone. "I've been in this damn Navy for over a year now and look where I am," Flynn wrote. But he showed no desire to quit the program. "[*T*]hey're going to have to kick me out before I'll quit." To revive his confidence, Flynn attended daily and Sunday masses. He thanked his mother for her prayers, which "help because I've been getting the breaks in flying, as I am way ahead of most of the class. . . ."[6]

Flynn's persistence paid off. He rose to honor student status in ground school (an achievement that earned him extra liberty), and in the cockpit grew confident and aggressive, even playful. During wingtip-to-wingtip flying, he took to tapping the wing or rudder of the plane next to him. He enjoyed "flat-hatting," an aerobatic sequence in which he dove upside down to 1,000 feet, pulled out upside down, and rolled over while ascending. Flynn took inexperienced cadets into the air, letting one poor fellow spin out of control for 4,000 feet until, as the more knowledgeable pilot, he regained control at 2,000 feet above the deck — a stunt that gave the cadet "a pretty good 'wringing out,'" as Flynn described in his August 10 letter home. Flynn also received his first flight in a combat aircraft, arranging a backseat ride in a Grumman TBF Avenger, the Navy's single-engine torpedo-bomber workhorse. Flynn thrilled at the plane's airspeed and wrote home on August 27 that its bombsight was "most interesting."

Pat Flynn graduated from Livermore in mid-September 1943 and boarded a first-class Pullman car for a four-day train ride to the Naval Air Training Center (NATC) in Corpus Christi. En route he made an important decision: during secondary flight training, he would apply for a commission in the Marine Corps. "The Marine flyers get a lot more action than the Navy," he explained to his mother in a letter on September 12. "[*Of*] course a lot more get killed but the war will probably be over by then anyway, since Italy folded."

Even so, combat training at Corpus would not exactly be a safe way to spend the last few months of the war. "At Corpus more are killed than are washed out," Flynn noted. And he shared with his mother his aspirations of becoming a fighter pilot: "Requirements are to have a lot of guts (a little on the reckless side) and be able to fly. They have a little follow the leader game called a 'rat race' to find out if a guy will make a fighter pilot."

At NATC Corpus Christi, not all training was done in airplanes. Flynn "flew" the simulated aerial combat machine — a chamber that introduced and enhanced aerial fighting techniques — and the Link Trainer, a mechanical cockpit that simulated instrument flying. Of course the real test for instrument flying took place in the air, where Flynn and the other aviation cadets spent countless hours "under the hood." While flying dual with an instructor, the cadet's field of view was blocked out by a canvas curtain that covered the student canopy of the SNJ trainer airplane, forcing the trainee to rely on flight instruments rather than references to the horizon.[7] Instrument training was a primary objective in the NATC training syllabus, evidenced by the over 30 hours of instrument flying Flynn experienced in his five months at Corpus Christi. During that period, Flynn spent dozens of hours in the SNJ and the Vultee trainer (the most widely used basic trainer produced in the United States during World War II) practicing tactical maneuvers, training in gunnery and bombing, night flying, flying on oxygen, and honing his navigation skills.[8]

The high number of accidents occurring at Corpus Christi shocked Flynn. "Just lost another one of my buddies since Pre-flight, 1 hr. ago," he wrote on October 6. "Flying formation and hit another plane." Flynn accepted this and several other accidents involving his friends "as a lesson to be damn careful as I'm in formation now. As a rule it's all due to carelessness though." Flynn also maintained his focus on achieving a Marine Corps commission. Recognizing that over 50 percent of the class would apply for — but only 12 percent would gain — admission to Marine Air, he prepared himself for rejection, as his October 17 letter described. But his discovery on October 23 that he had been accepted showed his unbounded elation. "Dear Mom — *I made the Marines!!* Now if my acrobatic [*sic*] flight grades are good enough I should get Fighters."

The news of Flynn's commission was followed soon after by advanced squadron assignment. He wrote on November 20: "Yippee!! I got Fighters and will train at Kingsville [*Texas*] about 50 miles from the main station. . . . I leave in the morning." Flynn hoped to fly the Marines' premier fighter, the Vought F4U Corsair, "in a class," he emphasized, "with the British 'Spitfire.'"

⊱━━━✥━━━⊰

Instructors at the auxiliary air station in Kingsville, Texas, stressed section and division tactics. Flynn marveled at the complexity of division tactics, which he described on December 25 as "the art of keeping a huge group of planes in close formation and evading attacking aircraft and anti-aircraft fire and still being able to concentrate the divisions [*sic*] fire-power on the target." Aerial gunnery, ground strafing, and dive-bombing practice in the SNJ — as recorded in Flynn's flight log — stretched his skills. Wing-mounted .30-caliber machine guns were fired at target sleeves pulled by tow planes. In "fighter opposition" drills, two planes "shot" at each other with cameras mounted in the plane's wings. Dive-bombing proved tricky — the catch, Flynn wrote, "keep[*ing*] the speed down to 250 MPH. It ain't healthy to get over 300 MPH and pull out very fast from a dive."

At the Naval Air Station (NAS) in Corpus Christi on February 12, 1944, Flynn was commissioned as a Second Lieutenant in the United States Marine Corps Reserve. On February 18, he reported to the Marine Barracks at NAS Jacksonville, Florida, for two months of operational training in the F4U Corsair and the FG-1, a Corsair variant manufactured by the Goodyear Aircraft Company.

Few planes in military aviation history were as loved and revered by their pilots as the F4U. Referred to by the Japanese as "Whistling Death," the gloss-blue Corsair boasted a massive 18-cylinder Pratt & Whitney XR-2800 Double Wasp engine, the most powerful piston engine then available, enabling the plane to achieve speeds of 446 mph. To harness the engine's power, a propeller 13 feet and 4 inches in diameter, the largest fitted to a fighter plane to that point in history, was bolted to the front of the aircraft. The propeller's size forced design modifications that resulted in the Corsair's most distinctive feature, the inverted gull-wing. Recognizing that a straight low- or mid-level wing design would not provide sufficient ground clearance for the prop's big blades, Vought engineers "bent" the inside of the Corsair's wings so that the plane's landing gear, situated at the wing dip, would create the necessary propeller-to-ground distance. Ultimately, the inverted gull-wing modification permitted a shorter, lighter landing gear and, more significantly, created an aerodynamic shape that increased the aircraft's speed.[9]

Some 33 feet in length with a wingspan of almost 41 feet, the Corsair was a fighter-bomber capable of carrying a formidable ordnance load. The plane's six Browning-Colt M2 machine guns fired .50-caliber rounds into a three- to six-foot circular pattern at a ratio of up to 80 rounds per second. In addition to its 2,350-round ammunition capacity, the Corsair could carry two 500-pound bombs or a single half-ton bomb. Pacific Theater aviators mounted 3.5- and 5-inch high velocity aerial rockets (HVAR) on the rails beneath the Corsair's outer-wing panels. By the end of the war, napalm tanks carried on the Corsair's under-wing bomb pylon were proving especially effective for close air support. When ignited, the napalm "jelly" — a combination of gasoline and naphthetic and palmitic acids — spread a wall of flame that reached 250 feet in length.[10]

At NAS Jacksonville, Flynn underwent intensive combat training. Navigation and communication courses, lectures and demonstrations on ammunition, guns, and bombing, and tests on aircraft recognition and combat tactics filled his hours. According to his flight log, Flynn spent nearly 100 hours in the Corsair, practicing formation flying and night flying, flying on oxygen, and instrument flying. Long hours of gunnery drills and glide-bombing, strafing, and air-combat methods introduced the untested aviators to the rigors of the Pacific War.

In May 1944, Flynn was assigned to Marine Corps Air Station (MCAS) Cherry Point, North Carolina, to prepare for an overseas combat assignment. Before reporting to Cherry Point, however, Flynn traveled to Washington, D.C., to spend an evening with his high school sweetheart, Frances Gassen. The two had not seen one another since December 1941, when Frances' family, opposed to her maintaining a relationship with Pat, forced the two to break up. In January 1942, Frances had passed the Civil Service stenography and typing examination, and in March, she had joined the

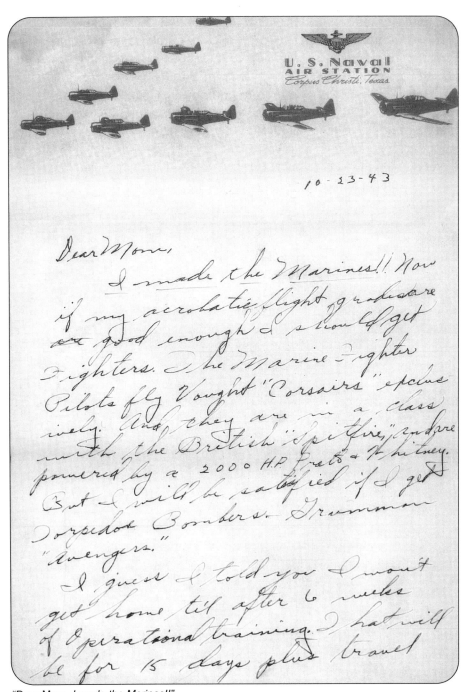

"Dear Mom, *I made the Marines!!*"

thousands of other "Government Girls" bound for federal jobs in the nation's capital. She was assigned a clerk-typist position in the Navy Department's Bureau of Supplies and Accounts, and in her free time played bass drum for a "Government Girl Band" that performed at veterans' hospitals and war-bond rallies. Having lost hope in rekindling her relationship with Pat, Frances was surprised to receive the telegram from him inviting her to meet with him at Union Station in Washington. They went dancing and took a walk together, and, as Frances later wrote in her memoir, "talked for hours about everything and nothing [*while*] trying to act very nonchalant."

The two reunited again in late June 1944. Pat wrote his parents that he and Frances "had a good time" and "a lot of fun together," but cautioned them that "no serious ties" existed between the two. It was not until September that Pat, on the verge of marrying a Greensboro, North Carolina, girl he had been dating, bared his soul to Frances. "I am going overseas and don't know if I will be coming back. I love you and wish things had worked out between us." Elated over Pat's feelings toward her after almost three years of separation, Frances arrived at Parris Island two days later, where the couple made plans for a November 11 wedding in Washington. When Pat was unable to arrange leave for that date, the wedding was postponed to the 17th, when the two were married at St. Ann's Catholic Church by a Father Phelan. Two Naval Reserve personnel from Frances' office served as best man and maid of honor. After a brief 10-day honeymoon, Frances returned to her Navy Department job and Pat caught the train back to North Carolina. The next day, according to his flight log, Pat was back in the air taking gunnery practice in an FG-1 Corsair.

⟨⟩⟩⟩=++=⟨⟨⟨⟩

In January 1945, after spending the Christmas holidays in South Dakota, Pat reported for temporary duty at the Aviation Combat Conditioning Program, Camp Pendleton, California. Shortly thereafter — as his official Marine Corps chronological record (NAVMC 545A-DP) indicates — Flynn received orders to join VMF-111, "The Devil Dogs" Squadron, which was at that time flying missions against Japanese garrisons on the Marshall and Caroline islands in the central Pacific. On February 13, six days before the Marine amphibious assault on Iwo Jima, Flynn shipped out from San Diego on the USS *Bollinger* for the two-week cruise to

Pat Flynn at the Naval Air Station in Jacksonville, Florida, 1944.

Eniwetok Island, amidst the 30 small islands of the Eniwetok Atoll at the western edge of the Marshall Islands.

The Marshall Islands, a large group of atolls over 2,500 miles from the southern Japanese island of Kyushu, became a Japanese mandate in the aftermath of the post-World War I Versailles Peace Conference. In the 1930s, Japanese engineers constructed an airstrip on Roi Island in the Kwajalein Atoll (the world's largest coral atoll), and in 1941-1942 built island defenses on Roi, Namur, Eniwetok, Garu, Kwajalein Island, and Ensetto in the Marshall atolls, as well as on Langar Island and other islands in the Carolines. A series of Allied amphibious landings in

February 1944 led to Japanese defeats and the capture of Kwajalein, Roi, Namur, and Eniwetok. As part of Admiral Chester W. Nimitz's island-hopping campaign, Wotje, Maloelap, Mille, and Joluit atolls in the Marshall chain and Ponape Island in the Carolines were bypassed by Marine units. U.S. planes pounded the isolated Japanese garrisons on these islands for the remainder of the war.[11]

Historian Robert Sherrod writes in *History of Marine Corps Aviation in World War II* that air operations against the Marshalls were "tiresome and monotonous and without much glory, but the Marines were assigned to this rear-area task and they carried out their assignment faithfully if not always cheerfully."[12] Pat Flynn left no account of his feelings about the Marshall Islands, but he must have found the duty more exciting and worthwhile than his long months of aviation training.

Although the islands' Japanese defenders had been cut off and isolated, they had no intention of surrendering or offering weak resistance to American air attacks. The Japanese antiaircraft (AA) installations in the Marshalls could prove deadly, and our Pacific aviators were not immune from non-combat-related operational accidents. In January 1945, three VMF-111 pilots had failed to return from an instrument hop; in May, two more had been killed in a mid-air collision. In March 1945, the same month that Pat Flynn had arrived at Eniwetok, a B-24 bomber carrying Army Lieutenant General Millard F. Harmon disappeared between the Marshalls and Wake Island, sparking speculation among Marines that Japanese fighter planes continued to patrol the skies above the atolls.[13] Some of the Marshall Islands may have been leapfrogged by the Allies, but they were by no means pacified. Rear-guard assignment or not, there were dozens of ways to die in the central Pacific in the spring of 1945.

Pat Flynn spent his first month with VMF-111 responding to alerts, logging instrument and night hours, taking gunnery practice, and, in his spare time, sea shell hunting and skin-diving. As part of an experiment in F4U tactics, the squadron participated in dive-bombing missions, first performed by Corsairs in attacks against Japanese installations on the Mille Atoll in March 1944. The squadron experimented with high-speed descent dive-bombing techniques throughout 1944-1945, discovering in the process that the F4U could perform effectively and safely at dives of up to 85 degrees (though most dives were conducted at a 70-80 degree downward angle).[14]

Second Lieutenant Flynn's first taste of combat came on April 11, 1945, as part of a 17-plane dive-bombing mission against the airfield, barracks, oil tanks, and antiaircraft emplacements on Ponape Island, 360 miles southwest of Eniwetok Island. Each pilot dropped two 500-pound bombs from 2,000-2,500 feet and then strafed targets with .50-caliber guns. Prior to the attack, the Japanese were distracted by a Navy PB4Y-2 Dumbo seaplane, a diversion that focused the enemy's antiaircraft fire on it rather than the fighters. Facing light ground fire, the Corsairs damaged the airfield, destroyed a barracks, and probably knocked out an antiaircraft installation. The entire mission lasted four and a half hours.[15]

Flynn did not fly another attack mission until June 6, when, in preparation for a transfer to Okinawa, he struck Garu Island in the Mille Atoll. From interrogations of enemy POWs, U.S. Navy intelligence learned that the Japanese defenders on Mille rushed to their foxholes and gun emplacements at the sight of any American plane, including cargo planes and seaplanes. Consequently, noted VMF-111's after-action report, the Dumbo escorting the six-plane strike from Majuro Island "stayed well out of sight" while "the Corsairs got right down on the deck . . . still out of sight of the target." Armed with a 1,400-pound napalm tank and two 100-pound incendiary clusters per plane, Flynn and his wing-mates, flying "just above the tree top level," destroyed ten huts and set off two "large" explosions, probably the result of direct hits on Garu Island's ammunition stores. Flynn flew another napalm strike on June 8, this time against Ensetto Island in the Mille Atoll.[16]

The Marshall Islands missions provided, in the words of Robert Sherrod, "invaluable training" for young, untested Marine aviators bound for busier combat assignments.[17] And ready or not, Flynn received orders on June 12 to join VMA-312, a battle-tested Corsair squadron based at Kadena Airfield on the war-ravaged island of Okinawa.

Few World War II battles matched the ferocity and savagery of the Battle of Okinawa. A small island in the Ryukyu chain only 350 miles south of Kyushu, Okinawa had been selected as the staging area for a planned Allied invasion of Japan, scheduled for late 1945. Referred to by one historian as "the greatest land, sea, and air battle of all time,"[18] the Okinawa campaign, code-named ICEBERG, involved over half a million men and 1,457 ships, making the armada the largest assembled in the Pacific during the war. Expecting fierce Japanese resistance on L-Day ("landing day," which fell on April 1, 1945 — April Fool's Day and

The men of VMF-312, Okinawa, summer 1945. Pat Flynn is in the back row, second to the right of the Corsair's engine. First row, l to r: Griffin, Shields, Hays, Haden, Gerham, Crow, Cole, Farris, Elliot, Deming, Pritchet, Gardiner. Second row, l to r: Griffiths, Meek, Crowley, Howland, C. Brown, Snyder, Diehl, Purvis, Sloan, Turner, Pitslaff, Temple, Currier, Brown. Third row, l to r: Wolf, Hopkins, Read, Gill, Shotwell, Lelich, Soha, Lockwood, Sterling, Flynn, Kelly, Russel, Davis, Smith, Corr, Solsenber.

Easter Sunday), naval gun batteries pounded Okinawa's beaches with the heaviest bombardment of the Pacific campaign. But the Marines and Army infantrymen wading ashore soon discovered that the Japanese Commander, Lieutenant General Mitsuru Ushijima, had given the Americans the beaches while his men entrenched themselves in Okinawa's rugged interior. As U.S. units pushed inland, they confronted a honeycomb of mutually supported pillboxes, tunnels, and caves coordinated into interlocking fields of fire. Soldiers and Marines fighting for control of Sugar Loaf Hill, Dakeshi Ridge, Kakazu Ridge, Kunishi Ridge, Wana Ridge, and dozens of other well-fortified Japanese positions suffered heavy casualties. Offshore, American sailors were exposed to Admiral Matome Ugaki's "Floating Chrysanthemums," the deadly kamikaze fighters that sank 36 ships and damaged 368 more during the three-month battle.

On June 16, Pat Flynn arrived at Kadena Airfield and reported to Major J. Frank Cole, the VMF-312 Commanding Officer who had replaced Major Richard M. Day after Day was killed in action on May 14. During the first two months of the campaign, VMF-312 — which displayed black-and-white checkered markings on its rudders and cowlings — racked up an impressive record of aerial kills. On May 25 alone, "The Flying Checkerboards" downed 16 Japanese aircraft. On June 10, they became the first land-based fighter squadron to attack the Japanese mainland, where the pilots of 312 focused much of their attention during the final months of the war.[19]

Kadena Airfield, in the words of World War II aviator Samuel Hynes, was "a sort of village" ruled by "a village life" all its own. Officers lived four or five to a tent at the top of a rise overlooking the 1,500-foot runway. A dirt road moved up from the runway, passing through the enlisted men's tents on its way to Officer Country. Kadena offered the semblance of normal base life: the quartermaster's clothing store; officers' and enlisted men's mess halls; a mail room in the Operations office; a Red Cross tent that provided tobacco, writing paper, and chocolate; and a primitive open-air movie theater complete with cartridge cases for seats. Hynes remembers Kadena as "an odd community — a village with no women or children, in which only one business was conducted — but it had a wholeness, and it felt familiar and comfortable and not, like the rest of the island, exotic and foreign."[20]

Yet, for all its amenities, Kadena remained a dangerous place. New

Lieutenant Pat Flynn on Okinawa, summer 1945.

arrivals found themselves digging foxholes, because the still-active Japanese air force routinely harassed American forces — sometimes during movie showings, according to Hynes. Air raids increased as the Japanese position on Okinawa weakened in the month of June. Less than a week after Flynn's arrival, the enemy launched its last organized air attack of the Okinawa campaign, with American positions and ships experiencing 30 air raids on June 22nd alone. Vice Admiral Harry W. Hill, Commander of Task Force 58, recognized the importance of Marine combat air patrol (CAP) missions on June 21-22 in defending the fleet from kamikaze attacks.[21] The Marine CAP fighters were charged with intercepting kamikazes before they came near their American targets. Radar picket ships — those ships (usually destroyers) that were strategically situated around the fleet's perimeter — identified incoming enemy planes and vectored CAP fighters to them.[22] Flynn flew his fourth Okinawa CAP on June

21, a nearly four-hour mission in which several "bogies" were sited in his patrol area. In the days that followed, he patrolled areas frequented by enemy aircraft, and on June 26, he engaged and chased a Japanese fighter, probably a Mitsubishi Zero, a Nakajima Frank, or a Mitsubishi Jack, until, Flynn noted in his flight log book, the plane was "lost in [the] clouds."

Between missions, Flynn accompanied Marine Infantry units on their mopping-up patrols. In a letter to his mother on June 18, 1945, he described the dangers of combat:

> Got the day off so went up to the front lines and went out hunting with a Marine patrol (Infantry). We found several snipers in fields and caves. One Marine got killed. We killed all we found. One Jap surrendered but when he got close tried to heave a grenade. Before he hit the deck he had 6-.45 cal. holes in him. Just can't trust those people.
>
> It's a lot of fun in a gruesome sort of way. But it was quite an experience. I've got a lot of respect for those kids in the Infantry. It isn't the cleanest way to fight a war, and plenty rugged.

In later years, Flynn retained vivid memories of bloated, maggot-infested Japanese corpses burned black by flame-throwers or napalm, the odor of flesh rotting in the tropical heat, the sounds of thousands of buzzing flies. After witnessing Marines rummaging through enemy clothing, Flynn pulled some objects from a corpse's pockets, discovering a family portrait of the dead soldier, his wife, and his young child. Flynn remained non-judgmental about the occasional explosive behavior of Marine infantrymen, including the most brutal behavior he had witnessed in World War II, Korea, or Vietnam: the bayoneting of an Okinawan woman by a battle-hardened Marine Corps Sergeant who, as Flynn said in later years, "enjoyed" the act.

Flynn's travels with the Infantry earned him some spoils of war, including several Japanese swords and a Nambu Type 96, 6.5-mm light machine gun, with a 30-round ammunition clip. After the war, Flynn fired the 20-pound weapon while on leave at Dog Ear Lake in South Dakota, a demonstration that earned him a stiff warning from the Tripp County Sheriff's Department.

In late June 1945, Flynn and his fellow VMF-312 pilots began flying strikes against mainland Japan. The plan for the amphibious invasion of Japan, code-named OLYMPIC, had been presented to Pacific Commanders in May, and on June 22, the day that Lieutenant General Mitsuru Ushijima committed *sepaku* — the Japanese ritual suicide — in a cave overlooking the ocean, American planners turned to organizing the assault. The Joint Chiefs of Staff established November 1 as D-day for the invasion of Kyushu. OLYMPIC strategists anticipated ferocious enemy opposition in a manner consistent with the strategy employed by Ushijima on Okinawa — the abandonment of the beaches to the invaders but a suicidal defense of the interior. Thus, to beat down Japanese resistance, an enormous American invasion force was being assembled. Over 436,000 troops would land in the first stage of the assault, followed closely by another 357,000. With the addition of 22,000 air-support personnel, the total number of American fighting men in OLYMPIC would exceed 800,000, dwarfing the 150,000 soldiers involved in the Normandy invasion.[23]

In an effort to weaken Japan's defenses, carrier- and land-based aircraft, including B-29 Superfortress bombers flown from the Mariana Islands, began attacking the small islands of the Okinawa *Gunto* — as the group of islands in the Ryukyu chain were called — and the main Japanese islands of Kyushu, Shikoku, and Honshu. Marine F4U pilots from Okinawa's airfields, now filled to overflowing with an assortment of military aircraft, attacked both Japanese coastal and inland targets.[24] Samuel Hynes' account of attacks on Mayako, Ishigaki, Kikai Shima, and other Japanese islands provides a glimpse of the combat conditions Flynn faced in the summer of 1945. The strikes against Japanese islands were characterized by large flotillas of planes whose pilots spent the majority of their mission over open water. Hynes wrote:

> And then the island appears ahead, the planes slide into attack formation, the high-speed descent begins, the first plane peels off, and you really see the island for the first time, in your bombsight . . . and little clouds of AA bursts hang in the air as you dive past. . . .[25]

Pat Flynn, in the field with Marine infantrymen on Okinawa, June 1945.

Flynn spent long hours in the air during June 1945, a month in which VMF-312 flew a squadron record 3,409 hours. On June 23 and 28, he flew with strike forces that attacked enemy airbases and shore installations on Ishigaki Island and Kikai Shima. Flynn also logged additional CAP hours and flew his share of "barrier patrol," protecting radar picket boats and other ships against kamikaze attacks. In recognition of his 20th combat mission and his performance during airstrikes and CAP missions, Flynn was awarded the Distinguished Flying Cross and his first of three Air Medals earned in World War II.[26]

Yet for Flynn, the events of July 1 and 2 proved the most memorable — and terrifying — of the war. On July 1, Flynn took off in a ten-plane patrol charged with CAP duty over southern Kyushu. An hour and 15 minutes into the mission, he aligned his plane for a strafing run against a Japanese ship. As he dove, his F4U was struck and its engine severely damaged by antiaircraft fire. He tried to hold his plane at 6,000 feet on his way back to Okinawa, but discovered that he was losing oil. His engine began laboring and then made, in Flynn's words, "a loud clanking noise." Suddenly, the plane caught fire. Flynn transmitted a distress signal, trimmed up the plane, stepped out of the cockpit (cutting his mouth in the process), and jumped, "falling free for some distance before pulling the rip-cord." Flynn's burning plane exploded as it slammed into the East China Sea.[27]

Flynn suffered his own impact trauma, for just before he hit the water, a strong wind gust caught his chute. He was dragged through choppy four-foot waves for about 100 yards, his parachute harness cutting into his hips, groin, and shoulders. With his "Mae West" inflatable life jacket keeping him afloat, Flynn wrestled from his harness, deployed evergreen dye into the water to mark his position for search and rescue aircraft, inflated and struggled into his portable life raft, and gathered his chute. Sick from swallowing mouthfuls of sea water, he took a big drink from his canteen, only to discover that the vessel's loose cap had allowed sea water and dye-marker fluid to mix with the fresh water. In Flynn's words, he went from sick to "very sick almost immediately."[28]

As Flynn fought nausea in his bobbing raft, he witnessed another member of his squadron, First Lieutenant Howard H. Heylinger, ditch his damaged Corsair only 75 yards away. Rigging his parachute into a makeshift sail, Flynn maneuvered his raft over to Heylinger's, where the two men were discussing their options when a Dumbo seaplane appeared overhead.

No rescue materialized, for the Dumbo pilot apparently determined that the water was too rough for a landing and/or takeoff (a determination that Flynn later questioned in his after-rescue statement). Before returning to its base, the Dumbo crew dropped a two-man raft with oars, water, and emergency rations.[29]

By nightfall, Flynn and Heylinger were floating in the East China Sea some 20 miles from Kyushu. They tied together the three rafts and situated themselves in the two-man raft, securing a parachute at the back of the raft to act as an anchor and prevent them from drifting toward nearby Tanega Shima, an island that they feared was occupied by enemy troops. However, the chute did not prevent their movement toward the island. Pulled along in what Flynn described as "a very strong drift," the two were dragged nearly eight miles from their original location.[30] Tired, hungry, and thirsty, Flynn and Heylinger huddled together to fight the night cold. "We tried to sleep," Heylinger recalled, "but we were too cold and wet. Everytime [sic] a wave splashed over us we had to bail out the raft to keep from sinking. I guess we only had about 15 minutes sleep together."[31]

At first light, the two Americans found themselves within a few hundred yards of the beach of Tanega Shima, where Flynn's worst fears were realized. The island was occupied by Japanese troops, whose huts and outdoor breakfast fires were clearly visible from the raft. For Flynn, surrender was not an option. Horror stories of the enemy's treatment of Allied POWs abounded in aviation circles. Stanley Weintraub writes that "[t]o be downed alive was a harrowing experience, as it was known that the Japanese were brutal, even sadistic, captors."[32] Staying as low as possible, the undetected Marines began rowing. They paddled for six hours, eventually drawing within a mile of small Mage Island at about noon. Flynn noted that "[t]he water was considerably rougher and choppier than it had been on the previous day," an observation that, considering the Dumbo pilot's behavior on the day of the crash, must have eroded Flynn's morale. But within minutes, he and Heylinger spotted a Dumbo in the distance, lazily circling the area around Mage Island. Flynn fired two red flares, but neither was spotted by the pilot, who altered his course and headed out to sea. An hour later, the plane reappeared and Flynn fired the final flare. The pilot appeared to have missed the signal, but then suddenly turned in their direction. The Dumbo crew flew over their heads, dropped dye to mark their location, circled back, and landed near the rafts.[33]

But the rescue nearly ended in tragedy. As the Dumbo idled on the rough ocean, heavy waves drove Flynn and Heylinger's rafts against the plane's fuselage. Heylinger was thrown into the water, while Flynn, after being momentarily trapped between the raft and plane, found himself underneath the plane. Underwater, he kicked free of the raft and swam upside down until surfacing ten feet behind the plane, where he clung to the torn raft. Heylinger was even luckier. After being thrown, he swam to the opposite side of the plane, where a wave lifted him toward a whirling propeller that missed him by an arm's length. Both men kicked clear of the plane, which circled and returned with its engines shut off to prevent another near miss. Flynn and Heylinger struggled aboard. They had been in the raft for 23 hours.[34]

On the Dumbo, the rescued aviators drank five glasses of water each and were treated to mugs of black coffee and slices of apple pie. After landing at the seaplane's base, Flynn and Heylinger cleaned up, were fitted with clothes, and, later that evening, were transported back to Okinawa where they were reunited with their fellow VMF-312 aviators. On July 3, Flynn underwent a physical, and on July 4 he learned that he had been awarded the Purple Heart for the hip injuries he had suffered during his bailout and water landing.[35] In an undated letter to his mother, he shared his relief at surviving the ordeal. "My getting shot down over Japan and spending 23 hours in a raft close enough to damn near see the whites of their eyes has made a better Christian of me."

After the war, Flynn learned how fortunate he had been to avoid capture by the Japanese on Tanega Shima. On the same day that he had parachuted from his burning Corsair, another VMF-312 aviator, First Lieutenant Samuel S. Smith, bailed out when his engine failed. On July 2, Smith was captured by the Japanese on Takana Shima in the Ryukyu Islands and held for four days in a coffin-sized cell in a hillside cave. His captors stripped him and handcuffed him so tightly that his thumbs remained numb for weeks. During his two months in captivity, Smith was transferred to four different prison camps, eventually arriving at Camp Omori near Tokyo where he endured physical tortures. He underwent beatings with "fists, sticks or anything handy," including a steel lock. Smith survived the beatings and the near-starvation diet and was repatriated on September 6, 1945.[36]

Though Flynn's ordeal was in no way comparable to Smith's, Flynn was kept out of the air for nine days. He flew again on July 11, patrolling and conducting airstrikes against Japanese shipping and mainland cities, and on July 15, he joined a three-squadron, 32-plane joint strike against Kushira Airfield on Kyushu. Armed with 500-pound bombs and MK 149 rockets, the Marine pilots damaged antiaircraft positions, barracks, warehouses, antenna towers, powerhouses, water tanks, and Kushira's runway.[37] Enemy ground-to-air fire remained fierce, Flynn noting in a letter to his mother on July 24, 1945, that "my buddies are getting the hell shot out of them over Japan. . . . I saw one of the planes, a fellow I roomed with on Eniwetok, explode from a direct hit from a. a. right in front of me last week." Another VMF-312 pilot "got a hole in his wing big enough to drop a barrel through."

On August 8, two days after the atomic-bombing of Hiroshima and one day before the attack on Nagasaki, Flynn — now flying from 312's new base at Awase Airfield — flew in a 19-plane rocket strike against targets on Kyushu. Diving at 40-degree to 50-degree angles from 10,000 feet, 312's pilots hit two airfields and other targets in the town of Kawashi. Flynn again chased an enemy fighter, but, as was the case with his first sighting, lost the plane in heavy clouds.[38]

For VMF-312 and the other F4U squadrons based on Okinawa, World War II ended on August 12, 1945, three days after the attack on Nagasaki, when Marine Air combat missions ceased. On that day, every available plane on the island took off and rose into a giant V formation that passed over the fleet. In his flight log, Flynn recorded the event as a "Photo Hop for News Reel Pictures." That night, the skies over Okinawa were lit in a display of antiaircraft and machine-gun tracer rounds, as Flynn and his battle-tested comrades celebrated the war's end by drinking and reveling deep into the night.[39]

On August 14, upon receiving word of Japan's formal suspension of all military activities against the Allies, President Harry S. Truman ordered a cessation of American offensive operations in the Pacific. VMF-312 continued its patrol duties, fulfilling orders that Marines remain on guard against the possibility of enemy "treachery."[40] The author of Marine Air Group (MAG)-33's September report observed:

The tension of a hard-fought war still lingered among the

personnel, but it gradually died down as the days brought us closer to the final surrender of Japan aboard the USS *Missouri*, one of the United States' greatest Battleships. It was during this period that we finally became conscious, both physically and spiritually, of the fact that the greatest War in all History was over.[41]

For Flynn and the men of VMF-312, postwar Okinawa provided two final — and deadly — surprises. In the early morning hours of September 16, MAG-33 squadron Commanders learned of an approaching typhoon. At noon, the Commander of Awase Airfield, at the behest of the aerological officer, declared a Storm Condition I and ordered all personnel to prepare for the worst. Fortunately, the eye of the storm passed 20 miles east of Awase, though airfield instruments reported wind gusts of 100 mph.[42]

The typhoon of October 8-10, however, struck Awase head-on. Heavy rains on the 8th and 9th drenched the base. At 3:00 p.m. on the 9th, VMF-312 personnel left their tents and took shelter in Quonset huts. By 3:30, winds had reached 112 knots and visibility was reduced to a few yards. Though secured to the runway, planes were lifted off the ground. Tents were ripped from their stakes, corrugated tin was stripped from Quonsets, and plywood floors were peeled off their foundations. The storm rocked Awase for the remainder of the day, and it would be the following evening before conditions reached anything resembling normal.[43]

The storm wrought terrible destruction, damaging 44 of MAG-33's aircraft, 18 Quonset huts, and 3 mess halls. Some 162 tents were damaged, destroyed, or missing; 80 percent of the Group's service and engineering shops were destroyed, as was a radio-radar tower. Supplies were water-soaked, generators and power lines damaged, and the entire MAG-33 communication system disrupted for days.[44] Samuel Hynes recalled that after the storm,

> [*Okinawa*] looked like a battlefield, [*yet the*] violence of nature was something amiable compared to the violence of war, even though ten men had died in the storm. To survive a war, and then two typhoons — there was a kind of immortality in that.[45]

Several weeks before the second typhoon struck Okinawa, Flynn had tested his immortality, nearly killing himself in the process. On September

21, Flynn joined 15 other Marine pilots in a demonstration for liberated Americans from the Philippine and Japanese prisoner-of-war camps. "The Colonel who led us told us to give them the 'works,'" he wrote his mother on September 22, 1945. Flynn took the Colonel's order a bit too literally:

> Anyhow in one pass I got down a few feet above the ground over their quarters, didn't pull up in time and hit the flag pole in the center of their compound. I had the stick back in my guts but was too late. The pole ripped a hole in the belly of my Corsair about 4 ft. long. I got the plane back to the field O.K. But it will have to be junked. That was truly the most stupid thing I've ever done in my life. If I were 2 ft. lower when I hit it — blooey!!

Flynn took time in September and October to familiarize himself with the new Grumman F7F-3 Tigercat, a twin-engine plane that entered Pacific duty in the final months of the war. Flynn flew the large but fast fighter-bomber during several routine observation flights over southern Japan. "Fresh from the states," was how Flynn described the F7F to his mother in his September 22 letter. "I'm going to try to stay in the squadron as I'd sure like to fly that airplane." It would be another six years before pilot and plane reunited over the deadly night skies of North Korea.[46]

On November 17, 1945 — the first anniversary of his marriage to Frances Gassen — Second Lieutenant Flynn boarded the USS *Altamaha* and began a month-long voyage to the United States that included stops at Midway Island and Pearl Harbor. On December 16, he disembarked at San Diego, where, after more than ten months of separation, he was reunited with his wife.

Pat Flynn had experienced his first ordeals of mortal combat, but far greater dangers lay ahead.

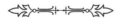

Chapter 3

Flying Nightmares

Flak, cables, and hazardous terrain combined to make these night missions some of the most difficult operations of the war.

John R. Bruning
Crimson Sky: The Air Battle for Korea[1]

IN 1949, First Lieutenant Flynn, his wife Frances, and their infant son Mark moved into a rural housing project near Pensacola Naval Air Station, where Flynn began a two-year assignment as an instructor for Naval Air Training Command (NATC). The 27-year-old aviator had spent the previous four years adjusting to family life and the demands of a Marine Corps career. After returning from Okinawa, he served briefly at Miramar Air Station before joining other vets at the three-month Marine Air-Infantry School at Quantico.[2] He underwent two months flight training at Corpus Christi, Texas, followed by an assignment to Cherry Point, North Carolina, where he flew F4Us and developed a reputation as a hardnosed football player, earning All-Navy honors as an offensive and defensive end in 1946.³

While at the 11,300-acre Pensacola Air Station, Flynn spent most of his time at Corry Field, training aviation cadets in instrument usage, aerobatics, and night flying in a two-seat SNJ. On average, Flynn flew between two and four hops a day. In a November 23, 1949, letter to his mother, he described the work as "adventurous" and superior to any "desk job." Lunch "on the job," however, demanded special skills, and Flynn found it "difficult swallowing a dry sandwich during an inverted stall." On a more serious note, he shared with his mother his concerns about the inter-service rivalries affecting the military. The creation of a separate U.S. Air Force in 1947 sparked disputes between the Air Force and Navy over air missions, aircraft technology, and control of the nation's nuclear strategy. Budgetary constraints resulted in airbase closings, and questions about the role of the Navy and Marine Corps in an atomic era created bad blood between those branches and the Army and Air Force. Army opposition to a separate amphibious force shrunk the Marine Corps to 74,000 men, a reduction applauded by President Harry S. Truman, who voiced his desire to keep the Corps as "the Navy's police force." Though worried that Marine Corps force reductions might affect his future, Flynn left his mother with one piece of reassuring news: he was hanging up his football cleats for good, his two seasons with the Pensacola Goslings resulting in career-ending knee and shoulder injuries.⁴

Instructor duty was never routine, though some students proved more memorable than others. In May 1951, for instance, Flynn flew with broadcast pioneer and Naval Reservist Arthur Godfrey. A lifelong champion of American aviation and an experienced pilot in his own right, Godfrey arrived at Pensacola determined to win his Navy wings. He eventually met the requirements for becoming a naval aviator, though his flight training was significant for another reason: while at Pensacola, the radio and TV personality discovered singer Julius La Rosa, a young sailor on the USS *Wright* who performed regularly at the Pensacola Officers and Enlisted Men's clubs.⁵ Before he departed Florida, Godfrey dined with Flynn, his wife, and several other couples at the Officers Club.

When not assigned weekend shore patrol, Flynn loaded Frances and Mark into the family's red Pontiac convertible and took them to Friday-night showings at the local drive-in theater. On Saturdays, he rose between 3:00 and 4:00 a.m., loaded his spear gun and fishing and diving gear into

Pat Flynn at Marine Corps Air Station (MCAS) Cherry Point, North Carolina, 1947 or 1948.

Pat and Frances Flynn after a football game at Marine Corps Air Station Cherry Point, North Carolina, 1946.

the car, and drove to the Pensacola marina. Steering a rental boat into Pensacola Bay or the Gulf of Mexico, Flynn would fish for redfish, black snapper, grouper, drum, warsaw, flounder, ling, marlin, bonito, mackerel, and bluefish. Occasionally he trawled for scallops and shrimp. An accomplished diver, he snorkled with his homemade spear gun for grouper, bluefish, pompanos, or sea bass in the waters around McGree Jetties, Pickens Docks, Pickens Jetty, Caucus Shoal, Gulf Beach, Pensacola Beach, or Santa Rosa Island. When fishing was slow, Flynn strapped on a homemade aqualung that he and Lieutenant John Vernon "J.V." Hanes had designed during their tour at Cherry Point. The Gulf of Mexico's deep-water port since the era of Spanish colonization, Pensacola was the final resting place for sunken galleons and British sloops. With oxygen on his back and weights around his waist, Flynn descended and examined the hulks that dotted the ocean floor, evidence of the rich colonial and maritime history of the Pensacola coast. Considering that scuba diving was in its infancy (Jacques-Yves Cousteau designed his first aqualung in 1943) and Flynn was diving in waters populated by sharks and 85-pound barracuda, it is little wonder that Frances spent her Saturdays anxiously pondering her husband's whereabouts.[6]

Frances (l) and Pat Flynn (second from l), dining with radio-television pioneer Arthur Godfrey (fourth from r), Pensacola Naval Air Station, Florida, September 1950.

Pat Flynn as a flight instructor at the Pensacola Naval Air Station, Florida, 1950.

Flynn shared his fishing stories with sailors, Marines, and the local citizenry. He wrote weekly columns and produced fishing guides and maps for *Gosport*, the base newspaper. His articles offered advice for novices or experienced anglers and promoted diving around Pensacola, an area renowned for its variety of saltwater fish. The *Gosport* editors lamented Flynn's transfer to California in 1951, noting that he had "proven to be an invaluable aid to fishing enthusiasts and will be sorely missed."[7]

On Sundays, the Flynns attended mass at a nearby parish, returned home for a large brunch, and gathered in the living room for afternoon relaxation. Televisions were becoming standard equipment in many American homes, but the Flynns had not purchased a set. Their Sunday pastime consisted of reading the newspaper and listening to popular radio shows like "The Shadow," "The Lone Ranger," "The Green Hornet," "Fibber McGee and Molly," and "One Man's Family."

But on Sunday, June 25, 1950, the Flynns, like millions of other Americans, listened intently to the breaking news from Korea, where troops of the Democratic People's Republic of Korea (DPRK, or North Korea) had invaded the Republic of Korea (ROK, South Korea). Pyongyang radio broadcast a declaration of war against South Korea, where ROK troops were in full retreat before the advancing force of the North Korean

Pat Flynn, the hunting-fishing editor of *Gosport* (the NAS Pensacola newspaper), with a Saturday catch, 1950.

People's Army (NKPA). Supported by Soviet-made T-34 tanks, Communist troops faced little resistance as they rolled toward Seoul.

In New York City, a hastily convened session of the United Nations Security Council (minus the Soviet Union, which was boycotting Council meetings in protest of Nationalist China's Council membership) condemned North Korean aggression and demanded an immediate withdrawal of NKPA units. U.N. Secretary General Trygve Lie denounced the invasion as "a violation of the principles of the [*U.N.*] Charter" and "a threat to international peace," and on June 27, the U.N. asked member nations to come to the aid of the government of South Korea.[8]

Five months earlier, Korea had possessed little strategic value to either the U.N. or the United States. In a January speech outlining American policy toward Asia, Secretary of State Dean Acheson, while conceding the need for economic assistance to South Korea, did not include the Korean peninsula within the U.S.'s Pacific defense perimeter.[9] Asia received scant attention from the State Department, where the "Europe First" strategy adopted by the Allies in World War II remained a priority following the Sovietization of Eastern Europe. Fearful of a Red Army invasion of Western Europe, Washington officials balked at using American forces in "secondary operations" in Korea or elsewhere. As the NKPA drove U.S. soldiers into a precarious defense perimeter around Pusan in southeastern Korea, many American officials maintained the belief that the North Korean attack was a Kremlin-inspired diversion to distract NATO forces prior to an all-out invasion of Western Europe.[10]

But by September, Truman and General Douglas MacArthur, the head of U.N. Command (UNC), had to act if they were going to save South Korea from Kim Il Sung's version of Stalinism. On September 15, U.S. Marines of the 1st and 5th Regiments of the 1st Marine Division executed a daring amphibious landing at the South Korean port of Inchon. Within days, the war's momentum swung in favor of U.N. forces. NKPA troops surrounding Lieutenant General Walton Walker's Eighth Army in the Pusan Perimeter broke and retreated toward the 38th Parallel. The U.N. advance matched the speed of the NKPA retreat. Seoul was liberated on September 28, Pyongyang was captured on October 19, and by late October, ROK troops had reached the Yalu River border between Manchuria and North Korea. Walker's Eighth Army, supported by U.S. Navy and Marine attack aircraft, Air Force fighters, and medium and heavy Air Force bombers, led the thrust above the "waist" of Korea. On Walker's right, Major General Edward Almond's X Corps, comprised of the 7th Infantry Division and the 1st Marine Division, fought across northeastern North Korea. In November, confidence ran high within the UNC staff, who saw no reason to doubt MacArthur's prediction that American boys would be "Home by Christmas."[11]

Hope for quick victory disappeared in late November, when the People's Republic of China (PRC) burst into the war. At the Battle of Chongchon, the Chinese People's Volunteer Forces (CPVF) struck the Eighth Army while six divisions of the CPVF 9th Army Group attacked U.S. Marine units at the Chosin (Changjin) Reservoir.[12] Outnumbered U.N. forces began falling back as hundreds of thousands of Chinese troops poured across the Yalu. As temperatures plunged toward zero, the 12,000 Marines of the 1st Marine Division, outnumbered five to one, found themselves surrounded. U.S. Marine, Navy, and Air Force pilots played a pivotal role in the Chosin breakout, strafing and napalming Chinese units as the Marine column marched and fought 78 miles to an evacuation point in the Hungnam coastal enclave. Flying day and night, Marine Air units displayed exceptional accuracy in their close air support, leading many Marine infantrymen to credit the Corps aviators with saving their lives. After the war, Chinese Generals ranked the men of the 1st Marine Division as the best American fighters in Korea.[13]

By mid-December, U.N. forces, though still retreating, were being chased by a dazed Chinese army. Nearly 31,000 Chinese were dead or missing. Poorly clad Chinese troops suffered from frostbite, and their food, ammunition, and medicine were in short supply. American artillery and air power undermined the morale of CPVF soldiers. A series of Chinese offensives proved costly, and ferocious U.N. counterattacks in the first four months of 1951 eventually drove the enemy back to the 38th Parallel.[14]

Although the UNC suffered a temporary disruption following Truman's relief of MacArthur in April 1951, a fifth Chinese offensive collapsed in late May on the outskirts of Seoul. Exhausted CPVF troops established a front near the 38th Parallel, where they faced a stiff U.N. coalition force that included troops from the United States, South Korea, Great Britain, France, Belgium, the Netherlands, Canada, Australia, New Zealand, South Africa, Greece, Turkey, the Philippines, and Thailand. Truce talks started in July 1951, but the stalemated front remained anything but peaceful; battles at Bloody and Heartbreak Ridges in the weeks preceding Flynn's arrival in South Korea were as fierce as any in the annals of modern warfare.[15]

As war raged in Korea, Pat Flynn fulfilled his NATC duties, providing instrument training to, among others, Ensign Harlo E. "Ed" Sterrett, who, while a member of VF-653, would later be shot down over North Korea and live side by side with Flynn in a POW camp on the Yalu River. In June 1951, Flynn was promoted to Captain and received orders to report to the Marine Corps Air Station in El Toro, California. He and his family enjoyed a leisurely vacation en route to MCAS El Toro, spending two weeks in South Dakota and some memorable days in Yellowstone Park.

At El Toro, Flynn was assigned temporary duty with VMF-235, an F4U-4 Corsair squadron. He practiced diversionary tactics, re-familiarized himself with bombing, strafing, and rocketing methods, and took several long-distance hops. According to his flight log, Flynn made 24 flights, none of which prepared him for the unforgiving terrain or severe climate of the Korean peninsula. In September, he received orders to join VMF(N)-513, an all-weather night squadron in South Korea. On October 17, Captain Flynn said goodbye to his pregnant wife and young son and, for the second time in six years, crossed the Pacific Ocean to enter combat.

Eight days later, Flynn arrived at VMF(N)-513's base at K-1 Airfield near Pusan, one of the four Korean airfields used by the squadron in 1951-1952. Flynn learned quickly that 513's mission was as dangerous as that of any squadron flying in Korea. Operating within the 1st Marine Air Wing (MAW) but under the coordination control of the Far East Air Force (FEAF), "The Flying Nightmares" performed night armed reconnaissance behind enemy lines, conducted night combat air patrol (NCAP), and shared air defense of the Inchon-Kimpo-Seoul area. The squadron's primary mission was the interdiction of Chinese supply routes during the hours of darkness, a task made difficult by hazardous terrain, enemy flak, and inclement weather. When Flynn joined 513, the Squadron was conducting over half of the night tactical work of the FEAF. Living by the motto "Be Sharp, Be Aggressive, Make It Pay," the 513 aviators fought intensely — and at a high cost. Between 1950 and 1953, 63 of their aircraft were lost, the majority to antiaircraft fire, pilot disorientation during low-level attacks, and operational accidents.[16]

VMF(N)-513 had arrived in Korea in October 1950 with radar-equipped F4U-5N Corsairs modified for cold-weather operations and

Eight Marines of VMF(N)-513, in front of an F7F-3N Tigercat in South Korea, 1952. Pat Flynn is on the right.

equipped with the latest-model APS radar systems (mounted in domes beneath the planes' starboard wings). The 513's seasoned fliers proved invaluable to the FEAF's Fifth Air Force, whose pilots were not prepared or equipped to conduct night close air support (NCAS) or nocturnal convoy attacks. The Corsair's APS-6 and APS-19 radar systems, on the other hand, detected approaching aircraft, "mapped" the terrain ahead for up to 80 miles, and picked up ground-based beacons, a feature that provided Marine aviators with azimuth (the angular distance along the horizon to an object) and distance readings for up to 100 miles.[17]

Occasionally VMF(N)-513 employed the MPQ-14 ground-controlled radar bombing system, which improved the efficiency of close air support during night hours or periods of poor visibility. During an MPQ-14 mission (Flynn completed several in 1952), the pilot flew at an unusually high altitude of 14,000 to 20,000 feet. His plane was directed over the target area by ground radar operators who picked the targets, locked onto the incoming attack plane, and computed the drop release point based on the plane's course, speed, and altitude. As the pilot maintained altitude and airspeed, the ground controller acquired control of the plane through its gyro control and released the bomb at the computed point. The MPQ-14 system made it possible for the pilot to strike enemy positions without making visual contact, a procedure that reduced the dangers of antiaircraft fire and pilot disorientation.[18]

Despite its value during poor weather, radar and bombing technology provided little assistance to aviators tasked with low-altitude night reconnaissance. In the early stages of the war, Communist Commanders learned that the U.N.'s overwhelming air superiority made the movement of troops and supplies during daylight too costly.[19] Thus, CPVF convoys moved at night, a tactic that determined 513's mission, described by the squadron Commanding Officer in October 1951:

> The primary mission of this squadron in Korea has been the interdiction of the enemy's road nets at night, i.e., to deny the enemy the use of his roads and other lines of communication at night. The basis of this squadron's success in this is found in the skill and aggressiveness of the individual pilot, who, working alone with or without the aid of a flare plane, must seek out and destroy the enemy's trucks, locomotives, rolling stock and other means of transportation.[20]

Captain Flynn was given several weeks to orient himself to the 513 mission. He checked out in the F4U-5N, and the squadron Operations department briefed him on flight procedures and radio and ground procedures. The Intelligence section briefed Flynn on tactical situations and furnished him with survival gear, maps, and navigation equipment. As a way of introducing Flynn to the night shift and the Korean terrain, Commanding Officer Lieutenant Colonel Robert R. Davis assigned Flynn several NCAP missions over Seoul.[21] Flynn familiarized himself with the ordnance used by 513 aviators, who, on a typical night strike, carried 800 rounds of 20mm high-explosive and incendiary explosive ammunition, a 110-gallon napalm tank, six 100-pound general-purpose bombs, and two flares to illuminate target areas. On occasion, rockets were employed, though the preferred weapon for destroying enemy armor was napalm, which incinerated everything in a 275-feet by 100-feet radius.[22] On his first attack mission in Korea, flown at 2300 hours on October 30, 1951, Flynn attacked a highway bridge at Sohung, expending his entire load of napalm, six bombs, and 800 rounds of ammunition, according to his flight log and the squadron's diary. Records show that he also conducted similar missions near Sohung and Kaedong during the first two weeks of November, and that on November 14, Flynn destroyed a barracks and some warehouses and damaged a bridge near Koksan.

Night interdiction posed unique dangers. "Korea was probably one of the most difficult countries for effective tactical aviation in the world," writes historian Warren Thompson. "Korea is 100% mountains, and it never ceases to amaze historians as to how the night fighters could be so effective under these circumstances, particularly when given the amount of anti-aircraft fire."[23] Mountain ranges of 5,000 to 9,000 feet harbored valleys and gorges that served as Communist communication and supply routes. In the dark and often in poor visibility, VMF(N)-513 pilots searched slopes and valleys around Sohung, Singosan, Koksan, Sariwon, and Sinmak for truck convoys, a tactic that demanded refined instrument skills and impeccable judgment. Pilot disorientation could, and on several occasions did, lead to the deaths of crews.[24]

Poor weather complicated missions. One ex-513 aviator, Norman Flinn, remembered the Korean winter of 1951-1952 as "one of the nastiest winters I have ever flown in."[25] Winter weather took its toll on ground crewmen, who worked outside without hangars to shield them from the elements. Maintenance crews received their only break in mid-February of

1952, when, according to the squadron historical diary, the 1st MAW grounded VMF(N)-513 during a two-day blizzard.

In Korea, Pat Flynn learned to coordinate night attacks with flare-dropping patrol planes that illuminated roadways for bombing and strafing runs. Although C-47 Skytrains served as 513's flare-droppers until June 1951, during Flynn's tour, Navy PB4Y-2 Privateers drew the majority of flare duty. During a typical night mission, the four-engine patrol bomber (call sign "Fat Face") rendezvoused with a night intruder (call sign "Flytrain") over a supply route. Pilots from the Privateer and the 513 plane searched for truck headlights, or, if the night was clear and moonlit, scanned North Korean roads (many were covered with white crushed rock) for trucks moving without headlights. An attack pilot flew at about 8,000 feet. If he sighted a target, he would either drop down to about 3,500 feet and release one of his parachute flares to mark the target for Fat Face, or direct Fat Face to release flares at a designated point. Upon hearing the sound of an approaching plane, Chinese drivers extinguished their lights and sought cover under trees or anything else that provided protection from napalm, bombs, rockets, and 20mm shells. Above the convoy, the parachute flares ignited between 2,500 and 3,500 feet, the burning magnesium emitting a greenish light that was concentrated downward by reflectors attached to the flares. If the zone proved target-rich, the PB4Y crew, maintaining an altitude of 6,000 to 7,000 feet, dropped additional flares — carried in a plywood crate in the bomb bay — down through the tunnel hatch. A Privateer carried as much as two tons of flares and could circle over a target area for hours, with the crew releasing flares at a rate of one every five seconds.[26]

When the target was sufficiently illuminated, Flytrain dropped beneath the flare canopy to about 1,500 feet and oriented himself to the terrain. If a pilot discovered a truck convoy beneath him, he would try to destroy or disable the first and last truck in the convoy in an attempt to bottle up the remaining vehicles. Calling on Fat Face for additional flares, Flytrain might make several sweeps of the road to destroy the remaining trucks. Strafing was initiated at 1,500 feet and broken off at minimum altitude. Pilots released 100-pound bombs at about 500 feet, larger bombs from 1,000 feet. Napalm tanks were released as low to the ground as possible, usually no more than a few hundred feet above the target. A truck exploding with an orange light signaled the destruction of an ammunition supply. Thick black smoke signaled a fuel-truck explosion. Troop convoys were, in the words of one night fighter, "brass-ring" targets. To avoid being bracketed by antiaircraft fire, a pilot varied his bombing-strafing maneuvers. After expending his ordnance and/or completing his reconnaissance mission, a new intruder would arrive, while Fat Face patrolled the target area for the new arrival and any intruders that followed.[27]

But working under flares posed serious problems, recalls night fighter H. E. Roland. A single flare provided insufficient illumination for banking and pulling up, and "[b]eyond the cone of light was a dark area that could contain a hill. Thus, there was always the uncertainty, that as we pulled up to turn back for another run, we would hit the ground." Roland believes that most of the aviators killed on night missions crashed in the darkness beyond the flare lights. And the flares themselves created their own dangers for the pilots, who occasionally pulled out of a dive to "find a flare coming through [the] windscreen."[28]

To further complicate their night attacks, 513 pilots contended with steel cables, strung by the Chinese above well-traveled roads, which could foul a plane's engine — or worse.[29]

On November 17, 1951, near Koksan, Pat Flynn attacked his first convoy. The squadron historical diary and Flynn's flight log show that in six passes beneath the flares he destroyed three trucks with bombs, napalm, and ammunition. He destroyed another truck on November 19, three more near Singosan on November 23, and two near Singosan on November 28. Flynn received additional night combat air patrol (NCAP) assignments over Seoul and responded to scramble orders from the Joint Air Command.

By late November, Captain Flynn had adapted fully to the 513 regimen. He slept through the morning hours and attended afternoon squadron meetings in the group briefing room of the MAG-12 Operations building. After each exhausting mission, Flynn went through a mandatory debriefing by MAG-12 Intelligence, who expected accuracy and thoroughness of reporting. Pilots reported all observations made in enemy territory, with vehicle sightings and antiaircraft emplacements receiving paramount attention. Pilots were expected to accurately identify the type of AA fire and the location and number of guns in question, information that was crucial to the maintenance of up-to-date flak maps.[30]

Although the Korean terrain posed special challenges to night fighters, the most dangerous aspect of any interdiction mission was ground-to-air fire. The Communists established flak traps, complete with Soviet-manufactured antiaircraft weaponry, along their supply routes. The Chinese antiaircraft force was comprised of three AA divisions, four AA regiments, 23 AA battalions, one searchlight regiment, and one radar company. Air watchers stationed on hills called out or radioed warnings of approaching American aircraft. Gunners positioned themselves on hills or mountaintops overlooking supply routes, and in some cases, actually fired down on approaching aircraft as they wove their way through a valley. As the war progressed and the Chinese detected patterns in intruder tactics, the odds of aircraft being struck or shot down over enemy territory steadily increased.[31]

Flynn encountered a variety of ground-to-air fire. Antiaircraft guns ranged in size from small machine guns to 90mm cannons. Truck-mounted 12.7mm and 23mm guns were probably the most common forms of air defense, though pilots of the 513 were exposed to 20mm and .30- and .50-caliber rounds. In addition to truck-mounted guns, the enemy placed stationary flak traps at heavily patrolled road intersections, where Communist officers attempted to trick U.S. pilots by stringing together lines of lights that, from 1,500 feet, appeared as a truck convoy. If the pilot took the bait, he found himself diving into an AA ambush, fired on by gun placements hidden under camouflage or within shadows of the surrounding hills.[32]

Enemy gunners found it difficult to track their targets at night. To compensate for their "blindness," they relied, according to the squadron historical diary, on pattern firing — wherein each gunner fired into an area in the hope that a pilot would fly into the hail of bullets, or on random firing — in which a gunner targeted parachute flares or bracketed an occasional sighted aircraft. H. E. Roland notes that night fighters identified the types of antiaircraft guns by observing their tracers. Explosive shells from heavy twin-mounted guns floated up as pairs of orange balls. Low-caliber shells formed red tracers. "If the tracers floated up, you had nothing to fear," writes Roland. "If they were streaks of fire snapping by the cockpit, they had your range. . . . Then they would cut loose with everything" and the pilot would find himself "'dazzled' with streams of tracers. . . . In that demonic glow the vertigo problem could become intense."[33]

Some of the heaviest antiaircraft opposition occurred in the fall of 1951, just as Flynn was familiarizing himself with 513's mission.[34] By then, according to CPVF General Nie Rongzhen, the Chinese army had upgraded its antiaircraft defenses.

> We had invented many ways to safeguard our transportation from being interrupted by air raids. Our major methods included . . . deploying more anti-aircraft artillery pieces to key positions, bridges, and transportation hubs. We organized the ground forces along the transportation lines to fire at low-flying enemy planes. . . .[35]

One of Pat Flynn's hairiest flying moments took place on the night of February 8, 1952. Flying out of K-18 Airfield near Kangnung in an F4U-5N, Flynn began patrolling over the main Communist supply route south of Singosan. After destroying one truck near the village of Sinauyangri, he was joined by a PB4Y-2. As the two planes proceeded south toward Sepori (approximately 20 miles north of the 38th Parallel), Flynn spotted a convoy of 12 to 15 trucks moving through a valley. Flynn ordered Fat Face to release his flares while he lined up his Corsair for a bombing-strafing run through what Marine officials later described as "the narrow confines of the valley." Receiving "intense" and continuous automatic weapons fire from 20mm, 37mm, and .50-caliber guns, Flynn lowered his flaps and reduced his airspeed to achieve better bombing accuracy. The "undaunted" pilot made seven sweeps and expended his entire ordnance while receiving flak and dodging a cable strung across the valley. By the time he finished his final pass, Flynn had destroyed seven trucks (three of which were fuel tankers) and a tank. Three other trucks received extensive damage. In recognition of his "alertness" and "superb airmanship" on that cold night of February 8, Flynn was awarded a Gold Star in lieu of his second Distinguished Flying Cross.[36]

VMF(N)-513 maintained a heavy flight schedule in the winter of 1952. From dusk to dawn, aviators from the 513 patrolled the four designated sectors of North Korean air space. Air crews spent up to two hours in a sector. "We were to relieve one another on station so there would be no gaps in coverage," recalls 513 pilot Ray Stewart. The "no-gap" policy proved effective; the movement of CPVF supplies was reduced to 25 percent of capacity when night fighters and flare planes patrolled a sector.[37]

Flynn's flight log shows that between January 8 and February 20, he flew 20 combat missions consisting of interdiction runs, MPQ-14 close air support, and night combat air patrols. On March 4, according to the squadron historical diary, he destroyed five trucks and damaged six more. A week later, while recovering from a strafing run on a convoy near Singosan, the left elevator on Flynn's Corsair was struck by a 37mm antiaircraft shell, the first of two direct hits Flynn received in March and April.

The dangers of night missions did not end for Flynn when he left the target sectors. Rain, snow, fog, and high winds complicated landings. Poor visibility, especially during the rainy season, prevented a pilot from locating a runway until he was on top of it. Under those circumstances, pilots relied on instruments and landed by means of Ground Controlled Approach (GCA). One 513 pilot recalled his anxiety when, halfway down his slope, he lost radio contact with the GCA controller. If the pilot was not relocated by the controller, he would add power, raise his flaps and his landing gear, and "climb out to a safe altitude, turn and navigate back to the homer, and start the whole ordeal all over again — with little confidence that they would do any better the next time." In the communication between pilot and controller on a poor night, "[t]he name of the game was trust," noted a night fighter. If a pilot detected uncertainty or hesitancy in a controller's voice, "even though he had good dope, we wouldn't believe him." A confident-sounding controller, on the other hand, relaxed the blinded pilot, and "he could drive us into a hillside with a happy smile on our faces."[38]

Upon landing, Flynn and his fellow night fighters debriefed, attended to administrative details, and retired to their quarters — which, at K-8 Airbase near Kunsan (Flynn's last assignment before being taken captive), was north of the runway and hangars and east of one of the rice paddies that encircled the base. The officers' quarters consisted of small woodframe buildings that housed half a dozen men. Each officer occupied a small room heated by a wood stove. Kunsan is located on the Yellow Sea, so Flynn went to sleep to the smell of the ocean, a pleasant reminder of his fishing trips in the Gulf of Mexico.[39]

"Anyone who had not lived the experience could never truly understand it," wrote a 513 veteran, describing the life of a night fighter. "A chance visitor to the squadron area at 1:00 p.m. would be discouraged to see a long line of seemingly idle aircraft and very few men anywhere, except within the shop buildings. Office spaces sat empty." High-ranking officers were probably disappointed at the uninspired welcoming ceremonies at a 513 base, where "drivers couldn't be found, airplanes arrived unmet on the squadron apron, and the officers were all snoring in peaceful bliss behind drawn shades in a Quonset hut."[40]

Crews and support personnel of the 513 inhabited a world of their own. Those on the day shift rarely encountered the night fighters, who "represented . . . noise during the outdoor movie or a rude awakening from a good sleep at 2:00 A. M." Night fighters rarely attended parties organized by "lousy day pukes" and proved persistent at getting supply requisitions filled at odd hours of the day. In the end, "Marine aircrews, pilots and R.O.s [*radar operators*] alike, were a decidedly mixed bag of eccentric characters and personalities. . . ."[41]

Whenever he received a short R&R (rest and recuperation), Captain Flynn hunted and fished, vacationed in Japan, or visited the St. Columban Mission Cathedral at Chunchon, where he formed a lifelong friendship with Columban Father Patrick Joseph "Paddy" Burke. Like Flynn, Burke loved bird hunting, so the two made several trips in pursuit of geese and pheasant. During one hunt, Burke shared the story of his friend and fellow Columban priest, Father James Maginn. When NKPA forces burst across the border on June 25, 1950, Maginn could have escaped but stayed behind with his parishioners at their small east-coast mission. On July 4, NKPA soldiers seized Maginn and over the next three days beat and tortured him. On the third day, he was executed.[42]

Frustrated at his inability to locate Maginn, but buoyed by a tip from an elderly Korean woman, Father Burke asked Pat Flynn to help. After locating what they believed to be the grave, the two men dug and discovered Father Maginn's remains. The missionary had been shot in the head and buried with massacred ROK troops. Maginn was reinterred at the cathedral in Chunchon. The story of Father Maginn's execution and the excavation of his remains changed Flynn, who later commented that he had been "in the presence of a martyr." The experience shaped his behavior in May 1952, when, with his own head on a chopping block, Flynn faced the prospect of his own martyrdom.[43]

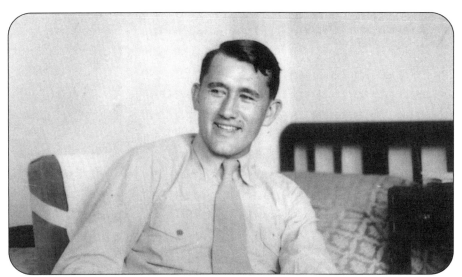
Pat Flynn, on R&R in Japan while stationed in Korea, 1951 or 1952.

In March 1952, Flynn began flying the F7F-3N Tigercat, a plane that he had been introduced to on Okinawa in 1945. The F7F was a large, twin-engine, heavily armed fighter-bomber characterized by its thin fuselage, cantilever shoulder-mounted wing, long nose, and tricycle landing gear. Remodeled as an all-weather nocturnal predator, the -3N model included the SCR-720 radar unit and a second seat for a radar operator-navigator. The plane's two Pratt & Whitney Wasp Model 2800 engines produced 4,200 horsepower, enabling the Tigercat to fly at 435 miles per hour with a climbing rate of 5,000 feet per minute. Its 4,000-pound ordnance capacity dwarfed that of the B-25 Mitchell bomber, and its 1,200-mile range exceeded all World War II-era Navy fighters. Four 20mm cannons mounted in its wing roots made the Tigercat a formidable fighter plane.[44]

The F7F fit Flynn's personality, as "Chief" had earned the reputation among his comrades as an aggressive pilot who, on occasion, recalls 513 aviator Norm Flinn, "carried things a bit too far." He did not hesitate to carry heavy ordnance loads or conduct bombing runs at tree-top level. Flinn and other Marine aviators described Pat Flynn as a "very good pilot" who "had excellent control." He had a way, recalls Navy aviator Harlo Sterrett, of putting younger pilots "at ease" with his openness, his kindness, his "fine sense of humor," and his stimulating conversation.[45]

Korea, 1952: Pat Flynn in the cockpit of an F7F-3(N) Tigercat.

The support of his Marine brethren and his deep religious faith carried Flynn through one of his worst days as a Marine Corps aviator.[46] Prior to a mission on the afternoon of April 22, 1952, Flynn took on his F7F, in addition to extra fuel and a full ordnance load, a crate of flares for delivery to an airbase north of K-8 (probably K-13 or K-16). Flynn asked the ground crew to stow and secure the flare crate in the fuselage behind the cockpit. A short time later, two Marines, Ray Bourgholtzer and Bud Dillberg, drove Flynn and his radar operator, 30-year-old Master Sergeant John Francis McAvoy of Key West, Florida, to their Tigercat. As Flynn was getting out of the jeep, Dillberg made the standing remark directed at departing aviators: "Don't crash and burn." Flynn and McAvoy strapped in, completed the takeoff check, taxied into position, and received clearance from the tower for takeoff. It was 1555 hours.

Flynn rose off the runway, retracted his landing gear, and climbed to about 200 feet. As he increased his airspeed to over 120 knots, the nose of the plane began to rise, despite pressure against the control stick and full nose-down elevator trim tab. Recognizing his problem, Flynn steered the plane to the left to clear the ground personnel working on the airfield. He throttled back, hoping to drop the steadily rising nose, now at 30 degrees above the horizon. Suddenly the control stick lodged at full back and the nose of the plane began pitching straight up, reaching about 60 degrees. (Later, Flynn and others concluded that the flare crate had broken loose and slid back toward the tail cone, rolling into the control stick linkage and jamming the plane's elevator controls.) Flynn threw both engines into full-throttle and ordered McAvoy to bail out. He quickly rolled back the canopy and unbuckled. The plane reached about 700 feet, stalled, and began flipping over. Flynn scrambled from the plane, at which point McAvoy was, in Flynn's words, about "half out of the rear cockpit" on the left side of the fuselage. As Flynn tumbled toward the ground, he clawed at the D-ring on his parachute. According to eyewitnesses, the chute, with two large holes in its canopy, opened low to the ground. Flynn swung once, and then landed hard on his back in a rice paddy. The last thing he remembered before hitting the ground was the individual rice stalks rushing at him "at an incredible speed." Flynn was found unconscious in the rice paddy, saved by his (crushed) helmet and the soft Korean mud. A second parachute was not sighted; McAvoy was unable to exit the cockpit and died in the crash.

Miraculously, Flynn suffered no broken bones. He spent a day in the hospital, treated for shock, a concussion, bruises, and a sore back. During the late afternoon on April 23, Flynn examined the area around the crash site, where he found an eight- to nine-inch-deep body impression in the rice paddy that had broken his harrowing fall.

Flynn's body healed quickly. Surprisingly, records show that he flew night interdiction on April 24, destroying six trucks and damaging another. But emotionally, Flynn had suffered a deep wound, the death of McAvoy weighing heavy on his mind and spirit. In a letter to his mother on April 29, 1952, Flynn described the "tragic accident" that took the life of John Francis McAvoy, "a wonderful man." K-8's Catholic chaplain "gave him absolution at the scene . . . minutes after the crash," and on April 28, with Flynn in attendance, celebrated a memorial mass for the dead Marine. Flynn thanked his family for their prayers and asked them to remember John McAvoy as they prayed. He briefly described his April 24 mission, and then abruptly ended the letter, concluding, "Too much thinking isn't good in this business."

But the thinking would continue. It would intensify in the depths of solitary confinement, where the deaths of not one, but two men gnawed at Pat Flynn.

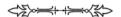

Captive

> I gave my back to those who beat me,
> my cheeks to those who plucked my beard;
> My face I did not shield
> from buffets and spitting.
>
> The Lord God is my help,
> therefore I am not disgraced;
> I have set my face like flint,
> knowing that I shall not be put to shame.
> Isaiah 50: 6-7

CAPTAIN FLYNN rose from his bed rested and contented. It was May 14, 1952, and after almost seven months of combat duty, his tour in Korea was nearing an end. He had flown only two combat missions during May, his first a flak-suppression mission that silenced two Chinese anti-aircraft batteries.[1] Flynn assumed that his assignment for May 14, his 62nd and last combat mission of the war, would be a routine sortie against a truck convoy. His buoyant attitude was evident to all those who encountered him. After spending several hours with Flynn that day, Captain Russell Stoneman observed that his squadron comrade "seemed to be in the best spirits and gave no sign or indication of being under any mental or physical strain."[2]

Early in the afternoon, Flynn received his assignment. He and his radar operator, Master Sergeant Norva H. Frank, were listed on the VMF(N)-513 flight schedule as "Mission 1206," with the call sign "Flytrain 06." They would conduct night intruder operations in an F7F-3(N) Tigercat against Communist supply routes Red 18, Red 19, and Red 20 in the area between Sinmak and Sariwon. Crews of the 513 were well acquainted with the target areas; Flynn himself had flown five interdiction missions in the Sinmak-Sariwon sector in the preceding weeks, as was recorded in his flight log and the squadron historical diary.

Flynn and Frank took off from Kunsan's K-8 airfield at 1645 hours. Because of field hazards at K-8, they flew to K-6 near Pyong Taek (about halfway between Kunsan and Seoul) to take on their ordnance. Upon landing, Flynn was greeted by Captain Stoneman, the officer in charge of the 513 detachment at K-6, who asked Flynn if he would consider taking a civilian observer on his mission. Flynn, who had on several occasions carried observers on night reconnaissance over North Korea, readily agreed to Stoneman's request.[3]

Stoneman's guest was Dr. Irving Shaknov, an analyst for the Navy's Operations Evaluation Group (OEG), the predecessor organization to the modern Center for Naval Analysis (CNA). Born to Jewish immigrant parents in Boston in 1922, Shaknov was, like Flynn, 29 years of age and a World War II veteran. In the early 1940s, Shaknov, considered one of Boston's "brilliant young scientists," had compiled an impressive academic record, earning a Bachelor's degree from the Massachusetts Institute of Technology (MIT) at age 19. He had enrolled in MIT's ROTC program and, upon graduation, was shipped to the European Theater as an ordnance officer with the U.S. Army's 9th Armored Division. After arriving in England, Lieutenant Shaknov requested a transfer to the 140th Tank Battalion. He participated in the Normandy invasion and the Battle of the Bulge, where he was captured near St. Vith, Belgium, by a German patrol. He escaped his captors and saved the life of a wounded American officer, a feat that earned him the Bronze Star. Following his discharge from the Army in March 1946, Shaknov enrolled in Columbia University, earning a Ph.D. in physics in 1951. He joined OEG, a group of scientists working under the direction of MIT's Division of Defense Laboratories on problems brought to them by the Office of the Chief of Naval Operations.[4]

In 1952, Shaknov and several OEG analysts traveled to South Korea to evaluate the effectiveness of U.S. interdiction of enemy convoys. After several observation flights in PB4Y-2 Privateers engaged in flare drops, Shaknov and his colleagues concluded that theories about the ineffectiveness of night interdiction were misleading. Far Eastern Air Force data that indicated a ten percent truck kill ratio did not, in the opinion of OEG, account for the low-altitude tactics employed by Marine night fighters, who, when locating a convoy under the flare ceiling, destroyed a high percentage of trucks with napalm and 20mm cannons. In contrast to the Marines, Air Force B-26 crews, who bombed from 5,000 to 6,000 feet, found it difficult to locate and destroy trucks. From his position in a Privateer, Shaknov decided that if convoy location methods were improved, destruction rates would climb for both Air Force and Marine squadrons.[5]

Determined to get a closer look at road interdiction, Shaknov had flown to K-6 on May 13 and, after a discussion with MAG-12 headquarters, secured a flight in an F7F-3N Tigercat. Meanwhile, H. H. Porter, an OEG analyst traveling with Shaknov, examined the record of VMF(N)-513 and grew concerned about the dangers of low-altitude night interdiction. Intelligence sources had reported heavy antiaircraft activity in the Sinmak and Sariwon complexes. But in the end, Porter, comfortable with the low rate of VMF(N)-513 losses over the preceding months and relieved that Shaknov would be flying with Captain Flynn, he supported Shaknov's decision. "The pilot," Porter later wrote, "was one of the best."[6]

At 1830 hours on May 14, Captain Stoneman introduced Flynn to Shaknov. Flynn learned that his passenger was from MIT, but little else about Shaknov's confidential mission was discussed. Stoneman and Flynn took the scientist to the flight line to brief him on his parachute, the rear cockpit of the F7F-3N, and emergency procedures. When Flynn and Shaknov felt satisfied with the flight check, they separated, agreeing to meet again at 2100 hours, one hour before takeoff. After informing Master Sergeant Frank that he had the night off, Flynn accompanied Captain Stoneman to the movie at the K-6 theater.[7]

At 2210 hours, Flynn and Shaknov took off in their Tigercat, bureau number 80597, fully loaded with napalm and 20mm cannon rounds. Visibility was three to five miles. As they crossed into North Korea, the two were greeted by small-arms fire made visible by tracer streaks that, as Flynn wrote in his 1968 unpublished essay, "A Red Rose for Valor," "criss-crossed far below, bounced up and faded. We were over the front lines on schedule, two hours before midnight, May 14, 1952."

Flynn was a seasoned veteran of night warfare and, though conscious of the dangers lurking below, allowed his thoughts to wander. He visualized the upcoming reunion in South Dakota with his grandfather, Joseph Gordon, the man who taught him the art of outdoor survival. Flynn later wrote in "A Red Rose for Valor" that he had envisioned greeting and laughing with his grandfather: "Behold your Grandson Long Elk, descendant of Chief Spotted Tail," he would say, adding, "Your prophecy was wrong — the crooked arrows of the Communists did not find me."

After charging the plane's guns and arming the napalm, Flynn conducted an intercom check with Shaknov, who insisted that the Marine refer to him by his nickname, "Spike." Flynn ribbed Shaknov about his duties, noting, as Flynn wrote in 1968, that it seemed like "a rough way" for a civilian scientist to make a living, but praised him for his courage in accompanying Flynn over enemy territory.

The squadron historical diary shows that 35 minutes into the flight, Flynn and Shaknov rendezvoused with "Flytrain 05," Captain L. W. Phillips and his radar operator, whose flak-suppression mission consisted of locating and destroying any antiaircraft positions firing on Flynn's plane. Close by was a Privateer, whose call sign was "Lightning Bug X-Ray" or "Fat Face," which would drop the parachute flares to illuminate the road for Flynn's sweeps. Together, Flytrain 05, Flytrain 06, and Fat Face were to destroy enemy trucks and AA sites on the road between Sariwon and Sinmak.

At 2250 hours, Fat Face identified a convoy moving near the city of Sinmak. Years later, Flynn retained vivid memories of the moment, as he wrote in "A Red Rose for Valor":

> "Tighten your seatbelt, Spike," I passed back, "we're going into the lion's den. Call out the flak and hang on!"
> Throttles full forward.
> The trees and shadowy features of the terrain slashed by below as we roared unto the color-blind stage; from utter darkness to the stark gray-white of the land beneath the avenue of parachute flares. I eased down to tree-top level and lined up on

> the road. The traffic was there — like main street at quitting time. I pressed the trigger.
> The 20 mm cannons hammered out high-explosive incendiary shells that sparkled alongside, across, and back through the trucks. I pulled up over a ridgeline as the red "meat balls" of anti-aircraft fire tracked in on us — and much too close.

With two trucks burning behind him, Flynn requested that Fat Face drop enough flares for one more pass over the convoy. Five flares lit up the night sky over Sinmak as Flynn, flying on a northwest to southeast course, maneuvered for a final strafing run. At approximately 200 feet above the deck, he lined up his plane with the road, completely unaware that the Chinese were manning a lethal flak trap along his descent path.

Just as Flynn began strafing, his plane, according to an airborne observer, was engulfed in a barrage of an estimated forty 20mm antiaircraft guns. As the shells splattered against the Tigercat's fuselage, the Chinese gunner of what Flynn believed to be a 90mm gun began firing. A shell struck the rear of the starboard engine nacelle — one of the streamlined cones that enclosed the F7F's engines and extended several feet behind the plane's wings. It set off a "blinding, wrenching explosion" that turned the engine into "a mass of orange-red flame," tore away the back of the wing from the nacelle to the wing root, and shattered the plane's canopy.

Dr. Shaknov was seriously, if not mortally, wounded by the blast, while Flynn, the victim of a broken right eardrum, experienced instant vertigo and nausea. As he fought to keep the crippled plane aloft, he transmitted the message "*I'm hit!*" followed by "*Bail out! No, stay with it!*" He began a steep climb toward 2,000 feet, jettisoned the canopy, unbuckled, jettisoned his ordnance, and called for a heading.[8]

About 45 seconds later, Shaknov, his voice weak and strained, attempted to communicate with Flynn. Realizing the severity of Shaknov's injuries, Flynn told his passenger to "wait" while he attempted to steer the burning plane toward an emergency landing south of enemy lines.[9]

Flynn described the next moments in "A Red Rose for Valor":

> Fuel shut-off to bad engine, propeller feather, trim, and full left rudder — which isn't enough. Reduced throttle helps. My napalm fire bombs, now impacting below, light up the night sky as we stagger across an onrushing ridge.

I fight the battered aircraft towards the south and safety. And then I see the white-hot glow of the magnesium fire. The wing is burning off.

Flynn continued to climb as the fire burned into the wing's main spar — the long, longitudinal metal support that carries the ribs of a wing. While he was talking to Shaknov, the plane underwent a complete electrical failure, preventing any further communication between the two. About ten seconds later, and approximately six minutes after being struck by antiaircraft fire, the starboard wing of Flynn's Tigercat fell off, spinning the plane upside down.[10]

The unstrapped Flynn dropped out of the cockpit at approximately 2,000 feet. He immediately opened his chute, and after about three seconds, came to the ground some 15 to 20 miles southeast of Sinmak and about ten miles east of the town of P'yongsan. Flynn heard his Tigercat explode on impact and realized that Shaknov had been unable to free himself. To this day, Dr. Irving Shaknov remains the only OEG/CNA analyst killed in combat, a statistic noted on a plaque near the conference room dedicated in his honor at the Center for Naval Analysis building in Alexandria, Virginia.[11]

Flynn was disoriented and terrified. He had landed awkwardly on a steep embankment, leaving him with broken bones in his left foot and a dislocated left shoulder that produced numbness in his hand. Worse still, he had the misfortune of rolling onto a road and in full view of a convoy of trucks filled with enemy soldiers. Headlights fell on Flynn as he wrestled out of his parachute harness, by which time the lead truck had closed to within 50 yards. He limped into the darkness, crawling up a hill between bushes and trees as he dodged small-arms fire.[12]

As Flynn evaded Chinese soldiers, a search by his VMF(N)-513 comrades was already underway. Captain Norm Flinn, Flynn's close friend and fishing partner at NAS Pensacola, was scheduled to follow Flytrain 06's interdiction mission along the Sariwon-Sinmak road. When he learned of Flynn's downing, Flinn took off immediately in his F4U-5N Corsair, dumped his ordnance on targets in the coastal city of Haeju, and sped toward what K-6 personnel designated as the approximate crash site. Flying at 500 to 3,000 feet in a systematic "square search pattern," Flinn spent nearly 90 minutes scouring a 40- to 50-mile radius around Sinmak. Focusing his attention on wooded areas that provided hiding places, Flinn identified only a few fires — nothing that indicated Pat Flynn's location or condition.

When Captain Flinn returned to K-6, MAG-12 launched four more F4Us to search the Sinmak area. From sunrise to sundown for the next two days, an intensive search for Flynn was conducted by the aviators of VMF(N)-513 and other Marine squadrons. Norm Flinn himself spent six of the next seven nights and eight of the next eleven days searching the Sinmak area for signs of his friend.[13]

Some 13 years later, in a letter to Flynn written on May 3, 1965, Norm Flinn described the frustrations faced by night search crews flying at low altitudes over the rugged Korean countryside:

> I never saw anything I thought significant to you. I am sure in my mind that I could never have found you in that country and under those circumstances unless you had found some way to signal me. It was so black on the surface, and required so much attention to avoiding hills, navigating, and staying within the desired area, that I now feel that nite search in a 150 kt min., single place, fixed wing A/C as my F4U held little chance for success. . . .

On the ground during the early morning hours of May 15, Flynn's chances for an evasion and helicopter rescue were evaporating. He had temporarily lost his pursuers, a feat that required him to sneak around a manned Chinese position atop a mountain ridge. Yet he felt himself being surrounded. To fight panic, Flynn began talking to himself and at one point offered a quick prayer, asking for his Grandpa Gordon to "conjure up another vision" that would show him the way out of the tightening trap. But a growing concentration of troops made it impossible for Flynn to get out of the area. "Wherever I went there were more enemy. I would get away from one group and run into another." At about 3:00 or 4:00 a.m., he came upon a large abandoned foxhole, or slit trench, near the top of a steep hill. He quickly cut and gathered some brush, crawled into the trench, and did his best to camouflage the opening. Exhausted, thirsty, and suffering from severe pain in his shoulder and foot, Flynn began the long wait for morning, when he could signal a search plane that would direct a rescue helicopter to his location.[14]

At approximately 7:30 a.m., Flynn heard the sound of approaching footsteps. Suddenly a Chinese soldier, fooled by the trench's camouflage, fell into the trench, landing on his feet directly behind the American. Flynn whirled around as the startled enemy soldier discharged his World War II-era Japanese rifle. The point-blank shot somehow missed Flynn, who tried to communicate his surrender while the soldier struggled to remove the jammed shell casing from his rifle. In the midst of this stand-off, a group of enemy soldiers, drawn to the sound of the rifle's report, surrounded the trench, their rifle muzzles staring down on the American's head. Flynn's eight-and-a-half-hour race for freedom had ended; his ordeal of captivity had begun.[15]

Flynn was dragged from the trench and knocked to the ground by young, bandoleer-belted Chinese soldiers who blindfolded the "air pirate" and tied his hands behind his back with wire (probably telephone wire). A Chinese officer carrying a holstered pistol and a briefcase-like bag approached Flynn, shoved him to the ground, and began kicking him down the steep hill. In his enthusiasm, the enemy officer lost his balance and tumbled for a short distance. He jumped up and directed his anger and embarrassment at Flynn, beating and kicking the pilot the rest of the way down the hill. The officer's violence toward Flynn was probably intensified by the satisfaction that he had captured a U.S. Marine night intruder. "Night fighters were the big enemy of the Chinese," recalls Russ Stoneman. "We were the ones who dropped the napalm. The bad stuff."[16]

At the bottom of the hill, a long rope was tied around Flynn's neck. Five soldiers began pulling their prize down an oxcart trail, the remainder of the Chinese squad scanning the skies for U.S. aircraft. On the first of what would be a two-day march north, Flynn felt the crunch of broken bones in his left foot, now swelled tightly in his boot. "If I only had a crutch," he thought to himself. His left shoulder "was a big dull ache," and his "hands were getting no circulation — the wire was too tight on my wrists." Two hours into the march, the column halted and Flynn's blindfold was temporarily removed. The Chinese officer took some papers from his briefcase and held them up to Flynn's eyes. Before him were copies of signed statements by two U.S. Air Force officers who had "confessed" to using biological weapons against the Chinese and North Koreans. The moment marked Flynn's first recognition that his captors would press him for a germ-warfare confession to be used as fabricated "evidence" in the Communist propaganda war against the United States.[17]

On the second day, the Chinese removed Flynn's blindfold. The officer now forced a faster pace, keeping his men and their prize near natural fortifications that provided protection from American planes. "The oxcart trail," Flynn recalled, "followed along rice [*paddy*] dikes in the valleys and skirted the terraced steppes of the low, rolling hills. Farmers paused and squinted as the dusty procession single-filed past." Ordered to remain completely silent, Flynn thought about his fateful decision to make the second pass over Sinmak. He cursed himself for his decision and wondered if he would live to see his infant daughter, who had been born just six weeks earlier.[18]

In the late afternoon, Flynn and his captors entered the outskirts of a village that had been recently attacked by American planes. The day was hot and the air motionless. Houses with mud walls and straw-thatched roofs blended with the colors of the surrounding hills. As the column proceeded into the village, Flynn's nostrils were greeted with what he described in 1968 as the smell of "burned straw, cordite, and recent death." His eyes fell on bomb craters, split bomb-casings, collapsed walls, and smoldering fires.

Flynn was ordered to halt before a large mud hut adorned with the flag of the People's Republic of China. Villagers gathered around him. A well-groomed Chinese officer emerged from the hut and approached Flynn, stopping directly in front of him. While glaring into Flynn's eyes, the officer received a short debriefing from the column Commander. He then began shouting at Flynn, and as the crowd of Korean villagers grew larger, spit in his face and slapped him hard across the mouth. The officer said something and backed away, and within seconds Flynn was being pelted with soft manure and rocks, a particularly well-aimed stone striking him in the ear and drawing blood. A hoe-wielding woman charged at Flynn but was restrained by some soldiers. An elderly man, on the other hand, was allowed to approach the American. As Flynn wrote in "A Red Rose for Valor," the Korean held up the lifeless body of an infant, with "the top of [*its*] head . . . blown off." The soldiers then dragged Flynn away from the frenzied crowd.

The next day, Flynn experienced the first of several terrifying moments he endured as a prisoner of war of the Chinese Communists. The ordeal began when the village Commander was informed of the rosary and Miraculous Medal (a religious sacramental honoring the Immaculate Conception) that Flynn carried in his flight suit. The Chinese officer decided to conduct a test of the American's faith, a test Flynn later discussed in three separate newspaper interviews in 1954 and 1966. Flynn was placed on public "trial" for the bombing of the Korean village and pronounced guilty by the Chinese Commander. At his sentence, Flynn was ordered to throw his rosary on the ground, trample it, and spit on it. Flynn refused, and continued to refuse when the order was repeated. The Commander barked an order to a subordinate, who produced a chopping block and a rusty ax. A soldier forced Flynn to kneel and pushed his head onto the block as the Commander repeated the order to desecrate the rosary. Flynn prepared himself for death:

> The first thing I thought of was that I was going to be a martyr. I thought of my family and how they needed me. But I knew if I gave in to the Reds, I'd be no good for my family or myself, and that I might lose my soul. This was it.[19]

But the ax did not fall, for the Chinese had no intention of executing a downed American flier who could prove valuable to the PRC's international propaganda campaign. Early the following morning, soldiers marched Flynn to an ox stable and tied him to a stanchion, where "thousands of flies" crawled over his face and body. He remained there the entire day, comforted momentarily when, seemingly from out of nowhere, a young Korean girl in a white dress appeared before him. She placed a fresh red rose at Flynn's feet, smiled at him, and walked away. The image of that moment, which Flynn believed to be a spiritual apparition, sustained him during the worst moments of his 16-month captivity. Years later, he was still struggling to understand the phenomenon, which he described in "A Red Rose for Valor."

On the fourth day after his capture, Flynn was transported north. Following night marches and truck rides, he arrived on May 20, 1952, at a POW camp that he believed to be located approximately 20 miles southeast of Pyongyang and about two miles from a large complex of Communist interrogation centers referred to by U.S. prisoners as "Pike's Peak." For the next two months, Flynn would undergo daily, intensive interrogations by Chinese air force officers determined to extract a confession that the American had perpetrated bacteriological warfare against NKPA and CPVF soldiers.[20]

China had accused the U.S. of germ warfare in 1951, but in the following year, with its military offensives having failed and truce talks in

Panmunjom at a standstill, it launched an all-out propaganda war to win international support for its bio-warfare claims. In late January 1952, just three and a half months before Flynn's downing, Chinese officials fabricated reports that U.S. fliers were dropping disease-laden ticks, fleas, mosquitoes, rats, spiders, crickets, shellfish, and chicken feathers on troops in North Korea. CPVF troops reported "milky mucus" falling from U.S. aircraft, and rumors spread among soldiers that the Americans were infecting Chinese units with smallpox, typhus, anthrax, cholera, typhoid, bacillary dysentery, and meningitis.[21]

Although enemy troops and Korean civilians were struck by typhus, smallpox, and other epidemics (the result of, among other factors, the movement of hundreds of thousands of unwashed, undernourished people across the Korean peninsula), no evidence exists that U.N. air forces engaged in biological warfare.[22] Nevertheless, in February 1952, PRC Chairman Mao Zedong, aching to win a victory of words against a foe he could not defeat on the battlefield, had authorized Premier Zhou Enlai to launch an aggressive, worldwide propaganda campaign charging the U.S. with germ warfare in North Korea. The Soviets helped coordinate the campaign, and North Korea and other Communist states joined the Chinese, who, by early March, were accusing the United States of "employing bacteriological weapons to slaughter the Chinese people." To support their charges, PRC officials reported that security forces inside China had collected paper bags containing fleas, spiders, and other insects dropped by American planes on the Chinese town of Fushun.[23]

On May 4, 1952, just 11 days before Flynn's capture, Radio Pyongyang had reported that two U.S. Air Force pilots, Lieutenant Kenneth Enoch and Lieutenant John Quinn, had confessed to dropping bacteriological weapons on Chinese targets. On May 16, a Peking newspaper, *People's China*, published Enoch's and Quinn's statements (shown to Flynn after his capture on May 15), in which the two Americans "admitted" their participation in germ warfare. In his "confession," Quinn described himself as "a tool of these [*American*] warmongers, made to drop germ bombs and do this awful crime against the people of Korea and the Chinese Volunteers. . . ." He praised the "patience" of his captors and shared his relief at getting "rid of this burden and to confess and repent. I have realized my terrible crime against the people."[24]

Other American confessions followed, earning Communist nations a propaganda coup that won them the sympathy of neutral states while placing U.N. forces on the defensive for the remainder of the war. No one would suffer the effects of the propaganda campaign more painfully than the 78 U.S. pilots accused of bacteriological crimes.[25] James Angus MacDonald emphasizes that from the release of Enoch and Quinn's statements

> until the end of hostilities captured aviators of all services were subjected to a degree of pressure and coercion previously unknown by prisoners of war. Prior to the turn of the year aviation and ground personnel received relatively the same treatment in Communist hands. After January, 1952, aviators were singled out for a special brand of treatment designed to wring bacteriological warfare confessions from them.[26]

Captain Flynn had been taken captive at the most inopportune moment, for his prewar training had been inadequate for Communist propaganda warfare. He and other captured aviators became subjects in sinister Chinese mental-torture experiments and political-indoctrination exercises designed to destroy POW resistance and turn U.S. pilots into propaganda puppets. The Korean War was a turning point in the treatment of POWs, writes Max Hastings, "the first major modern conflict in which a combatant made a systematic attempt to convert prisoners to his own ideology."[27]

At Pike's Peak, Flynn's interrogators went to work on their new prisoner. Each day between May 20 and June 25, when not isolated in solitary confinement, Flynn was questioned about his duties with VMF(N)-513 and indoctrinated to Marxist-Leninist principles. In his words, he "was interrogated immediately on germ warfare" and throughout this first phase of solitary, "germ warfare was the primary subject of interrogation."[28] To undermine Flynn's resistance to "brainwashing," the Chinese reduced his drinking water and limited his diet to one small meal per day, usually a bowl of boiled cabbage soup mixed with seaweed, soybeans, peanuts, and an occasional piece of fish or pork. On some nights he was moved to a 10- by 14-foot, unlighted, unventilated bunker occupied by several South Korean prisoners who spoke no English. It was the rainy season in Korea, and water seeped into the hole. The men breathed in the nauseating smells of sweat, urine, and feces. As the days passed, Flynn, unable to bathe or attend to personal hygiene, felt he was being reduced "to an animal state." In his deteriorating position the Chinese "began offering . . . various inducements to confess," including promises of improved living conditions and increased food rations. But Flynn rejected the Chinese offers and in turn experienced dramatic weight loss, from 200 to 125 pounds on his 6-foot, 2-inch frame.[29]

In his weakened condition, Flynn turned to prayer and repeated recitations of the rosary. After several weeks of captivity, he had concluded that, by themselves, patriotic values could not sustain his morale, military identity, and self-respect. He embraced religion as the rock of his resistance and clung to what he would later refer to as his most potent weapon against brainwashing — his faith in God. Flynn interpreted his plight as a mortal contest between Catholicism and Communism, with his opposition to an atheistic ideology precluding any collaboration with the enemy. To illustrate his stubbornness, Flynn later stated that he had "tried to convert them to religion — a method which didn't help my own cause too much."[30]

Flynn's cause was seriously tested by the torturous nature of solitary confinement, a condition described by a veteran of POW internment in Vietnam, U.S. Senator John McCain:

> It's an awful thing, solitary. It crushes your spirit and weakens your resistance more effectively than any form of mistreatment. Having no one else to rely on, to share confidences with, to seek counsel from, you begin to doubt your judgment and your courage. . . .[31]

To maintain his sanity in solitary, Flynn began the mental designing of a spear gun (that he would eventually construct in the spring of 1954), planned an escape, solved mathematical problems in his head, and imagined himself on hunting, fishing, and skin-diving trips. He avoided thinking about his family, though his interrogators constantly questioned him about his feelings toward his wife and children. The dreary monsoon weather dejected him, though "one pretty good flood" provided some dramatic diversion when the front of his solitary bunker caved in and he had to be dug out by several Chinese soldiers.[32]

Above and opposite: Pat Flynn's pencil drawings of his recollections of solitary confinement at (above) Pike's Peak Interrogation Center, summer 1952, and later at POW Camp 3 (opposite), summer 1953.

"NOT ALONE
(SUBJECT LIGHT SHINING DOWN THRU ROOF

During his 16-month captivity, Pat Flynn faced three Chinese interrogators, "Little Boy," "Quasimodo," and "Laughing Boy," who, in the words of a journalist writing about Flynn's ordeal, sought "to peel [*Flynn's*] mind like an orange and put it back together in their own design."[33] The interrogators were intelligent and crafty. After the war, one ex-POW described them as "well-educated — college graduates not only of their country but of our own country — people who had masters' degrees in economics and sociology."[34] Others were aeronautical engineers, communication specialists, and political scientists.[35]

Despite announcing their intention to abide by the Geneva Convention of 1949 and its articles on the humane treatment of prisoners of war, the Communists in actuality rejected international law and historical precedents.[36] "The Geneva Convention meant nothing to them," recalls William H. Funchess, an Army Lieutenant held prisoner in POW Camp 2 from September 1951 to September 1953.

> We constantly reminded them of it, but they would say "We are not signatories to the Geneva Convention. We do not have to abide by any of its provisions. We have our own policy, the lenient policy. We follow the lenient policy. You cooperate, you live."[37]

According to an authority on the experiences of Marine Corps POWs in the Korean War, the Chinese "lenient policy" was intended to control and manipulate U.N. captives. "Simply stated," writes James Angus MacDonald, "this meant calculated leniency in return for cooperation, harassment in return for neutrality, and brutality in return for resistance."[38]

Flynn's first interrogator at Pike's Peak proved especially brutal. Fluent in English, the diminutive, 100-pound Little Boy kept Flynn on short rations and confined him during daylight hours to a small, cave-like bunker that, over time, filled with the stench of human waste. There was no particular pattern to the interrogation sessions, so Flynn never knew when Little Boy would call for him or for how long he would grill him. On some occasions, he would stay only 10 to 15 minutes, while other interrogations lasted for hours. Little Boy often required Flynn to stand at attention, and, on one occasion, forced him to stand at attention on and off over a sleepless 24-hour period. If not standing at attention, Little Boy ordered Flynn to sit at attention, his legs crossed in front of him, his back straight and his hands crossed behind his back. When his posture failed, the Chinese guards struck Flynn with their rifles. They were eager to do the Americans harm, partly because they had been exposed to recurring propaganda statements that American troops had raped Asian women. But, Flynn recalled, "They didn't hit you very much, just a few times and only hard enough to loosen a tooth or two and draw a little blood in your mouth." To extract revenge, as well as amuse himself, Flynn began "cussing out" the guards in English. He discovered that "if you kept a smile on your face, you could call them anything you wished and they took it as a compliment."[39]

On several occasions, Flynn was kept awake for long stretches, forced to sit at attention while a guard rapped him with a rifle butt if he dozed off. In this sleep-deprived condition, Flynn was pumped for information about the organization and mission of the 1st Marine Air Wing in Korea, particularly the mission of VMF(N)-513. Air Force Colonel Walker Mahurin, an F-86 pilot downed and captured just one day before Flynn, described the mental tortures endured by exhausted aviator POWs charged with bacteriological warfare:

> Each night . . . I was so confused and tired that I could hardly think a rational thought. I knew that they would be at me the following morning, but I couldn't think clearly enough to figure out what to do or say when they came back.[40]

Each time Little Boy came back, he harangued Pat Flynn on the inhumanity, injustice, and immorality of the U.S. war in Korea. "About 90 per cent of the time he tried to make me see the light of why we shouldn't be in the war and to re-educate me to the wrongs of my ways," Flynn said in a 1965 interview. Little Boy's propaganda line included regular references to Flynn's slavish subservience to the "imperialist war mongers" and "war dogs and bloated running dogs of Wall Street." The interrogator slapped Flynn from time to time, a behavior that infuriated the flier. "I wanted to hit him so badly," he remembered. "I think I could have liquidated him right on the spot, but it wouldn't have accomplished anything."[41]

On July 13, the Chinese transferred Flynn to another location within the Pike's Peak compound where he was placed in solitary confinement in a small cave for the next 30 days. There Flynn faced some of the most intensive psychological tortures of his captivity. He was prevented from uttering even the smallest sounds. The Chinese guards insisted that he not groan, hum, or talk to himself. British POW Anthony Farrar-Hockley, captured while fighting with the legendary British Gloucestershire Battalion at the Battle of Imjin River in April 1951, remembered that in solitary, "[e]xcept during examination for one's offences, the requirement was the silence of a Trappist monk from dawn to dusk."[42]

In this silence, Pat Flynn's morale sank as his physical state deteriorated. He was deprived of washing and latrine facilities and the smell of his cave, which he was allowed out of for only a few minutes each day, humiliated him. When questioned by his new interrogator, Laughing Boy, Flynn found it difficult to talk. He began "breaking" and his "spirit collapsed." For the first time, Flynn thought that he was losing his sanity. Sensing Flynn's fragile state, Laughing Boy, a "friendly" interrogator who claimed to have been educated in the United States, preyed on his prisoner's weakness. Laughing Boy insisted that Flynn was an innocent victim of the war, that he had been manipulated by his superiors and unknowingly dropped biological bombs on North Korea and "he used all sorts of arguments to convince me it was true." Flynn felt himself falling for Laughing Boy's charm. The interrogator urged Flynn to relieve himself of the "remorse" he felt for having carried out germ warfare. "He played the nice guy. He'd say things like 'I hate to see you here . . . I can get you out.'" His hypnotic voice and gentle encouragement to confess gave Flynn the feeling that he was talking to one of his "buddies," and "the temptation to tell him or sign was tremendous."[43]

Flynn was being pushed toward a breaking point, a victim of what Dr. Joost K. M. Meerlo, a post-Korea expert on Communist torture, described as "menticide." Menticide was brought on by "unremitting" interrogation, sleep deprivation, and "degradation of the victim by keeping him immobilized, in solitary confinement, living in filth, starved, thirsty and freezing, without permitting him to die." In such a debilitated emotional and physical state, the victim, "in six hours or in six months," eventually confesses.[44]

As part of his strategy to wring a confession from Flynn, Laughing Boy engaged the American in discussions about his family. Flynn, who had learned in the early days of his captivity that "you can't think about your family," refused to discuss his wife and children with the interrogator. Flynn's Native American heritage also became a central focus of questioning, the Chinese reminding Flynn of the Indians' "mistreatment" at the hands of a racist, war-mongering government.[45]

To resist the temptation to confess, Flynn fell back on his religious and spiritual resolve. "In fact," he testified after the war, "when the subject was changed to something else I would bring it back to religion to try to impress upon the interrogator the reason I couldn't give him my confession, the confession he wanted."[46] After explaining that his Roman Catholic faith prevented him from assisting any "godless cause," Flynn decided "to draw the line." He took a personal vow to avoid saying anything against his country, his uniform, or his religious heritage. "I told myself that I wouldn't say anything that I wouldn't be willing to see on the front pages of any paper in this country."[47] Unable to seduce Flynn into writing and signing a confession, Laughing Boy began limiting his interrogations to ten minutes per day. He declared that it was time to "get to the point," to which Flynn responded, "There is no point. You know how I feel about that."[48]

Flynn's intransigence infuriated the Chinese. "The interrogator informed me that I had been found guilty as a war criminal and that I was sentenced to death, which would be carried out in the immediate future, . . . providing I didn't give them what they wanted."[49] Flynn believed the Chinese threat. And so, in his mentally and physically exhausted state, in fear of "losing his sanity," he invited the Chinese to kill him.[50] "I actually was prepared for it and told them to go ahead with it, that they had their alternative and it was their show, that they were holding the gun, so to speak, and to carry out their threat."[51]

The Chinese appeared ready to discharge the sentence. Sometime in August 1952, Flynn was removed from his cave and placed before a firing squad. When the command to fire was given, Flynn heard only the clicks of firing pins in empty chambers. "My legs collapsed," Flynn recalled for an interviewer in 1966, adding lightly that the mock execution was "quite an exhilarating experience but then I'd already died once on the chopping block."[52]

Their efforts to extract a confession unsuccessful, the Pike's Peak Commanders ended their interrogations of Flynn on August 13, when he and 12 other prisoners were transported to a POW holding center in the village of Obul near the Yalu River, 35 miles from Pyoktong on the North Korean-Manchurian border. There, Flynn was placed in a Korean hut with four Air Force officers and Marine Master Sergeant John T. Cain, who, after the war, recalled that he and the others "owed much to Flynn," whose sense of humor kept the POWs "amused."[53]

Captain Pat Flynn's first round of solitary confinement and interrogation had ended. More was to come, but for the next nine months, he would be called upon to lead other POWs in frustrating the enemy while planning his escape to the sea.

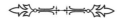

Chapter 5

Chief of the Annex

> Resistors bring the battlefield to the prison pen and oppose their captors by shunning cooperation or collaboration. This act places the resisting prisoner in extreme danger.
>
> Robert C. Doyle, *Voices from Captivity: Interpreting the American POW Narrative*[1]

WHILE HER HUSBAND was fighting for his life in North Korea, Frances Flynn was in Orange, California, fighting to maintain her spirits. The bad news about Pat had reached her on the early afternoon of May 16, 1952, when she heard the brass flap come down on the front-door mail slot. As Frances walked to the door, puzzled by the mail's early arrival, her eyes fell on the Western Union telegram lying at her feet. It could only be bad news, and as she read the message, her fears were confirmed:

DEEPLY REGRET TO INFORM YOU THAT YOUR HUSBAND CAPTAIN JOHN PATRICK FLYNN JR

USMC IS MISSING IN ACTION SINCE MAY 1952 IN THE KOREAN AREA IN THE PERFORMANCE OF HIS DUTY AND SERVICE OF HIS COUNTRY. I REALIZE YOUR GREAT ANXIETY BUT DETAILS NOT AVAILABLE AND DELAY IN RECEIPT THEREOF MUST BE EXPECTED. LETTER FOLLOWS
    G C THOMAS LIEUTENANT
    GENERAL USMC ACTING
    COMMANDANT OF THE MARINE CORPS

Numbed by the content of the message, Frances tried focusing her attention on the children while waiting for a visit from a Marine Corps officer or a chaplain. No one came to her home that day, nor did she receive a phone call from Marine Corps or Navy personnel. After tucking in her four-year-old son and two-month-old daughter for the night, she tried to sleep. Around midnight, she dozed off while clutching her rosary. She was then, in her words, "[s]uddenly . . . awakened by a gentle touch," and though she "could not make out a figure," she "could feel the presence of someone in the room." A gentle voice whispered, "Do not worry, everything will be all right." The presence disappeared as suddenly as it had appeared. From that moment, she never doubted that her husband was alive. "I felt a peace and quiet come over me," she told a reporter in 1954, "almost as though God had laid His hand on my shoulder, and I was sure John was a prisoner and that he would come back."[2]

On May 25, Frances received word from Marine Corps headquarters that her husband had been spotted bailing out of his crippled plane. Two weeks later, she received a letter from Lieutenant Colonel John R. Burnett, Commanding Officer of VMF(N)-513. Burnett wrote on May 19, 1952, that Flynn's MIA status was "a source of great sorrow" for him and for the "many friends" of "Chief" that flew with the Flying Nightmares.

> It is difficult to express adequately one's feelings under circumstances such as these because, as you undoubtedly know, a combat squadron is an extremely close organization, and each loss is very personal to every one of us.

Burnett provided Frances with reason for hope, noting that, prior to his disappearance, "Chief stated over the radio that he intended to bail out."

He praised Flynn for his "integrity and devotion to duty" and conveyed his "hope that the knowledge that your husband is keenly missed by his friends will in some measure alleviate your sadness."[3]

After consulting with the Marine Corps, Frances wrote two letters to her husband, the envelopes bearing the necessary but ludicrous address of the "Chinese People's Committee for Defending World Peace, Peking, China." Neither letter was delivered, American authorities explaining to Frances that the Chinese did not list her husband as a POW.[4] An Associated Press Wirephoto published on October 17, 1952, in the *Los Angeles Times* temporarily lifted her spirits. Asked to examine the photograph, which revealed U.N. POWs swimming in a water hole in North Korea, Mark Flynn identified a prisoner in waist-deep water as "Dad." Frances was less certain, though a photo of her husband skin-diving off the southern California coast bore a striking resemblance to the image in the Wirephoto. After the war, Frances' suspicions were confirmed when Pat informed her that he was not the POW in the photo.

As Frances Flynn pondered the Wirephoto in the fall of 1952, her husband was adapting to a Chinese prison compound on the Yalu River, Camp 2 Annex. The Annex was one of several camps and solitary confinement centers located in a steep gorge that prisoners referred to as "Obane Valley" or

One of Pat Flynn's pencil drawings of life in Camp 2 Annex, late 1952.

Pat Flynn's pencil drawings of life in Camp 2 Annex, late 1952.

Camp 2 Annex.

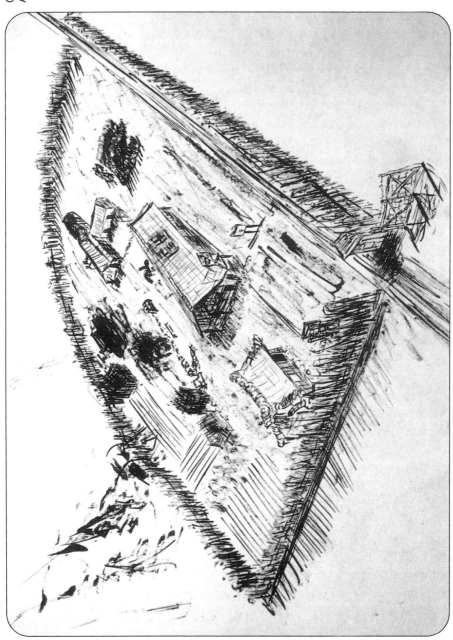

"No Name Valley." Over 140 men were confined in No Name Valley.⁵ On about October 15, Flynn and approximately 33 U.N. Command (UNC) prisoners, including the four Air Force officers and Marine Master Sergeant John T. Cain, were transported to the Annex and moved into an old schoolhouse, where the U.N. POWs were designated as 1st Platoon, C Company, under the command of senior officer Major William Wilson, USAF.⁶ Later, after the arrival of another detachment of prisoners, they were all moved into a large hut.

Following the arrival of a second POW platoon in mid-December, the population of the Annex grew from 34 to 63 men. The majority of the Annex prisoners were Americans, though soldiers and airmen from Australia, Great Britain, and the Union of South Africa were held in the camp. Prisoner housing consisted of one hut that slept about 40 to 45 men, a schoolhouse that slept 16, and a kitchen that housed the four or five men assigned cooking responsibilities.⁷ Flynn slept in the Annex hut, which had been built by prisoners from nearby Camp 2 in the summer of 1952. Army First Lieutenant William H. Funchess was a member of the work detail that shouldered large logs, some of them a foot in diameter and 20 feet in length, almost two miles to Obul, where the Chinese ordered Korean laborers to build the hut's frame. U.N. prisoners constructed the walls of the long, narrow building by tying together millet stalks with rice straw and placing the stalks vertically in the spaces between the upright frame logs. Stalks were placed about an inch apart and plastered with a mixture of clay, grass, and water to a depth of about four inches. The exterior was whitewashed. The hut's roof consisted of two layers of rice straw bundles laid upon lathes attached to pole rafters. The prisoners' beds, or *kangs*, were made of slabs of slate mounted about two feet above the hut's dirt floor. Flues running underneath the hut floor led to fireplaces that heated the slate during the winter months, a floor-heating system the Koreans call *ondol*.⁸

Prisoners were issued summer and winter uniforms. The bright blue summer uniform consisted of a cotton high-collar jacket-shirt and pajama pants. Winter wear consisted of blue "puffed" pants and jackets and white thermal underwear. Each prisoner received a summer and winter hat, the winter hats complete with earflaps. Clothes were changed on a regular basis, at which time prisoners were dusted with lice and flea powder.⁹

Flynn settled quickly into the routine of prison life, despite his occasional short-term isolation and interrogations. In the Annex, POWs were mustered at 7:00 a.m. To prevent the ingestion of water-borne contaminants, prisoners boiled water hauled from nearby streams, and on occasion, brewed morning tea. After calisthenics, a short walk, and a clean-up period, representatives of each squad drew rations from the camp kitchen and the prisoners ate breakfast, one of the two meals of the day. Sorghum seed, millet seed, tofu, soybeans (the primary protein for POWs), soybean flour, and cracked corn made up breakfasts. For supper, the men ate potato or cabbage soup served in their small green bowls, turnips, peanuts, onions, and — toward the end of the war — a bit of rice, chicken, goat, or pork. To flavor their evening meals, some POWs coated their bowls with garlic. Food portions were small and all prisoners suffered from malnutrition,[10] which was in direct violation of Article 26 of the Geneva Convention. The Veterans Administration's *Study of Former Prisoners of War* (1980) found that almost every POW, including Flynn, suffered a 40 percent to 50 percent weight loss. After the war, a thin-framed Flynn explained that the Annex food "was filling, but it did not do the job of keeping your strength up."[11] William Funchess's description of Camp 2 food was more forthright. "We were always hungry. We were always looking for something to eat — anything. We just wanted something to ease the hunger pains."[12]

During the day, the Chinese organized work details to unload supply barges on the Yalu River, collect firewood, dig root cellars, wash clothes, haul rocks, or dig latrines. Prisoners dug trenches to store food, which was covered with pine logs hauled down from the surrounding mountain slopes. To pass their free time, POWs played card games, including bridge, as well as chess, checkers, or backgammon, crafting their game materials with anything available. The Chinese encouraged the men to play basketball and volleyball and allowed prisoners to conduct "schools" where officers with expertise in mathematics, history, Spanish, English, and engineering shared their talents.[13]

When not laboring or enjoying free time, the prisoners, as part of their ideological indoctrination, were expected to conduct informal "political discussions" in their huts and read such works as *The Communist Manifesto*, *The Decline and Fall of American Capitalism*, and William Z. Foster's *The Twilight of Capitalism*. Copies of the *China Monthly Review*, *Shanghai News*, and *Daily Worker* were made available. Occasionally, POWs were brought together for formal Chinese-led lectures on the evils of capitalism and the glories of communism. Both individual and group education involved repetition, with the objective of indoctrinating prisoners to the ideology of Marx and Lenin, the teachings of Mao Zedong, the humanity of Josef Stalin, the corruption of the United Nations, the evils of Truman, Eisenhower, Dulles, and Churchill, the U.S. government's savage treatment of minorities, and the superiority of the People's Republic of China over the imperialistic, war-mongering United States. POWs who exhibited an acceptance of the Communist propaganda line were praised as "progressives" and benefited immediately from the captors' lenient policy.[14]

Albert D. Biderman, in *March to Calumny: The Story of American POWs in the Korean War*, contends that Communist indoctrination efforts were designed to elicit statements from American captives that later could be compiled "for propaganda output." Signed petitions and confessions, letters to families or hometown newspapers, and demonstrations of pacifism or neutrality proved valuable to the PRC's propaganda war. Yet propaganda materials were not always earmarked for export, for the Chinese, Biderman notes, were determined "to influence the prison groups, as in public 'self-criticism' statements and in material for POW newspapers and indoctrination sessions."[15] In addition to weakening the prisoners' patriotism, Chinese indoctrination sought to destroy rank and command structures and erode unit cohesion and military discipline. By dividing POWs, the Communists hoped to destroy their military identity and conquer their spirit, one prisoner at a time.[16]

Peace was a recurring theme of Communist indoctrination. Adopting methods employed by the Soviets during World War II, Chinese interrogators continuously emphasized the virtues of Marxism while avoiding use of the term "POW." Referring to U.N. prisoners as "newly liberated friends," the Chinese encouraged the Westerners to move rapidly in their "studies" and promised them early release if they cooperated in a progressive manner.[17]

Generally unsuccessful in their efforts to wrench confessions or statements from American officers, the Chinese pressured young enlisted men, many of them undereducated and a few of them near-illiterate, to condemn the "Wall Street Lackeys" responsible for the immoral war against peace-loving Communists. Korea POW Andrew Riker recalls that indoctrinators told "these 17- and 18-year-old kids that [*the Chinese*] way of life was better than the American way of life." Lecturers drew comparisons between the salaries of enlisted men and officers and railed against the injustices suffered by African Americans and other minorities. Indoctrination lessons were laced with exaggerated accounts of current events in the U.S. The Chinese, Riker notes, would "collect all the bad news that took place in the U.S. and pass it off as a typical day" in America.[18]

Pat Flynn was struck by the effectiveness of Communist indoctrination methods. Rather than fabricate American history or "tell you a lie in their propaganda," Chinese officers would "take the worst parts of American history and give it to you page after page." Because he was "hungry to read anything" and "their literature . . . [*was*] the only thing at hand," Flynn took great caution to avoid the seductions of Communist propaganda. "You brainwash yourself unless you hold onto your perspective and realize they are telling you only the bad parts of our history."[19]

William Funchess remembers Chinese lectures about class and race. "They were always promoting communism and the Communist doctrine. They tried everything known to man to convert us to communism, to turn us against one another, to turn enlisted against officers, to turn blacks against whites."[20]

Flynn found his racial background the subject of endless sermons by his interrogators. In a 1965 interview for the *Oakland Tribune*, Flynn, then a Lieutenant Colonel and a leading figure in POW and Code of Conduct training, reflected on the Chinese strategies. "They knock down my religion, talk about my family, talk about the fact that I was an Indian and how my people were mistreated in America."[21] But in Camp 2 Annex, Flynn turned the race card against his captors. Lieutenant Colonel William Thrash, one of four Marine POWs decorated with Flynn at the Pentagon after the war, remembered one of those moments during his temporary confinement in the Annex. In the middle of an indoctrination session, Chief Flynn suddenly stood up and interrupted the lecturer, demanding immediate recognition of his Native American heritage. Thrash recalls:

> He told the Chinese that he deserved special treatment because he was a monarch in America. "I'm a monarch in my country, and thus deserve special treatment!" he said. I think he'd gotten away with it, but we were all laughing so hard at what he was saying![22]

For Flynn, humor was a weapon of resistance and a force for unifying prisoners. Andrew Riker recalls that while organizing a work detail to unload a supply barge on the Yalu in June 1953, Flynn plotted a prank to provide the prisoners a few minutes of swimming on a hot summer day. "It had been real hot, and we were bugging the guards to let us go swimming," noted Riker. "There was no way they were going to do that. There were too many of us." Annoyed by the Chinese decision, Flynn informed the POWs that upon hearing the signal "Geronimo," the entire detail was to jump into the river.

> He yelled "Geronimo" and we all went swimming. You've never seen a Chinese fire drill like that one! [*The Chinese guards*] were all running around. They didn't know what to do.

The guards found no humor in the stunt, and "they all had loaded machine guns," Riker added. "One shot would have taken care of that." For their unauthorized dip, the POWs were given a four-hour lecture in Chinese and English on the irreverence of their actions.[23]

Pat Flynn's feistiness boosted morale, countered Chinese propaganda, and probably sowed divisions between Chinese officers and the compound's teenage guards. On several occasions, Ensign Harlo E. "Ed" Sterrett observed "the Chief," the recognized leader of the POW basketball team, displaying his signature rebounding technique against the guards. At each available opportunity, Flynn, who Sterrett described as "a rock and an inspiration to us all," would go up for a missed shot and bring down his elbows on the head of the nearest Chinese opponent. Flynn's blows "must have hurt," Sterrett recalls, "[*because*] the Chinese learned to stay away from him." Flynn's physical style won another kind of respect from the Chinese soldiers, who approached him to arrange a game between the prisoners and a team comprised of Chinese officers. The game was arranged, and "Needless to say," notes Sterrett, "our boys beat them badly, in score and otherwise, what with some of [*Flynn's*] elbows to the head and our guys being rather rough and aggressive in all ways."

The POW basketball victory pleased the guards, who, in Sterrett's words, "got a real charge out of seeing their officers manhandled so much by a group of not too physically well-off Americans."[24] From the reaction of the Chinese soldiers, it might be concluded that the Chinese officers' determination to spread discord among the POW ranks was a projection of their anxiety about discord within their own ranks. Flynn may have sensed or observed an enemy morale problem and provided his fellow POWs with a divide-and-conquer mission of their own.

Some of Pat Flynn's more memorable comic moments involved Chief Petty Officer Duane Thorin and the pigs given to the prisoners in the spring of 1953 as part of a "fattening-up" program prior to an anticipated prisoner exchange. Flynn and Thorin, a farm-raised Nebraskan who the prisoners also addressed as "Chief," were the only Annex captives skilled in slaughtering and butchering livestock (Flynn had slaughtered a goat for the compound in the fall of 1952). But even their skills were tested as they struggled to kill the dangerous Korean "razorbacks." In what Thorin describes as "one of the good shows in the compound," he and Flynn roped the animals, being careful to avoid their sharp tusks, wrapped lanyards around their snouts, and pinned them to the ground with a knee. Because the pigs had been given names during their confinement in the compound pen, their executions — which were conducted with quick thrusts through the animals' carotid arteries — were elaborate ceremonies reminiscent of the guillotine executions of the French Revolution. The POWs took enormous pleasure in the execution of "Mao Zedong," but no performance drew louder howls and more enthusiastic applause than the deaths of the Annex's most notorious pigs, "Ethel" and "Julius Rosenberg."[25]

Pat Flynn's antics raised the prisoners' spirits, but the Marine's value to his comrades was never limited to his sense of humor. Hog slaughtering might prove entertaining, but pork meat and fat were, for some prisoners, the difference between health and illness — and, in some cases, life and death. Flynn and Thorin utilized as much as possible of the 100- to 150-pound animals, including their bladders, which, according to Thorin, were hidden away for use as canteens during a potential escape. Flynn wanted the POWs to drink the blood to increase their iron intake, but the majority of the prisoners declined. Flynn and a few others mixed blood with soups, stews, and ground soybeans. All in all, insists Andrew Riker, Flynn and Thorin "kept us alive with their knowledge of how to slaughter a pig." The butchers' impact spread beyond the boundaries of the Annex, for, in Riker's words, Camp 2 Annex "fed all the prisoners in the other compounds around us."[26]

From the moment he had arrived in the Annex, Flynn was recognized as the camp co-Commander — or, depending on the circumstances, the

Commander or Senior Officer Present (SOP). When the Annex prisoners grew confused over who to address as Chief — Chief Flynn or Chief Thorin — Flynn, in Thorin's words, "called everyone together and straightened it out. 'This guy over here is a legitimate Chief. I'm just a regular Indian. Call me Pat.' He was called Pat from then on."

For all of his good nature and humor, Flynn maintained a military bearing. Thorin recalls that when Flynn headed up a work detail, it was obvious to anyone within hearing range that "some jarhead was . . . running the thing." The Marine barked cadence as he marched his men to a work site, and upon arriving, let no man shirk his duties. In the midst of an oppressive, propagandized environment where the Chinese did everything possible to erode enlisted men's respect for their officers, Thorin marveled at Flynn's ability to accomplish "whatever was necessary. Those that were too damned lazy and wanted to get out of [*work*], he had his different ways, according to the individual, [*of*] either making them work or encouraging them to." Thorin recalled one young American soldier suffering from a case of "give-up-itis" during the terrible winter of 1952-1953. Flynn's cure for the disease was to take hold of the GI and drag him into the snow, where he would have to get up and walk back in. "That man is alive today," Thorin stated, "simply because [*Flynn*] did that."

Captain Pat Flynn was SOP for only a few weeks of the eight and a half months he spent in the Annex, "but when it came to leadership," Thorin notes, "he was the guy keeping them in line."[27] Some 47 years after his repatriation, Andrew Riker said that to the men, Chief Flynn was "the highest ranking officer in the camp."[28]

Army Captain Joseph Kutys, who inherited the Annex SOP position after April 15, 1953, echoes Thorin and Riker's assessment of Flynn's leadership role. Still suffering from wounds to a leg that "was pretty shot-up" and infected, Kutys leaned heavily on Flynn's advice and counsel. Kutys maintains that when Marine Corps Major Walter R. Harris served as SOP between February and April 1953, he and Flynn, "a happy, go-lucky guy," shared decision-making in the Annex. "Sometimes one made decisions, sometimes the other did."[29]

❦

Prisoner morale was of primary concern to Flynn. He urged his comrades, especially the younger airmen, sailors, and soldiers, to avoid dwelling on anything "of an emotional nature." In a 1966 *Los Angeles Times* interview, he told how he had grown alarmed when he saw "perfectly healthy men pull into a shell, cry over the fact that they would never see their wives or families again and die. They just stopped eating. Stopped trying to live."[30]

Flynn viewed religion as an important means of maintaining morale. And oddly, although the Communists denounced religion as an opiate of the masses, they permitted the POWs to retain their religious articles — rosaries, religious medals, or small Bibles — and did not interfere with informal religious gatherings or services. As had been the case at the Pike's Peak interrogation center in the summer of 1952, Flynn made no effort to conceal his religious heritage, a comfortable balance of Roman Catholic beliefs and Lakota Sioux spirituality. Reflections on his Lakota heritage and his warrior ancestors bolstered Flynn's will to live and resist the interrogators' tactics. He set aside two to three periods a day to recite the rosary. He organized religious services for the Catholic prisoners, using the time to debunk Communist propaganda and warn them against committing mortal sin by cooperating with an atheist government. Many of those confined with Flynn credited his religious faith for sustaining him — and them — during the long months of pain and uncertainty in the Obul compound. A description of the impact of Flynn's religious faith can be found in Duane Thorin's 1956 novel about Korean War captivity, *A Ride to Panmunjom*. The book's "Captain Ghant" character is based on Pat Flynn and his experiences during the last two months of the war.[31]

Flynn and thousands of other U.N. prisoners also struggled to maintain their health during the winter of 1952-1953. Average January temperatures in the mountains of North Korea drop to about minus 5 degrees Fahrenheit, with lows on some nights reaching 40 below zero. The extreme temperatures placed the malnourished POWs, housed in drafty schoolhouses and barracks, in a precarious situation. The *ondol* heating system prevented men from freezing to death, but every prisoner, covered with only a blanket and a cotton comforter, experienced short nights. "During the cold weather," Flynn told an interviewer after the war, "it seems the food would keep you going until about three or four in the morning when all at once you would start to shiver and shake and you would keep doing this until meal time came again." Unable to sleep, most men in Flynn's hut rose and moved about or huddled around the hut's tiny wood stove. Those who stayed in "bed" piled on the blankets left by the men who were up and moving about. "But with no body heat, it wasn't until . . . we ate breakfast that we'd start to get warm."³²

A few years later, Flynn elaborated on the "peril and extreme privation" of his North Korean winter:

> In the winter of 1952-53 our compound contained 75 officers and enlisted members of the services of the United States and the British Commonwealth. Sickness and unhealed wounds were commonplace. Medical attention was not available. Food and clothing were inadequate. Heating the barn-like barracks was out of the question with the green logs we carried down out of the mountains. The situation was critical.³³

And yet at that critical juncture, Flynn wrote, the Annex prisoners grew more united. "Our mission was SURVIVAL." The needs of the sick and wounded were attended to, and food and clothing shared among the men. "An atmosphere of close fellowship prevailed" and a new resolve to resist the interrogators' harassment became evident. Morale ran high, Flynn observed, as "each man in the group took pride in his individual contribution. He had his own problems. Yet he went outside of himself to help others."³⁴

POWs even found a way to amuse themselves during the winter season by pelting the Chinese guards with snowballs. "The only trouble," Flynn reflected, "was they usually cut off our tobacco rations or used some other form of punishment" in response to the prisoners' high jinks.³⁵

Though weary of his living conditions and the occasional solitary confinement, Flynn controlled his feelings toward the enemy. On one memorable occasion, Flynn paid homage to "Peter Love," a popular and respected enemy soldier assigned to the Annex while recuperating from serious wounds incurred in the Chinese Civil War. The soldier recognized the prisoners' rank structure, and, through an interpreter, promised the POWs that he would respect them "as soldiers" if they respected him in return. In mid-May 1953, Peter Love arranged a work detail limited to Flynn, Thorin, and four other Americans. After supervising the POWs in the construction of a small dam, beach, and bathing area on the banks of the Yalu, Peter Love let the prisoners swim and bathe and fed them a lunch of rice cakes and tea. He marched the men back to the Annex, but halted them by the gate where, through an interpreter named Tsai, he made a short speech. After expressing his pleasure "to see good men from opposing armies work together to build a beautiful park instead of killing each other," Peter Love proclaimed his hope that the war would soon end and the Chinese and American soldiers could return to their homes. "Bad men cause the wars," he concluded, "and good men have to fight them."

Struck by Peter Love's sincerity, as well as Tsai's obvious displeasure with the speech, Flynn called the POWs to attention and ordered a hand salute. Peter Love returned the gesture. Flynn barked, "Detail, right face!" and marched the Americans into the compound. Duane Thorin remembers the demonstration of mutual respect as one of the remarkable moments of his captivity and described Flynn's action as thoroughly indicative of the Marine's leadership in Camp 2 Annex.[36]

Despite their regard for Peter Love, Pat Flynn and Duane Thorin, who had by this time developed a deep respect for one another, spent much of their time on the banks of the Yalu scanning the landscape in preparation for an escape the two had been planning for months. Any escape in 1952-1953 would have proved difficult, but by the spring of 1953, potential escapees faced a daunting challenge. The Chinese, concerned that the improved weather increased the likelihood of escapes, in April had constructed a 15-foot sapling wall around the Annex's perimeter. Three POWs botched a poorly planned escape mid-month and were captured within 14 hours. In response, the Chinese doubled the guard detail around the compound and placed the American SOP, Major Walter Harris, in solitary confinement.[37]

And whereas winter conditions had unified the compound, springtime brought out the worst in some prisoners, creating a poisoned atmosphere that affected Flynn and Thorin's plans. The arrival of warmer weather, the addition of pork meat and fresh vegetables to the POW diet, and the issuing of new uniforms and cigarettes had raised morale but had increased selfishness. "At this point," Flynn recalled, "the trouble started. Fights broke out between friends. 'Buddies' of a few months earlier threatened to kill each other. Discipline was almost non-existent. . . . We had lost our mission."[38]

Flynn and Thorin were careful not to disclose their escape plan for, as

Thorin remembers, "there were too many self-centered in the camp." The plan had won the approval of Major Harris, who, before his transfer to solitary confinement, oversaw the "escape committee," which approved and coordinated individual prison breaks. The men had weighed the strengths of two different escape routes, ultimately rejecting a shorter, but more predictable, 70- to 80-mile western route down the Yalu River to Korea Bay. Instead, Flynn and Thorin chose to strike eastward sometime in July. They were confident that if they crossed the Yalu River into Manchuria and traveled by night through difficult terrain, they could outwit and outrun Chinese search parties in their estimated 240-mile race to the Sea of Japan south of the North Korean-USSR border.

Flynn and Thorin drew up a map and estimated that their travel time to the coast, if they could hike four miles per night, would take 60 days. Because of his familiarity with naval operations on the Sea of Japan, Thorin believed that once he and Flynn reached the coast, they could steal a boat from a Korean village and float offshore until American patrol boats spotted them.[39]

But the escape did not transpire, due to a series of handicaps. Increased Chinese security inside the compound had decreased movement and communication. Several enlisted men who suspected Flynn's and Thorin's plan began begging the two to take them along. One of the enlisted men turned "stool pigeon" and began discussing the plan with other prisoners. Meanwhile, an unidentified POW cut a hole in the compound's sapling wall, an action that heightened Chinese suspicions of an impending break. And worst of all, a young "progressive" Private exposed the escape plan to the Chinese. The act of treachery led to the commitment of three Annex officers, including Captain Flynn, to solitary confinement.[40]

During the early morning hours of July 16, 1953, just 11 days before U.N. and Communist officials signed a truce to end the Korean War, a Chinese officer (either Tsai or an enemy soldier known as "The Sphinx") burst into Flynn's hut, thrust a flashlight into the Marine's face, and ordered him to get dressed. Flynn was led out of the hut, and several minutes later a guard returned to seize Flynn's soup bowl, a sign to the other POWs that Chief's absence would be long-term. Flynn was loaded onto a truck and transported about 40 miles west to the vicinity of Camp 3 near Changsong, where he was placed in solitary confinement in an abandoned, rat-infested room attached to an old farm house. The Chinese withheld his

Flynn's depiction of the morning of July 16, 1953, when he was removed from Camp 2 Annex and sent to solitary confinement.

food and water and broke up his sleep with intense, recurring interrogations.[41]

In the minds of the enemy, Pat Flynn's greatest offense was not his plot to escape from the Annex but, once again, his resistance to a confession of bacteriological warfare. With a truce and POW exchanges at hand, the Chinese pushed for a final victory in their propaganda war with the United States. Hence, Flynn faced what he characterized as a month-long period of "intense germ warfare" interrogation.[42]

Flynn's predicament was complicated by the earlier germ-warfare "confession," in January 1953, of another Marine Corps aviator, Colonel Frank H. Schwable, who, in his widely disseminated statement, had identified Flynn's squadron, VMF(N)-513, as a primary perpetrator of biological attacks on Chinese troops. To convince Flynn of the truthfulness of their charges about American biological atrocities, the Chinese offered Flynn a copy of Schwable's confession. The enemy hoped that a signed statement by a senior U.S. officer might persuade the Marine Captain to spare himself from further torture.

> They said it has been proven that it is true and that I do not have to worry . . . about myself, as far as having any misgivings about giving confessions because of the fact that high-ranking officers have given confessions.

For the remainder of his confinement at Changsong, Chinese interrogators pressed Flynn to "go ahead and confess and not worry about it. They said, 'It is not serious, just sign it and everything will be fine.'" They wanted Flynn's confession, and "they were going to get it, whether they got it within a month, a year, or twenty years."[43]

Flynn resisted and, as he had at Pike's Peak, simply challenged the Chinese to kill him. The enemy responded to Flynn's intransigence by ratcheting up the psychological torture, denying him food, water, and outside bathroom facilities and robbing him of even the most basic hygiene. Within days his exhaustion and filthiness began to undermine his morale. The Chinese tried him before a "court" of officers who found the American flier guilty of a list of trumped-up charges, including conducting germ warfare, plotting the murder of a Chinese officer in Camp 2 Annex, seizing weapons, planning a mass escape, and maintaining a generally "reactionary" attitude toward his benevolent captors. For his "crimes," Flynn was sentenced to 20 years in prison. The Chinese then placed him in confinement with a young Air Force airman.[44]

Flynn's Changsong experience is re-created in Duane Thorin's *A Ride to Panmunjom*. The character Captain Ghant is grounded in Flynn's detailed account of his captivity, which Flynn had shared with Thorin during a fishing trip off Baja California in 1954. Thorin's Ghant is a calm, patient, reliable, and greatly admired man. He exercises self-control before his interrogators and encourages a fellow prisoner to hold his temper in check. But Ghant's spirit is nearly broken during his final solitary confinement in the summer of 1953. His sleep is routinely disrupted, first by rats nibbling on his fingers and toes, then by the incessant harassment of one, two, or three interrogators. He grows fatigued under a hail of questions and begins to hallucinate. He endures unspeakable filth, a condition that begins to undermine his sanity. And, thus, in exchange for a bath, he agrees to write one paragraph of a larger confession.[45]

Yet in the end, the fictional Ghant refuses to collaborate with the enemy, finding a final residue of strength in his religious faith. In a climactic moment of resolve, Ghant tears up his confession:

> From then on, the torments of the enemy were powerless to hurt him. His body still became tired from lack of sleep, but his mind remained clear. His tormentors, once shrewd, were now pitiable, unseeing fools. Their shrewd threats bounced off the impenetrable armor of his Faith.[46]

For Captain Pat Flynn, the tormentors' final threat came on the morning of August 15 or 16, 1953, just hours after Flynn learned of the repatriation of American POWs. Flynn was dragged before a Chinese General who began harassing him. After a short but intense harangue, he walked Flynn to a pagoda on the side of a hill and pointed to the road below. Flynn saw a convoy of trucks taking Americans "down the road to freedom." The General informed Flynn that, "due to the new policy against war criminals," he could return home if he provided the Chinese with a germ-warfare confession. If he refused, he would begin serving his 20-year sentence. Impressed by the pomp and drama of an ultimatum from a Chinese General, Flynn concluded that the enemy was not bluffing. It was, Flynn later remarked, "the lowest point of my morale during the entire period of my imprisonment."[47] He tried to convince himself that "This can't be true; they wouldn't do this to me," but began to doubt whether he would ever be released. Nevertheless, he refused to sign a false statement, and, for his stubbornness, "was almost thrown out of the place" by the enraged General.[48]

On August 17, Flynn joined a larger group of captives and began a five-day trip southward, first by truck to Manpojin, and then by truck and train to Kaesong, a POW repatriation staging area near Panmunjom. At Kaesong, Flynn and 49 other "incorrigibles" were placed under heavy guard and isolated from the much larger compound of POWs being repatriated under the Communist-UNC prisoner exchange known as "Operation Big Switch." Flynn served as SOP for his camp and a nearby camp of 96 prisoners, most of whom departed for Freedom Village at Panmunjom on August 25. The remaining men under Flynn's command had been convicted and were serving their "sentences": 23 for breaches of camp regulations, 6 for waging biological warfare, and 13 for having served as guards at the U.N. prison for Communist captives at Koje-do Island, South Korea. (A series of violent revolts at the overcrowded Koje-do compounds had provided the Communists with a wealth of propaganda material.)[49]

At Kaesong, Flynn faced his final POW challenge. Two soldiers came to him, hoping to win the Captain's approval to assassinate a "bleeding progressive" among them whose collaboration with the enemy had caused untold suffering for U.S. prisoners. Physically, mentally, and emotionally drained, Flynn did not wish to confront the dilemma, but knew that he had little choice. Seeking a human sounding board from outside of his compound, he somehow skirted past the guards, walked out of his camp, and approached a POW washing himself in a rice paddy between two staging areas. The POW was Chief Petty Officer Thorin, who looked up to see a man who had "been through a pretty rough ordeal, a real ordeal." After some small talk, Flynn explained his predicament involving the collaborator and the potential executioners, noting that the two soldiers had every justification to kill the man. Nevertheless, as a holder of "a position of responsibility," he anguished about a violent act of revenge and the effect the assassination would have on the assassins. The conversation lasted only a few minutes, and Thorin was left with no indication of what Flynn's decision would be.[50]

Ultimately, Flynn denied the soldiers' request. Duane Thorin learned of Flynn's decision when Thorin was repatriated on August 30, the same day the collaborator in question crossed over to freedom. Thorin immediately informed U.S. personnel of the charges against the collaborator, emphasizing that the man had survived to this point only because a Marine Captain had dissuaded two soldiers from killing him. Thorin warned that unless some protection was granted the collaborator, he would not survive the trip across the Pacific Ocean. Neither he nor Captain Flynn cared for the fate of the man, Thorin stated, but they both feared that two good individuals might suffer the consequences of a rash, murderous attack on the traitor.[51]

On September 1, the weight of command was lifted from Flynn's shoulders when the first of the 50 men of Flynn's Kaesong compound began their ride to freedom at Panmunjom. On September 5, Flynn was loaded into the back of a truck for his own trip to freedom. At that moment, a Chinese interpreter took one last opportunity to remind Flynn of his 20-year

Pat Flynn (r), with Marine Lieutenant General Vernon McGee, at Flynn's repatriation at Freedom Village, Panmunjom, September 5, 1953.

sentence and the certain enforcement of the penalty should Flynn ever fall into Communist hands. Soon after that warning, Flynn's truck passed under an archway bearing the words "WELCOME! GATE TO FREEDOM!" A Chinese officer presented a list to an American officer, who called out the names of the men in the back of the truck. "Captain John P. Flynn, Jr., USMC" was announced, and, one year, three months, and three weeks after his capture, Flynn walked into Freedom Village. Marine Lieutenant General Vernon McGee, armed with a box of aviator wings donated by carrier-based Marine and Navy pilots, shook Flynn's hand and pinned the gold wings to his POW jacket.[52]

At that moment, a telegram was wired from Korea to Washington, D.C., and then on to 902 West Palmyra in Orange, California, where Mrs. John P. Flynn, Jr., was informed that her husband had been released from a Chinese prison camp.[53] The next day, Pat Flynn wired his wife from Inchon, South Korea:

> DEAREST FRANCIE NEVER SO HAPPY TO BE AN AMERICAN AS TODAY YOUR PRAYERS FOR ME HAVE BEEN ANSWERED ALIVE AND WELL ON MY WAY HOME BY BOAT TELL THE FOLKS LOVE TO THE CHILDREN FONDEST LOVE DARLING.[54]

Pat Flynn was a free man. His faith in God, maintains his hut mate Ed Sterrett, had carried him through.[55]

Chapter 6

God and Country

> If it was not for my religion I could not say what my actions would be.
>
> Captain John P. Flynn, Jr., testifying before the Court of Inquiry concerning the case of Colonel Frank H. Schwable, USMC, March 2, 1954[1]

*O*N JANUARY 1954, as Senator Joseph McCarthy's hunt for alleged American Communists reached the upper levels of the federal government, the U.S. Marine Corps established a Court of Inquiry to investigate the actions of Colonel Frank H. Schwable, the decorated aviator who had signed a 6,000-word germ-warfare confession while a prisoner of the Chinese. Though dedicated to protecting "the rights and reputations of the individuals involved," Marine Commandant General Lemuel C. Shepherd designated the Schwable case, in an interview published in the *Washington Post* on January 24, 1954, as "too important nationally to be dismissed with a perfunctory investigation...." Shepherd added that the court's purview included broad authority to examine the "unique psychological and mental factors" faced by American POWs held in Communist hands.

Department of Defense regulations prohibited a prisoner of war from disclosing any information beyond his name, rank, and serial number. Schwable's lengthy confession, which drastically exceeded that rule, prompted Shepherd to raise two important questions. First, "Shall there be recognition of the fact that each individual has a physical and psychological limit of endurance beyond which he has no control?" And, then, if so, "Where is this limit?" Schwable's behavior demanded a thorough military investigation, Shepherd noted in another *Washington Post* article on February 17, 1954, to prevent "future combatants [*from*] follow[*ing*] the immediate dictates of their own fears rather than taking necessary aggressive action inculcated through training and discipline." The court was to explore how Communist interrogators broke POW resistance, for, in Shepherd's view, such information was essential to the development of Marine POW-training programs.

Conducted between January and March 1954, the Schwable inquiry was, in the words of one military law expert, "absolutely, completely unique," an investigation without precedent in American military history. Though not a court-martial, the Court of Inquiry would gather facts and render opinions, and could conceivably make recommendations for future courts-martial. Because of its scope, the court's decisions would, in the words of a Washington reporter, "affect the lives of all military personnel in the future."[2]

Captain Pat Flynn was one of the 50 witnesses called before the court. His testimony exposed Communist interrogation and propaganda tactics and the captivity conditions faced by pilots charged with biological warfare. Moreover, Flynn's statements revealed the depth of his religious faith and the significance of that faith in sustaining him when patriotic values wilted under the strains of psychological torture. In his moment of national exposure, Flynn made clear that, at least in his case, religious faith was the best antidote to Communist interrogation.

Flynn was a member of the last group of "Operation Big Switch" POW repatriates who had arrived in the United States on September 23, 1953, after a two-and-a-half-week voyage on the USS *General Howze*. While on board, the ex-prisoners underwent physical and psychological examinations and answered questions about their capture and captivity. Intelligence officers accumulated data on living and deceased POWs to insure that none had remained behind. Repatriates were questioned about North Korean and Chinese atrocities and POW treason; the information from the debriefings was recorded in classified dossiers prepared for each man.[3]

In fact, Pat Flynn's most thorough debriefings had already occurred at Inchon on September 6 and 7, when officials from Marine Corps G-2 (Intelligence) and the Navy's Operations Evaluation Group (OEG) sought information on the fate of Dr. Irving Shaknov, Flynn's passenger on the fateful night of May 14, 1952. Flynn confirmed Shaknov's death, stating that, in his opinion, "there was only 'one chance in a million' that Shaknov got out of the plane." He expressed his desire to visit Shaknov's parents as well as his intention to recommend the MIT physicist for a posthumous award. It was at Inchon that American officials had first learned of Flynn's willingness to face execution rather than sign a false confession; an OEG report noted that "he consistently refused to sign a germ warfare confession, the charges being dropped when he stated finally that he would not sign and they could shoot him for all he cared."[4]

Frances Flynn traveled by train from Orange to meet her husband at San Francisco. September 23 was a foggy, dreary day. As the *General Howze* neared the harbor, the ship's passengers heard a message broadcast over the intercom system. "Gentlemen, if you will all look forward, you will see something you never thought to see again." Looming before the ex-POWs was the Golden Gate Bridge. As the *General Howze* docked, an Air Force band played "God Bless America" and tears filled the eyes of nearly every man on board.[5] After a lengthy photo session with some Red Cross girls, the repatriates finally debarked. Pat walked to the end of the gangplank, where he embraced Frances for the first time in nearly two years. Frances later said that she was struck by her husband's thin frame and the odor of tobacco on his clothing, evidence of the one vice Flynn had adopted in the Camp 2 Annex.

After a one-day train ride, Flynn was back home in Orange, where he began the awkward readjustment to freedom, family, and middle-class living. "Believe me," Frances later wrote to the author, "adjustment didn't happen overnight," an assessment that undoubtedly applied to the lives of all repatriated prisoners and their families. Flynn bonded quickly with his son Mark, who had retained clear memories of his father during his two-year absence. But Flynn's daughter, 18-month-old Colleen, remained suspicious of the man she knew only from stories and photographs. "He had expected his little girl to make up to him right away," remembers Frances, "and that is not the way things went." Even the family dog was confused by Flynn's return; "Punky" shook uncontrollably when Flynn arrived, and, for several days thereafter, cried whenever his master attempted to speak to him.

Gradually, Frances learned about her husband's ordeal. "I don't think he wanted to talk about it — trying to forget the hurt, humiliation and pain — so bits and pieces just came out from time to time." Sensitive about invoking any bad memories, she refrained from cooking rice, a prewar favorite of Pat's, but a dish that Frances assumed had been a prison camp staple. When her husband requested rice one evening, "it was then," Frances said, "that I learned . . . they seldom, if ever, were given rice." She made the mistake of serving pork, which, though cooked thoroughly, resulted in two days of diarrhea and stomach cramps for her husband.

> [Pork] was not served again for many years and then only rarely. Pat said that when they got one of those razor-back hogs they would eat all of it and the fat helped keep them warm during the cold winter.

It may be, as Frances Flynn suggests, that her husband's reaction to pork was a psychosomatic symptom associated with the physical and psychological stresses of captivity.

Frances also discovered that her husband's sleep behavior had been permanently altered:

> Pat had been home a couple of weeks when I learned not to touch him when he was asleep. I don't recall if I went to bed after he had gone to sleep or if I had gotten up for some reason and gone back to bed. I think I went to put my arm around him, and he came out swinging. Somehow I ducked and saved a fist in the face and almost fell out of bed. I was in shock and on the verge of tears and Pat was completely shook up and full of apologies. It took us quite awhile to get back to sleep after that,

but I had learned a very valuable lesson: to wake up Pat by touching [*him*] was putting him back in the hands of the enemy.

Frances passed on the lesson to her children, who learned to wake their father with muted voices from a distance of about ten feet. In later years, when Pat was hospitalized for heart ailments, Frances informed nurses about his sleep behavior and in 1975 overruled a nurse who attempted to tie his arm to a board as a means of holding an IV in place. Frances notes:

> He was frantic and I finally told the nurses that they would have to leave his arm free. It was O.K. while he was awake, but as soon as he drifted off to sleep that confinement put him back in prison camp in his subconscious. That was something he never got over.

After a two-and-a-half-week recuperation in California, Flynn and his family drove to South Dakota, where, in Frances's words, "it was go, go, go. Everyone wanted to see Pat, of course. And he received a hero's welcome everywhere he went." Flynn spoke to the residents of Colome, the Gregory Rotary Club, and the Gregory High School student body. On October 15, 1953, at a gathering attended by hundreds, he received the keys to the city of Gregory from Mayor Don Soper. At each engagement, Flynn spoke of the need to preserve peace "at any price," praised the joys of "living in a country that defended freedom of religion," and urged his fellow citizens to cooperate in the fight against communism. "Each and every one of us must be aware that these Communists mean business," he told a Gregory audience. His comments appeared in the October 22, 1953, issue of the *Gregory Times-Advocate*.

> We have the greatest country in the world here in the United States, but it will remain that way only if we are all aware of the danger that is facing us and each of us will be willing to do everything in our power to keep our country free.

⋄⊱≻═┼═≺⊰⋄

In November 1953, Flynn returned to El Toro, California, and joined Marine Training Group (MTG)-10, an aviation unit that provided refresher flight training for repatriated pilots.[6] On November 23, he rode in the co-pilot's seat of a twin-engine Beechcraft SNB-5 Expeditor, his first airplane flight since May 14, 1952. In December, he began jet training, logging flight time in the Douglas F3D-2 Skyknight, the stubby jet fighter that replaced the aging Corsair in Korea in 1952-1953.[7]

Flynn interrupted his jet training in early December 1953 to visit the parents of Dr. Irving Shaknov at their home in Boston. In a letter to Flynn dated December 11, 1953, Jacinto Steinhardt, director of the Operations Evaluation Group, recognized how difficult the experience of meeting the Shaknovs had been, but thanked Flynn for his "kind, understanding, patient, and sympathetic" attitude. "Your action in this matter," wrote Steinhardt, "adds to the already high opinion of Marine Corps personnel held by the members of the Operations Evaluation Group, particularly by those members of the Group who have had assignments with the Corps."

Upon his return to El Toro, Flynn learned that he would receive the U.S. Navy and Marine Corps Medal, an award for heroism in a combat theater not involving direct enemy confrontation. After a comprehensive review of the security dossiers of 194 repatriated Marines and recommendation letters from the part-time SOP in Camp 2 Annex, Major Walter R. Harris, Marine Commandant Lemuel C. Shepherd recommended to Secretary of the Navy Robert B. Anderson that Flynn receive the honor. In describing the selection process, Shepherd noted that Flynn and four other Marines were being honored after "a thorough intelligence processing of . . . records" revealed that their actions were "of exceptional nature, and in all respects in keeping with our highest principles."[8]

Shepherd praised Flynn for withstanding "severe and inhuman treatment," which included confinement in a hole, extreme mental torture, extended periods of solitary confinement, the constant threat of execution, and a trial and sentencing to 20 years imprisonment for war crimes. Major Harris lauded Flynn's leadership skills, his collection of materials for purposes of POW escapes, his organization of escape measures, and his devotion to "various projects to improve the living conditions in the [*Camp 2 Annex*] compound." On behalf of President Dwight D. Eisenhower, Secretary of the Navy Anderson accepted the recommendations and prepared for an awards ceremony at the Pentagon.[9]

Flynn flew to Washington, where, on January 11, 1954, he took part in the highly publicized ceremony in Anderson's Pentagon office — the first awards ceremony honoring Korea POWs who had displayed exceptional conduct. Recognized along with Flynn were Lieutenant Colonel William G. Thrash, Lieutenant Colonel John N. McLaughlin, and Major Walter Harris, the recipients of the Legion of Merit, and Master Sergeant John T. Cain, the recipient of a Letter of Commendation. As part of a larger effort by the Defense Department to rebuke the actions of POW "progressives" who had refused repatriation or had cooperated with their captors, Secretary Anderson lauded the five men for achieving a "shining moral victory" against a "diabolical enemy" seeking "to obtain their collaboration for his evil purposes." In his remarks before an audience that included the Secretary of the Air Force, the Air Force Chief of Staff, the Army Vice Chief of Staff, and reporters from *The New York Times*, the *Washington Post*, and Associated Press, Anderson portrayed the five as:

> proud veterans of the ideological war, who would not quit, who did not quit, who fought back with every ounce of their strength and every drop of their blood. Throughout those weary, hopeless years, when the only visible reward for valor was hunger and pain and death, they stood ready to die rather than compromise their faith, or bear false witness against their country and their fellow men. They resisted the torture, the threats and the blandishments to prove their belief that the disappearance of regular constituted authority does not relieve men from a continuing responsibility to their comrades, to their country, and to their moral principles.[10]

Following his remarks, Anderson pinned medals on the Marines and read the corresponding citations. Flynn's citation recognized him for "[e]xhibiting a high degree of courage and integrity" and demonstrating "unselfish loyalty and determination in refusing to compromise his personal honor and that of his country. . . ."

Flynn awoke on January 12, 1954, to discover his face on the pages of *The New York Times*, the *Washington Post*, the *Kansas City Times*, the *Omaha World Herald*, and California's metropolitan newspapers. John Barnett, a fellow Marine, recalls that the exposure of Flynn's POW record changed everything between Chief and his comrades. "Pat . . . really became a legend, and set such an example, because of his POW experiences."[11] Back in southern California, metropolitan dailies, Roman Catholic publications, and Marine and Navy newspapers ran stories about

Flynn's capture and captivity. Congressman E. Y. Berry of South Dakota spoke for the citizens of Flynn's home state in a letter to Flynn on January 14, 1954, recognizing their native son "for meritorious and heroic acts" while in Korea. "You have, indeed, more than earned the honors bestowed upon you, and we are all very proud of you," he wrote.

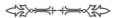

Flynn's heroism, however, had also earned him the unenviable task of providing testimony that could destroy the career and reputation of fellow Marine Corps aviator and hero of World War II Colonel Frank H. Schwable. The son of a Marine officer, the 47-year-old Schwable boasted an impressive military record. The U.S. Naval Academy graduate held four Distinguished Flying Crosses, ten Air Medals, and two Legions of Merit with a Gold Star in lieu of a third. When Pearl Harbor was attacked, Schwable was on an around-the-world tour as an observer for the Marine Corps. In England, he lived and worked with Royal Air Force pilots and attended the RAF fighter director school at Stanmore, where he gathered operating information on the British Mark IV aircraft interceptor radar system. In July 1942, Schwable was named Commanding Officer of the Marine Corps' first night-fighter squadron, VMF(N)-531. Pressured to meet deadlines under less-than-favorable conditions, Schwable prepared his men and their twin-engine PV-1 Vega Venturas for Pacific night combat. In September 1943, VMF(N)-531 began flying missions against the Japanese in the Solomon Islands. On January 12, 1944, Schwable shot down a Japanese Kate over Torokina Island, his first of four kills in the Solomons.[12]

Schwable's record had earned him an appointment as Chief of Staff of the Aviation Division, Headquarters Marine Corps. In April 1952, he was named Chief of Staff to Brigadier General Clayton C. Jerome, Commanding Officer of the 1st Marine Air Wing at P'ohang, South Korea. On July 8, Schwable and Major Roy Bley took off in a Beechcraft SNB on an inspection tour of the facilities of MAG-12 at P'yongt'aek. On their return flight, the two made a navigation error and found themselves over enemy lines, where 40mm antiaircraft shells ripped through the plane's fuselage, wounding Bley and damaging the fuel system. Both men parachuted to the ground, where they were captured by Chinese soldiers. Because he was on a routine inspection tour and had no intention of flying near a combat zone, Schwable was in uniform with his wallet and flight-clearance ticket on his person, providing Chinese interrogators with valuable personal and military information.[13]

For two weeks, Schwable misled his interrogators, claiming that he was new to Korea, had been shot down during his initial inspection tour, and knew little about U.N. operations. The ploy might have worked indefinitely, had not *The New York Times* and other newspapers run Schwable's biography, effectively informing the enemy that they were in possession of the Chief of Staff of the 1st Marine Air Wing. On July 24, 1952, Schwable was moved to Pike's Peak interrogation center, where, at that very moment, Captain Pat Flynn was enduring psychological torture from Chinese officers determined to extract his biological-warfare confession.[14]

Schwable was a prize catch for the Communists, who pressed him to confess to supervising tactical germ warfare against North Korean and Chinese troops and civilians. From September to November 1952, Schwable was isolated in an unheated mud lean-to and required to sit at attention, except during designated sleep periods. Deprived of adequate food and water, living in dirt and his filth, undergoing constant interrogation and mental torture, and convinced that he would eventually freeze to death, Schwable yielded to the interrogators' pressure in late November.[15] Over a two-week period, he fabricated a report, later referred to as the "Fleas, Flies and Mosquito Confession," that described U.S. plans for biological warfare and the conduct and effects of germ bomb missions. Chinese officers edited Schwable's draft; the revised document indicted the United States for inhumane actions against Asians. Distributed and radio-broadcast internationally, Schwable's signed "confession" of January 21, 1953, coupled with a similar document signed by Major Roy Bley, became an effective piece of Chinese propaganda. The two confessions, writes historian John Toland, were "a masterly coup for the Communists," who circulated the documents among the delegates of the U.N. General Assembly convening in New York City on January 23.[16]

Schwable's confession charged that in October 1951, the Joint Chiefs of Staff initiated bacteriological bombings. The document provided detailed information, written in a terse, military style, on the specific objectives of these missions. The confession stated:

> The effectiveness of the different diseases available was to be tested, especially for their spreading of epidemic qualities

under various circumstances, and to test whether each disease caused a serious disruption to enemy operations and civilian routine or just minor inconveniences, or was contained completely, causing no difficulties.

Various delivery methods would be employed by U.S. pilots, who would allegedly conduct bombing runs at night. According to the document, Okinawa-based Air Force B-29s had carried out the first "bacteriological bomb operations" in November 1951, followed by the F7F-3(N) Tigercats of VMF(N)-513 — Flynn's squadron. "By the end of January 1952," the confession declared, "night fighters of the 513th Squadron [were] making isolated night reconnaissance flights and conducting operations in connexion [sic] with bacteriological bombs. . . ." The document specifically identified Tigercats like the one in which Flynn had been shot down as the preferred delivery vehicles because of their "twin-engine safety."[17]

With Schwable's confession as its key article, the Marine Corps' Court of Inquiry convened on January 23, 1954. A day earlier, the U.S. Army had filed court-martial charges against Corporal Edward S. Dickenson — who, along with Corporal Claude J. Batchelor, had stayed behind temporarily in North Korea with 21 other American POWs who rejected repatriation after the war. The Dickenson court-martial gave the Schwable inquiry a tone of urgency, though the *Washington Post* did its best to differentiate between the two cases. Dickenson stood charged with attempting to "curry favor with his captors" and collaborating in a manner that may have "injured his fellow prisoners." Such allegations, maintained the *Post*, stood in sharp contrast to Schwable's behavior. It was a "terrible fate," the *Post* declared, "to be one of several captured American fliers who were subjected by their Communist captors to outrageous tortures prolonged over several months for the purpose of extorting statements concerning germ-warfare from them." The *Post* questioned whether "any board of officers," or, for that matter, "an American newspaper office," should decide the fate of pilots who had been subjected to the "technique" and "scientific perfection" of Communist Chinese interrogation.[18]

The Court of Inquiry deciding Schwable's fate consisted of three Marine Generals and a Navy flag officer. Major General Henry Linscott was a veteran of 30 years and an authority on military law. Major General

Christian Schilt held the Medal of Honor for heroism during the Nicaraguan rebellion in 1928. Major General Robert Bare directed the Marine Corps Development Center at Quantico, Virginia, and Rear Admiral Thomas Cooper served as Assistant Chief of the Navy Bureau of Medicine and Surgery.[19] The four heard testimony from the 50 witnesses in an improvised courtroom in Building Four, Henderson Hall Barracks, Arlington, Virginia. During the second day of the proceedings (February 17, 1954), Schwable, represented by Colonel Paul D. Sherman and a civilian lawyer, Mr. John H. Pratt, issued a 24-page report detailing the Communists' "diabolical, methodical, unrelenting system of breaking down a human being to the point where he can no longer resist." Schwable described the Communists' "new method," which, he argued, "only the Communist people thoroughly understand."[20] It was difficult for Schwable to judge the court's reaction to his report, for on the following day, Major Roy H. Bley, the co-pilot of Schwable's downed plane, learned that the court suspected him of "having dealings with the enemy." Bley immediately retained Colonel Sherman as his counsel.[21]

Many ex-POWs testified before the court, including Army Major General William Dean, commander of the 24th Infantry Division at the time of his capture, who expressed sympathy for Schwable and urged the court to consider the conditions experienced by Schwable and other "confessors." After concluding his testimony, Dean, the highest-ranking U.S. officer captured during the war, walked over to Schwable and shook his hand. Other witnesses included Navy Lieutenant Andrew Riker, Flynn's comrade from Camp 2 Annex, and Lieutenant Colonel William Thrash, decorated with Flynn at the Pentagon.[22]

Pat Flynn and Major Dee E. Ezell, described by *Washington Post* writer Stan Stavisky as "Leatherneck officers" who "begged for death rather than sign germ-warfare 'confessions,'" took the witness stand on the morning of March 2. The accounts of their ordeals received front-page coverage in the March 3 issue of the *Washington Post*. After his swearing-in, Flynn, described as a "jut-jawed combat flier," gave a summary of his capture and interrogations by Chinese officers before and during his detainment at Pike's Peak. The counsel for the court, Lieutenant Colonel Kenneth E. Murphy, questioned Flynn, who confirmed the layout of Pike's Peak, described the prisoners' holding bunkers, and discussed his interrogations in the spring and summer of 1952. Though he downplayed incidents of physical torture, he stressed the debilitating effects of the "rigid silence" requirement.

> While I was in the bunker, the second one, I am talking about, in solitary, I was never allowed to make any sound. I couldn't sing or talk to myself or make any sound. . . . It had the effect on my morale because I had too much time to think and the silence bothered me a great deal.[23]

Flynn emphasized to the court that his faith had sustained his physical strength and reinforced his resistance against signing a false confession. He described reasoning with a Pike's Peak interrogator, telling them that his religious convictions made it impossible for him to write and sign a confession:

> I tried to tell him that according to my religion, being a Catholic, that if I gave him this I would be guilty of grievous sin in that I would be aiding a godless cause and turning my back on my [Christian] faith.
> I went to great length to tell him that in the event I died before I got to a priest, which I thought there was a good chance of, I would forfeit my hope for eternal happiness.
> That is the point I spent a good deal of time talking on.[24]

Flynn described his death sentence for war crimes, and his captors informing him that if he maintained his stubbornness, the sentence would be carried out "in a matter of days." He told how he had resigned himself to death, thinking, "This is as good a way as any." He had reflected on the lives of the saints and, finding strength in the realization that "it isn't everyone that could be a martyr," prepared for "their going ahead with it."[25]

In a remarkable exchange with court counsel Lieutenant Colonel Kenneth E. Murphy on the effectiveness of Chinese interrogation methods, Flynn confessed that his captors had destroyed his patriotic resolve. "If it was not for my religion I could not say what my actions would be," Flynn testified. Although he considered himself patriotic, his "patriotic sense of values became distorted" under food and sleep deprivation, insidious mental tortures, misleading propaganda, and filthy living conditions. "I am ashamed to think right now what my patriotic values were because they weren't very good," Flynn confessed. Patriotic values, at least in Flynn's case, were "not sufficient" for resistance, and he feared he "was losing them."

"Yet you retained your moral values through the church?" asked Lieutenant Colonel Murphy.

"Yes," Flynn replied, "that is the only thing I had."[26]

After Flynn recalled the events of his trial and sentencing, Murphy turned to the issue of Schwable and Bley's confessions. Chinese officers had shared the confessions with Flynn in July 1953, less than two months before his release. Flynn explained the Chinese General's threat to prevent his repatriation unless he wrote and signed a similar confession, the General punctuating his threat by taking Flynn to a hillside and showing him a convoy of trucks loaded with soon-to-be-repatriated POWs.[27]

In his cross-examination, Colonel Paul D. Sherman asked Flynn if he had cooperated with the Chinese. Flynn admitted to providing information on conventional bombs, flight training, and VMF(N)-513 aircraft and armaments. On the other hand, he rejected the practicality of germ bombs, provided meaningless data on F7F-3(N) radar systems, and made several false, "fantastic" claims about group and squadron organizations that the Chinese accepted as true.

Flynn testified to the effectiveness of Chinese Communist interrogation methods. Because of his "sense of values" being eroded by the imprisonment, Flynn acknowledged that the interrogators began to get information, "gradually drawing it from me." He remembered "making excuses" for himself, "saying this can't be important" and getting to the point where he then believed it to be so. He concluded "that it would not be very important" to give the Chinese a little useless information, and thus he provided it, recognizing the precarious slope he was headed down. From the text of the testimony, one can discern Flynn striving for honesty and accuracy while expressing doubts about his behavior as a POW.

> I can't remember too well what I told them. It may have been important, and it may not; I don't know.[28]

But in his closing remarks, Flynn insisted that, despite his deteriorating psychological condition in solitary confinement, he rejected germ-warfare claims as a "farce" and had no intention of writing and signing a false confession.[29]

In the days following Flynn's testimony, the court heard from Dr. Alan M. G. Little, a State Department expert on Russian propaganda methods, and Dr. Joost K. M. Meerloo, a psychiatrist and former member of the Dutch underground interrogated by the Nazi SS during World War II. Both men testified to the effectiveness of Communist mental-torture techniques in destroying POW resistance. According to Little, American POWs served as subjects in China's "great experiment" to prove the effectiveness of their "propaganda pressure techniques." The "luckless aviators" were victims of the most intensive torture by the Chinese "shock brigade," whose method was to "combine degradation and mental torture with intensified indoctrination . . . in a manufactured sense of guilt." Meerloo reinforced Little's conclusions, charging that "Red 'menticide'" could force anyone, including the court's members, to write and sign a confession similar to Schwable's. In the end, the only way a captive could escape menticide — the "organized system of psychological intervention and judicial perversion in which a power tyrant synthetically injects his own thoughts and words into the minds and mouths of the victims" — was through "death or madness." According to Meerloo and Little, the application of Communist menticide extended far beyond the captor-captive relationship. Both witnesses warned of the dangers of mass indoctrination that, in Meerloo's estimation, was "a much greater threat to the free world than genocide."[30]

Apparently the testimony of Little, Meerloo, and the military witnesses swayed the court, which, after deliberating for six weeks, recommended no further action against Schwable. The Colonel, wrote the court, had "resisted this torture to the limit of his ability to resist [*and had*] reasonable justification" for writing and signing a biological-warfare confession. The court accepted the scientists' conclusions on Communist propaganda and interrogation, noting that under intensive mental torture, one of three things takes place: "The victim's will to resist is broken and he responds as the enemy desires; the victim becomes insane; or the victim dies."[31]

Flynn, who had harbored serious reservations about testifying about a fellow Marine and former POW, sympathized with Schwable. In an address to the South Dakota Legion Convention just two days after his testimony, Flynn discussed the many "misconceptions" surrounding the Schwable case. The Marine Corps, he argued, was simply attempting to establish a policy toward POW behavior. He warned the Legionnaires not to underestimate the hypnotic power of Communist propaganda, which, Flynn admitted, he also "was believing" for a time. "I didn't think I could, but I did. They pump it into you day and night . . . you hear nothing but that." And, again, in a message that he would reiterate many times in the years to come, Flynn credited his faith in God as the one factor that had enabled him to resist Communist indoctrination. "I believed that if I aided a Godless cause, I would, in effect, be turning my back on God." Convinced that the Chinese would eventually kill him, he refused to "forfeit eternal life for them," an act of stubbornness that prevented him from losing his "self-respect."[32]

Flynn issued a challenge to his audience. "Communism has but one purpose and that is to rule all mankind," he stated. "The only way to defend yourself is to know something about it." Flynn warned the convention delegates that the war was not over, it was just beginning. "There will be backfire wars for years to come."[33]

Two days later, Pat Flynn was back in California preparing for those wars — fierce ideological struggles characterized by nuclear threats and guerilla insurgencies in steamy Asian jungles.

Chapter 7

Cold Warrior

Crusades, even when failures, are emotionally satisfying. Wars of containment, wars of policy, are not. They are hard to justify unless it is admitted that power, not idealism, is the dominant factor in the world, and that idealism must be backed by power.

T. R. Fehrenbach, *This Kind of War: The Classic Korean War History*[1]

ARCHITECTS OF foreign policy during the presidencies of Dwight D. Eisenhower (1953-1961) and John F. Kennedy (1961-1963) sought to balance nuclear deterrence strategies with methods for fighting limited wars through conventional means. Eisenhower and his tough-talking Secretary of State John Foster Dulles envisioned a military with the strength, flexibility, and mobility to meet any form of Communist aggression. They were prepared to use nuclear weapons in an all-out war with the USSR or a localized "periphery" conflict in which tactical nuclear weapons would be added to conventional arsenals.² Writing in *Foreign Affairs* in 1954, Dulles, warning that the free world could not deter the Soviets "at every point where they might attack," urged a strategy founded on America's "special assets, . . . especially air and naval power and atomic weapons." A strategy devoted to "flexibility and the facilities which make various responses available" would guarantee the defense of the continental United States and Western Europe while deterring Communist aggression in peripheral regions of lesser strategic importance.³

Three years after the publication of Dulles's article, Dr. Henry Kissinger, writing for the Council on Foreign Relations, called for a re-examination of the flexibility debate, noting that America's obsession with an all-out Soviet attack on the continental U.S. left the country "vulnerable . . . to the preferred form of Soviet aggression: internal subversion and limited war."⁴ The Kennedy administration did re-examine flexibility, and in the process placed a greater emphasis on the country's preparation for fighting guerilla wars against Communist insurgents. General Maxwell D. Taylor, Kennedy's military advisor and later chairman of the Joint Chiefs of Staff, proposed a "Strategy of Flexible Response" to prepare U.S. forces "to react across the entire spectrum of possible challenge, for coping with anything from general atomic war to infiltrations and aggressions. . . ."⁵ Kennedy himself envisioned a flexible-response capability that included the deployment of special forces for fighting "wars of subversion" in underdeveloped African, Asian, and Latin American nations.⁶ Like his predecessor in the Oval Office, Kennedy was concerned about the vulnerability of U.S. allies on the periphery, especially in Southeast Asia, where, he believed, if one non-Communist country fell to insurgents, its neighbors would collapse like a string of falling dominoes.⁷

Pat Flynn's military career had spanned the Eisenhower-Kennedy years and was thus shaped by the geopolitical issues facing their administrations. After transitioning from propeller to jet aircraft in the mid-1950s, Flynn trained in the delivery of tactical nuclear weapons and, in an 18-month deployment to the U.S. Air Force, became familiarized with the mission of the Strategic Air Command (SAC). In 1958, he joined a Marine squadron charged with a nuclear mission, deployed for a Mediterranean cruise in 1959, and in 1960, attended the Air Force Command and Staff College to study Cold War strategy. In 1962-1963, Lieutenant Colonel Flynn served as an intelligence officer in the Far East and Southeast Asia, an assignment that exposed him to Maoism and the guerilla war in South

Vietnam. Through the years, Flynn's POW story and his Code of Conduct lectures had earned him the praise and respect of dozens of military and civilian audiences around the country.

After returning to MCAS El Toro following his post-Korea recuperation, Flynn joined Marine Training Group-10, where he and other ex-POWs polished their aviation skills and trained in straight-wing jet fighters. After logging over 86 hours in Lockheed TV-2 Sea Star trainers, Douglas F3D-2 Skyknights, and F9F-2 Panthers, Flynn was transferred in the summer of 1954 to VMF(N)-542, an all-weather Skyknight squadron based at El Toro. In addition to his aviation duties, Flynn served as assistant squadron maintenance officer and, in recognition of his POW record, lectured at the Marine Corps Survival School.[8]

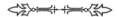

Marine Corps aviation in the post-Korea era was characterized by jet research and development. Flynn found jet propulsion exhilarating, but his return to full-time flying status was marred by a spate of tragedies involving several close friends. In the 18 months after Korea, four ex-POW Marine aviators — Richard Bell, Byron H. Beswick, and Arthur Wagner at El Toro, and Duke Williams, Jr., at MCAS Cherry Point, North Carolina — were killed in flying accidents. "Ding" Bell appeared to have passed out while flying solo over the Pacific Ocean during a training flight. He made no radio contact with El Toro tower prior to the accident, and neither he nor his plane were recovered. Just hours before his crash in California's Mojave Desert, "Buzz" Beswick was in good spirits, rattlesnake hunting with Flynn in the desert. While flying at 25,000 feet, Beswick radioed that he was in trouble and "passing out." Beswick's jet began spiraling downward as Flynn and other airborne pilots tried to communicate with him. They received no reply. Williams probably blacked out as well, though Wagner's death was classified as a drowning after he struck his head against the canopy and lost consciousness while ditching a malfunctioning aircraft in the Pacific Ocean.[9]

Flynn was deeply troubled by the death of Beswick, a warm and selfless man who had been shot down and captured on his 135th mission over Korea. Beswick had suffered severe injuries in a fire that engulfed his cockpit during the bailout. He was burned over his entire face and experienced temporary blindness, yet he never complained about his condition

Pat Flynn and an F3D Skyknight, MCAS El Toro, California, 1954.

and offered his clothing to sick prisoners.[10] To the end of his life, Flynn insisted that had Beswick, Bell, Wagner, and Williams received more thorough physical and psychological examinations following Korea repatriation, they would not have died in aircraft accidents. Writing several months before his death, Flynn recounted how, after the war, he and the ex-POW aviators discussed the "tensions from P.O.W. trauma and fear of flight as we were all shot down and had our P.O.W. confinement to brood on the experiance [sic]." Trauma and fear, he believed, explained the in-flight blackouts that led to the accidents involving his comrades. Flynn (who had lost consciousness while co-piloting an SNB during a training mission in early 1954) wrote that the aviators' "heart conditions" had yet to stabilize, and they should have been grounded or assigned to dual-control aircraft until medical tests cleared them of any maladies. "But no one wanted to be considered a 'chicken,'" he noted, adding that after Wagner's death, the U.S. Navy Department of Medicine either grounded the ex-POWs or placed them under close medical surveillance. "This whole matter was very embarrassing to [the Navy]," noted Flynn, and he and other ex-POW aviators, though convinced they were suffering the lingering effects of psychological trauma, "pledged to keep silent on this continuing problem."[11]

A Veterans Administration report published the year after Pat Flynn's premature death in 1979 lends credibility to his concerns about the long-term effects of POW trauma. In their *Study of Former Prisoners of War* (1980), the VA found that "medical repatriation procedures" and "repatriation examinations" for Korean War POWs were "not completely adequate." The study emphasized the higher occurrence of service-connected disability among Korea POWs and identified "anxiety neurosis" as a severe, prevalent, and recurring condition suffered by ex-captives. Symptoms associated with anxiety neurosis — general anxiety and nervousness, startle reaction (wherein ordinary stimuli like a ringing phone alarm the victim), insomnia and nightmares, phobias, psychosomatic complaints, memory lapses, moodiness, inferiority complex, obsession with the past, depression, apathy, and "survivor guilt" — resembled "K-Z" or "concentration camp syndrome," a condition experienced by Holocaust survivors. Anxiety symptoms intensify during the night hours, accompanied by nightmares that become "'acted-out' recollections of traumatic prison-camp experiences." The "residuals of physical and psychological disabilities suffered during captivity still affect the current health status of former POWs," noted the report's authors, who cited three separate post-Korea studies connecting the high ex-POW mortality rate, as measured in accidents, suicide, and homicide, to postwar psychological trauma.[12]

Flynn suffered from most, if not all, of the symptoms associated with anxiety neurosis. But in 1955, he had little time to dwell on the tragic effects of POW trauma. On March 9, he left VMF(N)-542 and joined VMF-314, an F9F-5 Panther squadron stationed at El Toro. A few weeks after his transfer, Flynn was promoted to Major, a rank that brought with it the added responsibility of squadron Operations Officer. While with VMF-314, Flynn took part in maneuvers over the Mojave Desert, where the squadron trained in gunnery, strafing, bombing, and rocket firing. In 1955, he participated in the OPERATION TEAPOT Nuclear Weapons Test at the Nevada Test Site, an exercise involving 100 aircraft and extensive night flying. TEAPOT proved critical to the Navy's assessment of tactical nuclear weapons and stimulated development of a nuclear capability for carrier-based aircraft.[13]

VMF-314 joined the rest of the 3rd Marine Air Wing (MAW) in November 1955 to take part in the Pacific Training Exercise (PACTRAEX), a large operation that involved the 1st Marine Division, U.S. and Canadian ships, and 300 U.S. Marine, U.S. Navy, and Canadian aircraft. VMF-314's Panther jets flew as aggressor aircraft, impressing the ground umpires with their attacks against "friendly" Infantry, tanks, vehicles, and planes.[14]

In August 1956, the Marine Corps loaned Flynn to the U.S. Air Force for an 18-month exchange assignment with the Strategic Air Command's 12th Strategic Fighter Wing at Bergstrom Air Force Base, Austin, Texas. Since the Korean War, when the Far East Air Force exercised "coordination control" over all special tactical operations, Marine Air had cooperated in joint operations with the Air Force. During the war, the Air Force and Marines minimized their disagreements over air-support doctrines — disagreements that had been rooted, write James A. Winnefeld and Dana J. Johnson, in "different conceptions of the proper role of airpower, the different training and equipment priorities that flowed from these conceptions, and the different employment practices shaped by the capabilities and limitations of the aircrews and equipment available."[15] In Korea, Air Force commanders accommodated the concerns of the Marines, who were determined to have their air assets available to conduct close air support for Marine ground troops. The Air Force granted the Marines some independence in planning and ordering air operations, an arrangement that resulted in an effective integration of Air Force-Marine control.[16] In Korea, an arrangement between the Fifth Air Force and the 1st MAW allowed combat-tested Marine aviators to join Air Force F-86 Sabre jet squadrons for several weeks of duty. In all, Marine F-86 Sabre pilots — including Korea ace Major John F. Bolt and future astronaut Major John Glenn — shot down 21 Soviet-built MiG-15s.[17]

After the war, the Air Force and Marine Corps instituted the pilot exchange program that Flynn became part of in 1956. At Bergstrom, Flynn was expected to broaden his understanding of Air Force operating procedures, technology, maintenance systems, attitudes, and practices, in addition to deepening his exposure to joint air operations and SAC's strategic nuclear mission. In assignments with the 559th and 561st Strategic Fighter Squadrons, Flynn flew his first swept-wing fighter, the F-84F Thunderstreak. The Thunderstreak evolved directly from an existing straight-wing aircraft, the F-84E Thunderjet. In Korea, the E model served as the Air Force's primary fighter-bomber and became the first American fighter-bomber outfitted for delivering small atomic bombs like the Mark VII, an implosion weapon that is considered the first tactical nuclear weapon developed for U.S. aviation.[18]

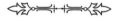

In many ways, Major Pat Flynn's Air Force training resembled his Marine flying schedule. Navigation training, tactical formation flying, aerial refueling practice, night-formation flying, instrument training, air-to-air and ground gunnery, dive bombing, and simulated aerial combat filled much of his SAC regimen. As the mission of the 12th Strategic Fighter Wing included a nuclear weapons capability, Flynn likely trained in the "over-the-shoulder" delivery technique that SAC fighter pilots used when releasing dummy nuclear bombs. To conduct the over-the-shoulder maneuver, the pilot streaked toward his target at low altitude to avoid radar detection. The pilot actually flew over and beyond his target, at which point he performed a steep ascent, releasing his dummy bomb in a vertical position but at an angle that would "throw" the bomb back toward the target. And, as the bomb curled back toward the target, the pilot completed a loop and accelerated from the area to avoid the effects of a nuclear blast.

Marine Major Pat Flynn climbing into the cockpit of an F-84F Thunderstreak of the USAF 561st Fighter Squadron, Bergstrom Air Force Base, Texas, in 1957. Flynn was on an exchange assignment with the Strategic Air Command's 12th Strategic Fighter Wing.

Flynn performed well in this and other areas of SAC training, for by April 1957, he had earned the designations of 561st Mission Leader and Instructor Pilot for the F-84F.

The Air Force respected Flynn's POW record, evidenced by the Code of Conduct and evasion-and-survival lectures he presented to Air Force audiences in the 1950s and 1960s. Flynn's reputation preceded his arrival at the SAC Officer Staff Commanders Course at Chanute Air Force Base in Illinois, in the fall of 1956. In the words of one Chanute writer, POW Flynn was a "major headache to the Chinese Communists" and "a first-class thorn in the side of his Commie captors." Flynn told Air Force pilots that if captured, "The best thing you can do is not think of your family at all." Instead, he emphasized, "Worry about self-survival, and keeping your strength and self-respect." In reference to the Code of Conduct for Members of the Armed Forces of the United States, an Executive Order promulgated by President Eisenhower in August 1955 to establish standards expected of U.S. servicemen in combat or captivity, Flynn reminded readers not to "feel that, just because you're a prisoner, you have no responsibility to the United States. You're still an American serviceman."[19] The Chanute interview marked one of Flynn's first public statements on the cardinal value of the Code of Conduct. For the remainder of his career, he contributed mightily to meeting Eisenhower's order that "each member of the armed forces liable to capture shall be provided with specific training and instruction designed to better equip him to counter and withstand all enemy efforts against him . . . during combat or captivity."[20]

Although he would receive another Air Force assignment in the early 1960s, Flynn and his wife and three children (Teresa was born in Austin in 1957) rejoined the Marine Corps in January 1958. His return assignment was with Headquarters & Maintenance Squadron-14, Marine Corps Air Station (MCAS) Edenton, North Carolina, where he logged 35 hours in the Grumman F9F-8B Cougar. Three months later, he was back with an attack squadron, VMA-225, based at Edenton until October 1958, when the squadron transferred to MCAS Cherry Point, North Carolina.[21]

Flynn joined VMA-225 just as the squadron was replacing its piston-engine AD-5N Skyraiders with the Douglas A4D-2 (later A-4) Skyhawk, a single-engine attack jet introduced to select Navy and Marine Corps squadrons in the fall of 1956. With the exception of the F4U Corsair, Flynn spent more time in the Skyhawk than any other aircraft. At a time when aviation experts were clamoring for large combat jets, Douglas chief engineer Ed Heinemann, designer of the Skyraider and A-26 Invader, unveiled the A-4, which weighed less than half of the 30,000-pound weight stipulated by the Navy for its new attack aircraft. Capable of undertaking a wide variety of combat missions, the A-4, affectionately referred to as "Heinemann's Hot Rod," was a remarkably responsive aircraft, evidenced by its selection as the aircraft of choice by the U.S. Navy Blue Angels precision flying team from 1973 to 1985. Though it had been designed to provide lethal close air support, the Skyhawk was also expected to carry tactical nuclear weapons; its long landing gear raised the plane high enough to accommodate the tail fins of an atomic bomb attached to its belly.[22]

For 25 years, the A-4 formed the backbone of the Navy-Marine light-attack mission. In the words of one Navy veteran, the A-4 "was a great joy for all carrier aviators who manned its cockpits . . . a jewel to bring aboard the carrier and steady as a rock in the landing configuration." It tracked well during high-speed bombing runs "and could be flown into highly accurate bombing and rocket attacks."[23] The A-4 compiled an illustrious combat record in Vietnam and was exported in large numbers to air forces in Indonesia, Australia, Malaysia, Singapore, New Zealand, Kuwait, Israel, and Argentina. Skyhawks were still flying in the late 1990s, a tribute to the toughness and reliability of one of the finest attack jets ever built.[24]

Pat Flynn began flying A-4s in late April 1958, and by October his flight log showed 132 hours in the jet. Although much of the training was routine, VMA-225 aviators were expected to master skills new to Flynn's repertoire: the "lofting" of dummy nuclear weapons in the Navy way (as opposed to the Air Force over-the-shoulder maneuver) and carrier launching and landing. In addition to conventional bomb, rocket, napalm, and gunnery training, Flynn and his comrades practiced the delivery of tactical nuclear weapons, lofting or "tossing" a simulated A-bomb, possibly a dummy Mark 28 series bomb — a one-megaton nuclear device designed for low-level delivery. (Introduced in 1958, the 2,000-pound Mark 28 became the standard jet-delivery weapon for the strategic and tactical aircraft of the Air Force, Navy, and Marines.)[25]

With the advent of guided nuclear missiles in the 1950s, the Navy and Marine Corps were under great pressure to demonstrate the utility of jet-delivered nuclear weapons. Budgets for the nation's missile program were increasing dramatically, from $800 million in 1950 to $7 billion in

1960. The Air Force's Atlas and Thor ballistic missiles were operational by the late 1950s, as was the Jupiter C missile, which by 1956 was achieving distances of 3,000 miles.[26]

Former Navy Commander Jerry Miller notes that in developing an effective nuclear weapons delivery method for attack jets, scientists, engineers, and aviators faced the daunting challenge of getting the bomb to target without sacrificing the delivery aircraft and its pilot. To provide an "escape envelope" for the pilot to avoid the pressure and radiation associated with an atomic blast, experimental squadrons developed the loft/toss maneuver, which began with the pilot flying at high speed and minimum altitude toward the target. At a calculated distance from the target, Miller writes, "the pilot initiated a pull-up using a prescribed G acceleration force and speed. . . ." At a calculated angle of climb — usually about 45 degrees to guarantee a maximum "throw" from the aircraft to target — the pilot released the bomb, which arced toward its goal. The pilot then performed an "aggressive escape maneuver" to minimize the effects of the bomb's detonation. The half Cuban-eight maneuver — in which the pilot made the first part of a loop, then rolled out and dove for minimum altitude while speeding directly away from the target — was the preferred escape method following mock nuclear delivery.[27]

Pat Flynn and his comrades spent long hours honing their lofting/tossing skills and escape maneuvers. Carrier launch and recovery procedures also required extensive practice. As is the case with many Navy and Marine aviators, Flynn remembered carrier launches and landings as the most strenuous moments of his flying career, a sentiment confirmed by a 1967 biomedical study conducted by NASA. In studies aboard the USS *Bon Homme Richard* and *Constellation*, NASA scientists discovered that pilots' heart rates during launch and recovery reached 125-130 beats per minute, as compared to 100 beats per minute during a bombing run that generated 4G stress during a pull-out. The results surprised NASA experts, who concluded that "non-physical stress in pilots is substantially less during bombing than during a carrier landing or launching."[28]

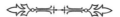

In October 1958, in preparation for their deployment to carrier duty with the U.S. Sixth Fleet in the Mediterranean Sea, VMA-225 aviators practiced field carrier landings on the Cherry Point runways, logging as many as eight or nine landings per day. In April 1959, Flynn began launch and recovery training on a carrier, and in May made his first night carrier landing, a terrifying experience for the most experienced of naval aviators. By the time of VMA-225's deployment in August 1959, Flynn had completed approximately 30 carrier landings, according to his flight log, and qualified for in-flight refueling in the A-4.

Major Flynn served as VMA-225's Operations officer, an assignment that gave him the opportunity to teach and assist the younger pilots. Richard "Dick" Hoffman, a Second Lieutenant when he joined the squadron in 1958, recalled how Flynn, "a very good pilot," took him "under his wing. He looked out for me, settled me down, and gave me confidence." Hoffman, who served as the assistant Operations officer, was "impressed" with Flynn's desire to put Marine Corps aviation on the "cutting edge of things . . . He was always interested in advancing the cause, doing whatever was good for the Corps' image."[29]

One example of Flynn's advancement of Marine Corps aviation took place on January 24, 1959, when he and another VMA-225 pilot (and fellow South Dakotan) Captain Clifford D. Warfield, established a cross-country flying record. Just prior to the record flight, the squadron had been training at the Naval Ordnance Test Station at China Lake, California, where they conducted tests to prove that the Navy's loft-maneuvering manual contained erroneous figures that failed to account for temperature when calculating bomb trajectories. Warfield recalls that in proving the shortcomings of the manual, VMA-225 put a "real feather in [*its*] cap."[30]

After completion of the China Lake tests, VMA-225 Commanding Officer Lieutenant Colonel A. R. Boag decided it was time to put another feather in the squadron's cap — the first non-stop, coast-to-coast flight without refueling in single-engine jets, from El Toro, California, to Cherry Point, North Carolina. On Saturday, January 24, 1959, Boag, Flynn, Warfield, and squadron Executive Officer Major G. F. Bauman filled their tanks with JP-5 jet fuel. The heavy fuel loads raised the A-4s' noses to an unacceptable height, forcing the ground crews to reduce hydraulic pressure on the nose gears and lower the nose sections of all four planes. With the adjustments completed, the pilots taxied their jets to the end of the runway, where fuel trucks topped off their tanks. The planes took off, but within seconds Boag discovered that his nose gear would not retract — the consequence of the hydraulic adjustments made prior to takeoff. Boag and his wingman Bauman peeled off and returned to El Toro, while Flynn and

Warfield, with the wind at their backs, set out to test whether a single-engine jet could fly coast-to-coast on those full tanks of JP-5.[31]

Following a direct route to Cherry Point, the two aviators maintained an altitude of 27,000 to 35,000 feet. Before the flight, Boag had designated NAS Memphis and MCAS Beaufort, South Carolina, as fuel checkpoints. If Flynn and Warfield arrived over Memphis with sufficient fuel, they were to proceed to Beaufort, where, if enough fuel remained, they could continue to their destination at Cherry Point. When the men reached Beaufort, approximately 270 miles from their destination, Flynn calculated their fuel requirements and made the decision to complete the flight. After 4 hours and 25 minutes and 2,082 miles, Flynn and Warfield touched down at Cherry Point and, in the process, entered the annals of aviation history. Their cross-country feat was recognized in the 1960-1961 edition of *Jane's All the World's Aircraft*.[32] Before the flight, recalls Dick Hoffman, "No one knew if it could be done," a mystery that made the record more satisfying.[33] Flynn ranked the non-stop flight as the most important aviation achievement of his 24-year Marine Corps career — a record, he boasted in later years, that undoubtedly caught the attention of the Soviet military.

In August 1959, Flynn bid farewell to his wife and four children (Sean was born in April 1959) and joined his VMA-225 comrades for a six-month Mediterranean Sea cruise aboard the USS *Essex*, "The Fightin'est Ship in the Fleet." The *Essex*, which relieved the Sixth Fleet's USS *Intrepid*, was a reconverted World War II-era aircraft carrier modified to accommodate nuclear weapons. Compared to the larger *Forrestal* and *Kitty Hawk* classes of carriers, the 41,000-ton *Essex* was relatively small in size — a fact that, according to Jerry Miller, former Commander of the Sixth Fleet, "greatly reduced the margin for error and operational efficiency." Miller salutes the aviators of *Essex*-class carriers. Those ships "were not large enough to continuously provide a stable landing platform, particularly when the direction of the wind is not the same as that of the heavy seas, a phenomenon that occurs occasionally."[34]

Pat Flynn thrilled to the sights and sounds of the Mediterranean. Liberty calls included Palma, Cannes, Barcelona, Naples, Rome, Florence, Athens, Thessaloniki, Beirut, Jerusalem, Genoa, and Venice. Flynn attended mass at St. Peter's, climbed the Acropolis, watched flamenco dancers in Barcelona, and distributed Christmas gifts to the orphans of Naples.[35] Wherever he went, Flynn absorbed European culture while sharing his Native American heritage with Continentals. Clad in full headdress and moccasins and following the rhythms of recorded Lakota drum music, Chief Flynn, referred to by one writer as a "Goodwill Dancer," performed traditional dances for hundreds of Europeans each month. "The people whose ancestors built the Coliseum and the Parthenon aren't easily impressed by monuments to the past," noted a stateside press release. "But reports from the Mediterranean indicate that the feather-wreathed head and moccasined feet of Major John Flynn are capturing the imagination and respect of hundreds of American friends overseas."[36]

Aboard the *Essex*, Flynn's trumpeting skills were in high demand. Under the sponsorship of the U.S. Information Office, the ship's musicians formed a jazz band, with Flynn as a featured soloist. During the intermissions of jazz gigs, he performed his traditional dancing to "the rhythms of the American Indian."[37]

Though sightseeing, exotic music, and foreign cuisine afforded a once-in-a-lifetime experience for the men of VMA-225, the squadron's two-fold mission — supporting NATO ground forces and SAC's nuclear objectives — was deadly serious. The Polish and Hungarian revolts (1956), the Suez Crisis (1956), the Lebanon intervention (1958), and ongoing U.S.-Soviet tensions over Berlin underscored the importance of the *Essex*'s presence in the Mediterranean Sea. In mid-December 1959, President Eisenhower, in Europe on a "peace tour" and to attend a summit of Western leaders in Paris, reminded the Sixth Fleet of its mission during a tour of the *Essex* Task Force. The *Essex* itself hosted 80 journalists traveling with Eisenhower, and on December 16, Flynn and other VMA-225 pilots participated in an air demonstration for the Commander-in-Chief.[38]

When at sea, VMA-225, the only Marine Corps squadron aboard the *Essex*, maintained a grueling flight schedule that Operations officer Flynn was responsible for overseeing. The squadron participated in NATO exercises, coordinating operations with both the Greeks and the Turks. It conducted conventional bombing and lofting exercises, rocket firing, close air support training, and airborne refueling, as well as hundreds of launches and recoveries. The squadron paid a heavy price for its efforts, for on the night of November 14, 1959, one of its own, Captain Paul J. Ermatinger, was lost at sea when he inadvertently taxied his jet over the edge of the *Essex*.[39]

Ermatinger's death dealt a heavy blow to the spirits of the men of VMA-225, but it also made them more determined to win the respect of

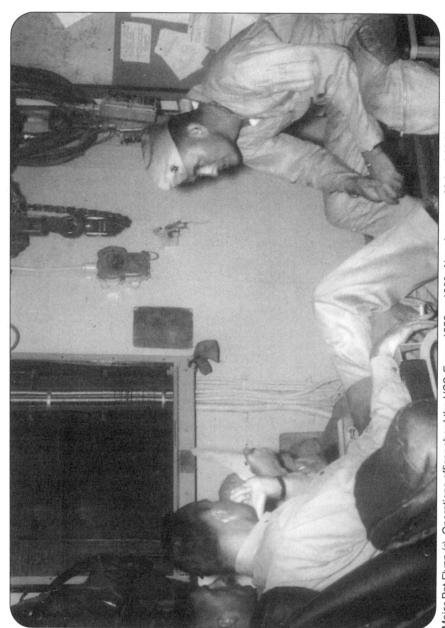

Major Pat Flynn (r), Operations officer aborad the USS *Essex*, 1959 or 1960. Also shown are Major J. V. Hanes (far l) and Major G. F. Bauman.

their Navy counterparts. Clifford Warfield remembered vividly the competitiveness brewing between the Marine and Navy fliers aboard the *Essex*. Too many Navy aviators "thought the Marines didn't know anything about carrier flying." Yet VMA-225 "performed well, much better than the Navy thought we would do." Flynn relished the inter-service competition, and pushed the younger pilots to meet the Navy challenge. "He was a great communicator, and very much a team person," noted Warfield. "He knew how to develop enthusiasm, how to motivate. . . . He had a reputation for being a great pilot. And everyone knew he wouldn't hold back. He was very competitive, a real competitor."[40]

Flynn played a leading role in the squadron's greatest inter-service victory, when, on January 23, 1960, every VMA-225 pilot became a "Centurion" — a title bestowed on an aviator following the completion of his 100th launch and recovery during a single cruise. Early in the cruise, Lieutenant Colonel Boag established a goal that each of his men would achieve the title of Centurion on the same day, a feat never accomplished by a Navy or Marine squadron. Boag's goal placed pressure on Flynn, who, as squadron Operations officer, was responsible for coordinating the launch and recovery cycle that would meet the CO's objective. What Boag desired, remembers Dick Hoffman, "was something unique," to establish a naval record by doing something "no squadron had ever done before." Flynn faced a challenge that "was tricky to work out, to get everybody to 100 on the same day." On occasion, one or two of the pilots would fall ill and miss flying opportunities, and it was up to Flynn "to get everybody caught up. Boag wanted the record, but it was [*Flynn*] who implemented it."[41]

When in early January it became apparent that the squadron could set the mark, Boag asked E. L. Feightner, Commander of Carrier Air Group 10, for his assistance and support in VMA-225's pursuit of naval history. Feightner forwarded Boag's request to the Air Operations department of the *Essex*'s Carrier Air Traffic Control Center. "Air Ops," responsible for coordinating all of the carrier's flying activities, promised its full cooperation. As of the last night recovery on January 22, 1960, all VMA-225 aviators had completed 99 landings.

The following day, Major Flynn made the squadron's first Centurion landing, followed by Bauman. Within hours, all 17 pilots had been recovered, making it "a clean sweep" by VMA-225, and a first in carrier aviation history.[42] The aviators gathered below the deck for a photograph, Boag

Above: Major Pat Flynn distributing gifts to orphans on the USS *Essex*, 1959 or 1960.

Opposite: "Centurions All." The men of VMA-225 after their historic landings aboard the USS *Essex*. Front row, l to r: Captain C. D. Warfield, Major J. V. Hanes, Major Pat Flynn, Lieutenant Colonel A. R. Boag, Major G. F. Bauman, and Captain S. J. Kittler. Back row, l to r: First Lieutenant R. P. Connolly, First Lieutenant R. T. Lawrence, First Lieutenant R. L. Hoffman, First Lieutenant M. T. Fountain, Lieutenant J. Kerwin, First Lieutenant F. M. Logan, First Lieutenant J. D. Sells, First Lieutenant M. L. Whitehouse, Captain J. E. Holland, Captain R. A. Plamondon, First Lieutenant B. P. Pike, Captain J. Enos, and Captain T. W. Nelson. Notably, Navy Lieutenant Joseph P. Kerwin (back row, 5th from l) was selected as a scientist-astronaut for NASA in 1965, and flew on the first manned Skylab (SL-2) mission in 1973.

displaying a VMA-225 flight schedule with the words "Centurions All" displayed boldly in the middle.

Pat Flynn's Mediterranean cruise ended on February 26, 1960, when VMA-225 landed its A-4s at Mayport Naval Air Station (NAS), Jacksonville, Florida. Flynn spent the next five months at Cherry Point, but in August 1960, returned to temporary duty with the Air Force, this time as one of eight Marine students in the Command and Staff College (CSC) of the Air University, Maxwell Air Force Base, Montgomery, Alabama. The Command and Staff College provided Flynn with a rich intellectual and cultural learning experience. Of the 51 foreign officers who were members of the class of 1961, two — a Saudi Arabian pilot and a Guatemalan pilot — were assigned with Flynn and nine Air Force officers to Wing III, Seminar 29. CSC instructors tested students' communication and problem-solving skills, and offered courses in international conflict, aerospace warfare systems, and Cold War geopolitics. High-ranking officers, foreign officials, intelligence analysts, engineers, economists, foreign policy scholars, and journalists lectured on NATO organization, command management, military doctrine and policy, general and limited warfare, and Cold War strategy.[43]

In fulfillment of his CSC research requirement, Flynn prepared a thesis paper that proposed changes in the survival kits issued to American fighter pilots. He documented the low priority given to survival-kit design and contents. "Development and modification of survival equipment for high speed jets must be oriented to the bailout situation," Flynn wrote, emphasizing that "forces encountered in high speed bailouts invariably result in partial and sometimes complete loss of survival equipment." The contents of survival kits could be improved by the inclusion of a small, malleable cooking container. "Most survival situations present favorable 'foraging' conditions," he noted, though it was up to individual pilots, many of whom were "not conditioned to subsist on certain plant and animal life unless it is prepared by cooking," to overcome their dietary fears. Flynn himself had "boiled small rodents, bugs, grasses, weeds, and 'things' that grow under rocks, and suffered no ill effects from eating them. Eating such provender raw is something else again." As the current Air Force survival kit did not include a cooking container, Flynn recommended adding a folded sheet of heavy aluminum foil, similar to that found in Navy and Marine aviators' kits. He recalled successful cooking experiments with the foil in 1958, adding that, as "a bonus value," the aluminum "offered high reflectivity for signaling purposes."[44]

Flynn graduated from the CSC on June 9, 1961. Following a ten-day cross-country drive, he arrived with his wife and five children (Timothy, the Flynns' last child, was born in Montgomery, Alabama, in 1961) at El Toro to begin a two-year stint as an assistant G-2 (Intelligence) officer with Headquarters, Aircraft Fleet Marine Force, Pacific. His nuclear weapons background earned him a temporary assignment at the Defense Atomic Support Agency in Albuquerque, New Mexico. Copies of Flynn's original orders show that in October and November 1961, Flynn attended to intelligence matters in Hawaii, Japan, and Okinawa. He went on to complete a weapons operation planning course at NAS North Island in San Diego in February 1962, and a month later, attended a top-secret counterinsurgency training course in Washington, D.C.

Flynn must have impressed the staff of the CSC, where, as a student, he lectured on his POW experiences. In September 1961 and again in January 1962, Flynn returned to the Air University and presented a series of Code of Conduct lectures to the members of the Squadron Officers School class of 1962. Colonel H. N. Holt of the Air University praised Flynn for "present[*ing*] just the arguments we needed to sell the Code." In addition to hundreds of Air Force officers, Flynn addressed officers from Bolivia, Taiwan, Colombia, Greece, South Korea, Laos, the Philippines, Thailand, and South Vietnam. His 1962 lecture, a one-hour presentation to 900 officers, was captured on videotape and used by the Air University for future Code of Conduct presentations. Entitled "The Code of Conduct Will Work," the lecture was an effort by Flynn to use his Korean War captivity experience as a means of demonstrating the "workability" of the Code. Flynn viewed his address as "an education program to promote a greater interest in the need for loyalty, leadership and high moral values during normal conditions as well as during war."[45]

Larry Willis, a Marine officer and student at CSC in 1962, recalled the excitement generated by Flynn's Code of Conduct lectures.

> The Air Force guys really talked about [*them*]. He had [*the men*] mesmerized, spellbound. There aren't many things that impress a fighter pilot, but Chief really impressed them. He got up on the stage and just awed them.[46]

Flynn kept a heavy lecture schedule for Marine Corps audiences, including a series of three Code of Conduct addresses to Marine Air Group (MAG)-16. In a letter of appreciation to Flynn's Commanding General, the MAG-16 Commander wrote that the addresses were "excellently presented and received with enthusiasm, . . . and the impact of hearing first-person experiences under these trying conditions was obvious. All present now have a deeper insight into the meaning of the Code of Conduct."[47] By the 1960s, Larry Willis notes, Flynn's Code of Conduct message had reached all levels of the Marine Corps. "He was held up as the example for us Marines. I knew him before I met him."[48]

In the fall of 1962, Flynn began a year-long overseas tour as Assistant Chief of Staff, G-2, Aircraft Fleet Marine Force, Pacific. Though based at MCAS Iwakuni, Japan, he traveled extensively throughout Southeast Asia, especially South Vietnam. His duties, according to two of his post-military resumes, included managing classified materials, supervising counterintelligence efforts, and providing top-secret briefings to flag and general officers and staffs responsible for planning operations against Communist forces in South Vietnam. Flynn was expected to monitor political activities in Vietnam, Laos, Cambodia, the Philippines, and Indonesia, and provide situation forecasts and unit profiles on Southeast Asian guerilla forces.

For the American mission in Vietnam, 1962 was a pivotal year. Historian George C. Herring writes that President Kennedy had made Vietnam "a test case of America's determination . . . to meet the challenges posed by guerilla warfare in the emerging nations." Kennedy and his team agreed "that the Vietnamese themselves must win the war," though the White House understood that it would take "the provision of American equipment and skilled American advisers" to defeat the Viet Cong and their North Vietnamese providers. In the months before Flynn's arrival in Asia, the South Vietnamese army (ARVN) and its American advisors mounted a two-pronged operation against the enemy, combining a military offensive with the implementation of the strategic hamlet program — a pacification program designed to isolate Viet Cong guerillas from South Vietnamese peasants.[49] Marine Corps helicopter units played a major role in the military offensive, transporting ARVN troops, food, arms and ammunition, medical supplies, and the dead and wounded in both the Mekong Delta and the northern provinces, an operation dubbed SHUFLY.[50]

Already motivated by his contribution to the U.S. effort in South Vietnam, Flynn received an added morale boost on October 19, 1962, when the silver oak leaves of Lieutenant Colonel were pinned to his shoulder boards. But four days later, Flynn's joy turned to frustration, the result of a titanic street brawl outside an Iwakuni bar. The fight further elevated Flynn's status among fellow Marines, and, to this day, is remembered vividly by many of Flynn's contemporaries, whether they witnessed the fight or not.

On the evening of Tuesday, October 23, Flynn and several officers had retired to the Iwakuni Officers Club for a few drinks. A 220-pound Navy Lieutenant Junior Grade with 17 years of service — and a black belt in judo — walked into the club and up to the bar, where he announced that he was ready "to whip a Marine." No one accepted the challenge, though as Flynn later learned, several Marines directed the Lieutenant to "try 'Chief' Flynn."[51] That other Marines would direct the antagonist toward Flynn did not surprise Frank Petersen, who served with Flynn at Iwakuni. Petersen was the Marine Corps' first African American aviator and the author of *Into the Tiger's Jaw* (1998). "No one could kick Chief's ass," recalled Petersen. "Everybody knew that."[52]

The ill-tempered Lieutenant approached Flynn and challenged him to a fight. When Flynn refused, the man insulted him, threw a drink into his face, and called him "yellow." Flynn admitted that he was yellow, left the Officers Club, and made his way to T. Harry's, an Iwakuni bar frequented by officers. The antagonist followed Flynn into the bar, insulted him again, and threw another drink in his face. "I accepted his challenge," Flynn wrote his wife several days later, adding that "[h]e is still in the hospital here at Iwakuni."[53]

Frank Petersen described the fight in front of T. Harry's as "one of the most talked about battles in Marine Corps history, a battle to remember." It lasted about 30 minutes, which played into Flynn's hands, Petersen adds, for "Chief Flynn was known in Marine circles for his extraordinary stamina and strength." The Lieutenant had gone for Flynn's left eye and "tried to gouge it out," then narrowly missed his groin with a kick that left a deep bruise on one of Flynn's thighs. In the end, however, boxing and street-fighting skills trumped martial arts training. Flynn kept jabbing at the man's face, and eventually the Navy Lieutenant was lying unconscious on the pavement. He was then, in Petersen's words, placed "into the meat wagon" and transported to the base hospital "where he stayed for a good long time." The doctor who treated the Lieutenant's broken jaw and sewed 26 stitches into his face accused Flynn of "savagery" and was "reputed to have said about the Navy guy" that he had "'never seen a man so brutally beaten in my life.'" Flynn required medical attention to repair his broken hands and a broken left arm that required a cast up to his elbow.[54]

Petersen first learned of the fight the following day, when he met Flynn in the Iwakuni officers' mess. "Chief," I exclaimed, "what the hell happened?" "Just an awareness test," Flynn replied, "just an awareness test."[55]

Marine and Navy authorities investigated the fight and exonerated Flynn. His opponent, on the other hand, was blamed for the incident and released by the Navy. Flynn found little consolation in the results of the inquiry or in the recognition that his "contemporaries & junior officers think I am the greatest. . . . I can feel sick at heart about the whole affair — I almost killed a man."[56] But Petersen, who would reach the rank of Lieutenant General before his retirement, viewed the Iwakuni incident as just another of the many lessons Flynn offered him and other Marines. "He was a class act. He did more things than were ever understood at the time." Petersen viewed Flynn as a natural-born leader and credited Flynn with teaching him, through example, "how to rise above all that racism" without being "confrontational toward the Marine Corps. . . . You had to follow him. Everybody respected him. Everybody loved him. I have never met another man with the sincerity, conviction, and strength of [*Flynn*]. Chief was a legend."[57]

Flynn's wounded body and spirit had little time to heal. On November 2, 1962, he flew on an intelligence-gathering mission to Da Nang, South Vietnam, where a Marine helicopter squadron, HMM-162, was flying ARVN troops, food, ammunition, and supplies to military outposts in support of Operation SHUFLY. Upon arriving, Flynn toured Da Nang, an old but thriving French colonial city and the second largest city in South Vietnam.[58] Marine Corps historian Robert H. Whitlow explains that with "its throngs of bicycles, and a noticeable dearth of automobile traffic, the city was certainly more Asian than European in appearance," though "the former French presence was evident in the architecture of public buildings, electric and telephone lines, paved streets, built-up waterfront, and an airfield."[59]

During several temporary assignments at Da Nang, Flynn accompanied Marine UH-34D Choctaw helicopter crews on their transport and supply missions into enemy territory. Flying over 90 miles per hour, the Choctaw could carry a squad of 12 ARVN troops 20 miles in 13 minutes. A fleet of 14 Choctaws could deliver an ARVN battalion of 165 men to a landing zone with their weapons, ammunition, and two days' supply of food. A half hour later, the helicopters could return with a second force and/or extract the original troop force. To muffle their approach, Choctaw pilots flew at tree-top level for the last two or three miles, the force from the helicopters' rotor blades driving the engine noise downward.[60]

Flynn flew in the co-pilot seat and, like the pilot, carried a side arm and wore (or sat on) armor pants and an armor vest to protect against the ground-to-air fire that was growing commonplace during the Marines' "administrative runs." Richard Tregaskis, an American journalist covering Marine operations at Da Nang in 1962-1963, in *Vietnam Diary*, described how guerillas ". . . could shoot up our particular aircraft with anything from a single homemade popgun to a section of heavy machine guns or a blasting battery of .57-mm. recoilless field pieces. . . ." Flynn witnessed the unloading of ARVN troops at landing zones and the delivery of supplies and ammunition to distant outposts near the Ho Chi Minh Trail on the South Vietnamese-Laotian border. He accompanied helicopter crews hauling pigs and five-gallon cans of *nuoc mam*, a strong-smelling fish oil used by the Vietnamese as a food seasoning and source of protein. Prepared in large vats and then fermented for a year, *nuoc mam* was, Tregaskis notes, "about as familiar in Vietnam as catsup is in the States."[61]

During a week-and-a-half assignment to Da Nang in May 1963, Flynn accompanied the Commanding Officer of HMM-162, Lieutenant Colonel Reinhardt Leu, as his squadron helilifted ARVN troops into the mountains of Quang Tri and Thua Thien provinces near the Laotioan border. Leu, who remembers Flynn as "a fine Marine" with a "colorful career in the Corps," placed his guest in the co-pilot seat, where Flynn observed ARVN troops in their multi-regiment drive against Communist infiltration routes on the Ho Chi Minh Trail. HMM-162's missions, whether troop transport, re-supply, or medical evacuation, were dangerous and flown in difficult terrain.[62]

In a May 14, 1963, letter to his wife written after a helilifting operation, Flynn described his feelings about the war in Vietnam:

> Today, flew co-pilot in helicopter deep into Communist territory and landed at an outpost. There is a war going on here. Had

Lieutenant Colonel Pat Flynn on an intelligence-gathering mission near the South Vietnamese-Laotian border, 1963.

picture taken with Vietnamese children at outpost. Children are the same everywhere — but they take a beating over here — in this jungle war. One of them offered me a fish he caught in the stream. Would have liked to take them all out with me. Poor, dirty, hungry, love-starved, homeless babies.

Nine days later, Flynn received a letter from Leu with the photographs of Flynn and the children enclosed. In his letter, Leu explained that the Viet Cong had attacked the outpost the day after Flynn's visit, killing 7 and wounding 25. Flynn forwarded the photos to his wife. "Children's parents were killed by the Commies," he wrote on May 23, 1963. "Poor kids. Am I so bad that I ached to take them all 'out' with me? But one cannot be sentimental in this business — can one?"

In addition to his intelligence duties, Flynn planned joint training exercises for the III Marine Expeditionary Force (MEF), comprised of the 1st Marine Air Wing and the 3rd Marine Division on Okinawa. In April 1963, exercise TEAM MATE tested the proficiency of the MEF staff, evaluated operating procedures, and exercised, coordinated, and perfected command and communication capabilities. During TEAM MATE, messages flowed into the command post requesting hypothetical aircraft strikes and reconnaissance and bombing missions in support of Marine ground units. During the three-day exercise, Flynn slept a total of two-and-a-half hours. "Didn't know I could do it," he mused in a letter to his wife.[63]

When on the base at Iwakuni, Flynn took enjoyment in playing trumpet in a jazz sextet made up of Marine and Navy officers. The group began playing at the Iwakuni Officers Club in December 1962, providing, according to the base newspaper, "music to suit almost every mood or taste, . . . from blaring impressions of 'When the Saints Go Marching In' to the smoothness of 'September Song.'" In reference to the quality of the unnamed sextet, the paper wrote that O-Club-goers had the "pleasure of hearing an unusual and extremely talented group of musicians" and a "brand of entertainment matched by few professional groups."[64]

In June 1963, Flynn took leave to revisit the spot off the coast of Kyushu where he had bailed out of his crippled F4U Corsair in the final months of World War II. He stayed on a small island near the crash site and visited an island near his rescue point. Flynn's guide during his three-day trip was a Japanese fisherman who, during World War II, had flown fighter planes for Imperial Japan. Flynn enjoyed his time with the

Lieutenant Colonel Pat Flynn (r), with unidentified officer, planning the TEAM MATE exercise, Okinawa, 1963.

former enemy who, before losing his leg in combat, had shot down two Corsairs and an F6F Hellcat. "What a great gentleman," Flynn wrote to his wife on June 26, 1963.

Flynn completed his Asian tour in October, and, following a short leave with his family in Gregory, South Dakota, reported to his new assignment with an A-4 reserve squadron at NAS Alameda, California. From 1953 to 1963, Flynn had served on the front lines of the Cold War. During the next three years, he would commit himself to Code of Conduct and survival training before joining civilian life and experiencing a short but volatile career in South Dakota politics. But one final brush with death awaited him, this time on the high, snow-covered peaks of the Sierra Nevada.

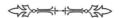

Chapter 8

Always a Marine

Now and then an innocent man is sent to the legislature.
Kin Hubbard[1]

IN NOVEMBER 1963, Lieutenant Colonel Flynn was named Executive Officer of the Marine Air Reserve Training Detachment (MARTD), one of two Marine Reserve squadrons based at NAS Alameda. In addition to his routine assignments at Alameda, California, Flynn participated in maneuvers at the Navy Bombing Target Areas, NAS Fallon, Nevada, where MARTD and Marine Air Reserve Squadron-133 — Alameda's other Marine squadron — conducted rocket and bombing practice. By the time he left MARTD in August of 1965, Flynn had logged nearly 200 hours in A-4B Skyhawks.[2]

In his public relations role, Flynn cultivated a positive image for MARTD and Marine Corps Air in general. He spoke to Bay Area and Sacramento Valley business, civic, and religious groups, who heard tales of his POW exploits and descriptions of Communist propaganda and indoctrination techniques. He participated in an

Armed Forces Week tribute sponsored by the Sacramento Rotary Club and Navy League, addressed local Lions Clubs, lectured at Bay Area high schools and colleges, and led tours of NAS Alameda for visiting Catholic dignitaries.[3] He organized a Bay Area model airplane show that was held on MARTD's runway, one of NAS Alameda's highlight events of the mid-1960s. A control-line and radio-control model enthusiast, Flynn worked with the Alameda Falcons Model Builders Club and the Western Associated Modelers to bring more than 400 flying models and 2,000 fans to the base on May 29, 1965. The day-long show and flying contest featured a performance by the 12th Naval District Band and displays of Marine fixed-wing aircraft and helicopters, aircraft ordnance, and a Mercury space capsule.[4]

When not promoting Marine Air, Flynn traveled the nation teaching his fellow warriors how to combat Communist interrogation and survive captivity. After a lecture at MCAS Yuma, Arizona, Brigadier General D. J. Preacher, grateful for the privilege of hearing Flynn's presentation firsthand, commended the speaker in a letter dated August 20, 1965, for "giving this lecture at every opportunity because it could prove to be of untold benefit should [*Marines*] ever be taken prisoner by the enemy." Back in California, Flynn held POW training sessions at Pickel Meadows in the Sierra Nevada near Bridgeport, where Marines under the direction of Flynn and others constructed a mock prison compound. At Pickel Meadows, Flynn, Lieutenant Philip Morris, and Sergeant Antonio Lopez introduced students to the interrogation techniques employed by Communist captors. "Here," wrote *Oakland Tribune* military writer Tom Flynn (no relation) on December 5, 1965, "Marines are shown what they might face in the hands of a Communist enemy should they be captured in Vietnam or elsewhere." Props in the camp complex exposed Marines to prison cells and tortures favored by Asian captors. After touring the complex, participants heard from Flynn, who instructed students how to maintain self-discipline and self-respect during confinement. Tom Flynn observed that "[*i*]t was from Flynn's experiences and those of other Marines who returned home that the POW compound became a reality," allowing "thousands of Marines" to benefit from the expertise of the instructors.

In addition to being the home of a POW training site, Pickel Meadows served as the Marine Corps Cold Weather Training Center (CWTC), where on March 22, 1965, Lieutenant Colonel Flynn was scheduled to conduct a routine lecture on winter survival and evasion methods. The trip to Pickel Meadows was anything but routine, and before it was over, Pat Flynn had cheated death one last time.

Flynn was to arrive at Pickel Meadows in a Marine SH-34 helicopter piloted by Captain Clifford E. Reese. Crew Chief Lance Corporal Roger Harcher and writer Tom Flynn, who had been assigned to cover Lieutenant Colonel Flynn's lecture for the *Oakland Tribune*, completed the passenger list. The four took off from Alameda at about 9:30 a.m. on a scheduled two-hour flight. Reese made radio contact with the Stockton tower after completing the first leg of the trip and maintained an eastward course.[5]

At 11:00 a.m., flying at 8,300 feet, Reese maneuvered the helicopter over the mountains north of Sonora Pass, when without warning, the helicopter experienced power failure. Lieutenant Colonel Flynn, realizing that the aircraft was going to crash, yelled out to Tom Flynn to brace himself for they were "going in." The helicopter, flying about 700 feet above the trees, fell into a steep right turn and plunged toward the south side of a mountain named, appropriately, Disaster Peak. As Reese struggled to avoid trees and huge boulders, the helicopter slammed wheels-first into a snow bank. The impact dislodged the main rotor blade, which struck the rear of the helicopter, narrowly missing Lieutenant Colonel Flynn and chopping off the back third of the fuselage. "Everything in back of Col. Flynn and me just disappeared," Tom Flynn recalled. The crash ruptured the fuel tank and scattered debris for a hundred yards across the southern slope of Disaster Peak.[6]

Miraculously, no one was seriously injured, though Flynn was masking the pain of a re-injured lower back that plagued him the rest of his life. Smelling fuel, the four scrambled from the wreckage and, looking back, marveled at their luck. Large boulders and tall trees surrounded the helicopter, which teetered on the steep mountain slope. But the survivors' joy was short-lived. It was cold, they possessed a minimum of food and winter gear, and during the power failure, Reese had no opportunity to transmit a Mayday distress signal and coordinates. Lieutenant Colonel Flynn had been bound for Pickel Meadows to conduct a survival lesson for Marine trainees. Captain Reese later commented, "We got the survival training."[7]

While a crew member shot off the first of a short supply of flares, Reese made several unsuccessful attempts to contact commercial jets with a small emergency radio. The Marines and the journalist searched the skies for rescue aircraft and retrieved any clothing, survival equipment, and

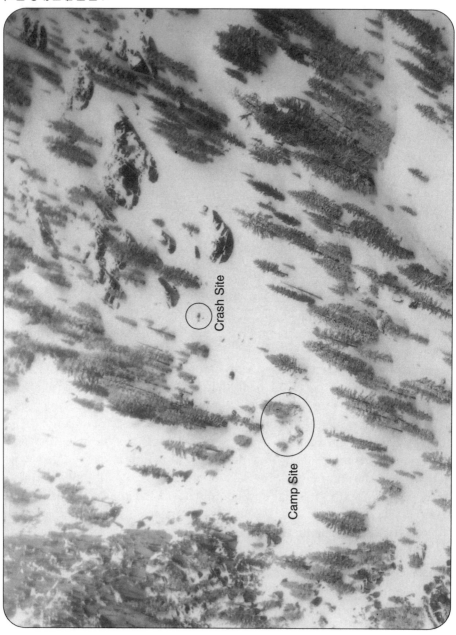

The helicopter crash site at Disaster Peak in the Sierra Nevada, March 22, 1965.

food they could find. Lieutenant Colonel Flynn, concerned that a snowstorm would move in during the night, ruled out any attempts at hiking to safety and ordered the men to prepare for a cold night on the mountain. He supervised the construction of a windbreak made from two parachutes and turned an inflatable rubber raft into a bed for four. Wood was collected for a fire that could burn through the night. Meals were out of the question, as the entire food supply consisted of three bullion cubes and three chocolate bars.[8]

While the four men prepared for near-zero temperatures, aircraft from NAS Alameda, Hamilton AFB, and Stead AFB searched the Sierras for signs of a wreckage. Joining the air search were Marines from the CWTC, mounted on "snow cat" tracked vehicles that operated in the deep snow and rocky terrain. Search parties combed a large area between Stockton and Bridgeport until nightfall, but found no signs of a crash site or survivors.[9]

Frances Flynn learned of her husband's disappearance from his Commanding Officer, who arrived at the Flynn home between 4:00 and 5:00 p.m. Frances immediately contacted Brother Robert "Bob" Nunes, a close family friend and the principal of St. Joseph High School, where Mark Flynn was enrolled as a student. Nunes distracted the three youngest Flynn children while Frances explained the situation to Mark and Colleen. To distract herself, Frances stayed up the entire night sewing a Confirmation dress for Colleen, whose 13th birthday fell on March 23.[10]

As darkness fell on Disaster Peak on the evening of March 22, Lieutenant Colonel Flynn and the others, their flare supply nearing exhaustion, manufactured flares from twisted rags soaked in fuel. As the four discussed their options, Lieutenant Colonel Flynn ordered them to guard their words and avoid saying anything that could induce panic. After sunset, Lieutenant Colonel Flynn, who would stay up the entire night tending the fire and scouting the skies for aircraft, began praying. As the temperatures dropped, he said he had "made no promises" to God, "because he had been spared so many times in the past that he felt it would be overdoing it to bargain with the Almighty again."[11] Several times during the night, Flynn spotted a wolf encircling the camp, a sign, he believed, that a snowstorm was imminent.[12]

At first light on March 23, the Air Force, Marines, and Navy, concerned that an advancing cold front would reduce visibility and trap the four men in the mountains, launched an intensive search. On Disaster Peak, Lance

The return to NAS Alameda, following the rescue on Disaster Peak, March 23, 1965. Top to bottom: Lance Corporal Roger Harcher (in baseball cap), Captain Clifford E. Reese, *Oakland Tribune* writer Tom Flynn, and Lieutenant Colonel Pat Flynn.

Corporal Harcher sighted a low-flying jet and launched a flare. It went undetected. At that point, Lieutenant Colonel Flynn, worried that he and the other stranded men would freeze to death in the snow, torched the remaining fuel in the helicopter's tank to attract attention. The wreck burned for two hours, a column of thick, black smoke rising up into an increasingly overcast sky. At 8:00 a.m., an A-4 Skyhawk piloted by Captain Jay Davis, an MARTD pilot and a close Flynn family friend, sighted the smoke column and transmitted the location. Shortly thereafter, a Marine Corps helicopter appeared above the slope and dropped blankets down to the men. At 10:00 a.m., as light snow began to fall on Disaster Peak, two Air Force helicopters lifted the four to safety. By day's end, snow was falling heavily, the first stage of an intense blizzard that enveloped the Sierra Nevada range for several days.[13]

Pat Flynn had dodged another bullet, though the prospect of freezing to death on Disaster Peak had shaken him. "This was one of the most precarious situations that I had ever been involved in," he told a reporter in the days following his rescue.[14] Colonel W. C. Lemke, the Commanding Officer of MARTD, praised Flynn for "demonstrat[ing] outstanding presence of mind" during the Disaster Peak ordeal, emphasizing that he had "effectively rall[ied] crew & passengers for survival and rescue under extreme climatic conditions." Flynn's "sound judgement and forceful leadership," Lemke wrote, "was solely responsible for prompt rescue and conversion of this near disaster into a favorable public relations incident." Good press coverage seemed to follow Flynn, "who helped project the Marine Corps image most favorably in this area."[15]

⋄━━┼┼━━⋄

Flynn's tour in the Bay Area ended in the summer of 1965, when he was ordered to a non-flying position as Assistant Chief of Staff, G-3, rear, 1st Marine Division, Camp Pendleton, California. In February 1966, in what would be his final assignment with the Marines Corps, he became Commanding Officer of Marine Air Control Squadron-4 (MACS-4). The mission of the 250 officers and enlisted men of MACS-4 included installing, maintaining, and operating radar-control facilities that provided air surveillance, control of aircraft and missiles for anti-air warfare, and navigational assistance.[16] Flynn inherited a squadron affected by location changes, personnel shortages, and equipment deficiencies. The squadron was, in the words of the Commanding General of the 3rd Marine Air Wing (MAW), in "chaotic condition." Flynn focused his energies on improving unit morale, administrative efficiency, and supply and matériel acquisition while ensuring that MACS-4's multi-million dollar equipment would function satisfactorily under stressful combat conditions. By the late spring of 1966, MACS-4 had gone from a "generally unsatisfactory" condition to that of "satisfactory," an evolution that, according to Flynn's superiors, reflected the Marine's "outstanding leadership, attention, skill and dedication to duty."[17]

Despite his success as commander of MACS-4, Flynn longed for command of an attack squadron. When in the spring of 1966 he learned that his transfer request had been denied, Flynn decided to retire. His announcement sparked a flurry of Code of Conduct speaking engagements. At El Toro, for instance, Flynn joined with 3rd MAW Chief of Staff Colonel H. G. Dalton and others to conduct a school for teaching commissioned and non-commissioned officers about the challenges and responsibilities they might face if captured. "A prisoner is dependent entirely upon his captors for his food, shelter and survival," Flynn reminded the audience. "The odds are stacked entirely against the individual. It's you alone who must make the choice between survival alone or survival with honor."[18]

It was fitting that Flynn's last official duty before his August 31 retirement was an acting role in a POW training film entitled *Before the Battle*. During the 25-minute film (co-written by Flynn), he related his personal POW journey to the six paragraphs in the Code of Conduct. The film was produced by West Coast Sound Productions of California, and after its completion in mid-August, it was distributed to various Marine units as an official training aid to illustrate Communist interrogation tactics and the means of resisting those tactics.[19] The impact of *Before the Battle* on Marine audiences is uncertain, but lectures on the Code of Conduct by Flynn and other POWs unquestionably strengthened the resistance of Vietnam War captives of all services. Ex-POW Senator John McCain noted that "fidelity to the Code was almost constantly challenged" by North Vietnamese captors. "Yet its principles remained the most important allegiance of our lives."[20]

Pat Flynn participating in the Code of Conduct training film *Before the Battle* at Camp Pendleton, California, August 1960.

On September 1, 1966 — 24 years, 1 month, and 14 days after entering the military — Pat Flynn entered civilian life. With Frances and four of their five children (Mark had enrolled in college in San Francisco), Pat drove to Gregory, South Dakota, where they moved into the home they had purchased from Frances's parents in 1962. After enrolling his children in school and reacquainting himself with family, friends, and the choicest fishing spots in south-central South Dakota, Flynn built a small repair shop. He operated an electrical equipment and household appliance repair business until May 1967, when he began crop-dusting. Flynn enjoyed the flying, and, on one occasion, took time to display his aviation talents by flying a plane — upside down — beneath the Platte-Winner bridge that spans the Missouri River west of Platte, South Dakota. But the back injuries he suffered in the aircraft accidents in Korea and California forced Flynn out of aerial spraying in the late 1960s. By then, he was suffering from intense, recurring back pain and partial paralysis in his neck, lower back, and left thigh.[21]

Yet it was more than physical ailments that explain Flynn's retirement from crop-dusting. In May 1967, Pat Flynn and his brother Dennis had traveled to Washington to meet with Senator George S. McGovern, Democrat of South Dakota. Pat, a lifelong Democrat, had appeared with McGovern during the Senator's visit with Tripp County Democrats in Winner, South Dakota, on March 28. In a letter to McGovern written after the event, Flynn thanked his fellow South Dakotan for inviting him to participate. He promised to work for McGovern and other Democrats and, in a reference to his own political aspirations, announced his intention "to press for the opportunity and privilege to serve my state and nation in the United States House of Representatives."[22]

But Flynn's support for McGovern changed dramatically after April 25, 1967, the day the Senator made a scathing public attack on President Lyndon Johnson's policy toward Vietnam. McGovern's remarks came one day after General William C. Westmoreland, Commander of U.S. forces in Vietnam, castigated critics of the war for encouraging the North Vietnamese enemy to believe that "he can win politically that which he cannot accomplish militarily."[23] On the floor of the Senate the next day, McGovern proclaimed that the nation's "deepening involvement in Vietnam represents the most tragic diplomatic and moral failure in our national experience." He dismissed any "Munich analogy" or "domino theory" about Asian communism and accused Vietnam policymakers of "unwittingly advancing the cause of communism while seeking to contain it." McGovern described North Vietnam's Ho Chi Minh as "an ardent nationalist" whose commitment to "the [*Viet Cong*] revolt in the south" was the result of an "insurrection in Vietnam [*growing*] out of local conditions which pitted one group of Vietnamese against another." He called for a suspension of bombing missions and a replacement of offensive ground operations with defensive "holding operations on the ground." McGovern encouraged President Johnson to "negotiate directly with the [*Viet Cong*]," who should "play a significant role in any provisional government resulting from a ceasefire [*sic*] and a negotiated settlement."[24]

In South Vietnam in 1962-1963, Pat Flynn had witnessed the destructive effects of North Vietnamese-directed insurgency on the South's political institutions and peasant society. But in 1967, he was just beginning to grasp the depth of McGovern's anti-war position. Flynn would covet McGovern's support in his potential bid for Congress, but not at the price of maintaining silence on the Senator's anti-war stance, a stance that was becoming increasingly unpopular with South Dakotans of both political parties.

Flynn was no warmonger. A veteran of three wars, he had witnessed unspeakable violence on Okinawa and in Korea and South Vietnam. But even in retirement, he remained committed to the containment of communism and the preservation of liberty around the globe. "Certainly, I share a deep abhorrence to armed conflict," he wrote, "but at the same time I resent any power that would destroy or withhold the right of self-determination."[25] From Flynn's perspective, George McGovern was a misinformed, divisive politician who aided Hanoi's war effort while undermining American military morale. In downplaying North Vietnamese communism and portraying Ho Chi Minh as a savior, McGovern raised North Vietnam's stature in the international community while weakening U.S. resolve to defend South Vietnam. "It is no secret that our posture in [*Southeast Asia*] has been seriously degraded by 'unilateral withdrawal' advocates in high government," Flynn wrote. "Though not representative of the will of the constituent[*s*] such a position reinforces the enemies' will to resist."[26]

In 1967, with McGovern's anti-war message attracting increasing media attention, Flynn traveled to Washington.[27] He and his brother met with McGovern in the Senate dining room. Dennis Flynn remembers that his brother "lost his temper with McGovern," and in a straightforward manner, "tried to persuade [*him*] to see his side."²⁸ Pat contended that McGovern's high-profile debate with President Johnson undermined the U.S. military position and hardened North Vietnam's resolve at a time when the U.S. was achieving military successes. He criticized McGovern for suggesting that the movement of U.S. forces be limited to the coastline, a proposal that, in Flynn's words, "gave the enemy new hope. . . ."²⁹ He accused McGovern of fracturing American foreign policy by advocating defensive strategies that contradicted the military's objectives in Vietnam.³⁰

Flynn's exhortation was, in his words, a "fruitless personal appeal" that made little impression on McGovern.³¹ The Senator remained cordial, though, and invited the Flynn brothers into his office for a photo opportunity. The picture arrived at Flynn's home a few days after he returned from Washington. On Agriculture and Forestry Committee letterhead, McGovern wrote that it "was good to have an opportunity to visit with you and Dennis when you were here in Washington."³² Ten days later the photo appeared in the *Mitchell Daily Republic*, a newspaper serving the Gregory area. The caption infuriated Flynn, who felt that he and his brother had been used by McGovern. Readers were told that the Flynns traveled to Washington "to discuss business problems related to the federal government and other matters now before Senator McGovern's sub-committee on Indian Affairs." Flynn peeled the photo from the page and scrawled a message across the top: "I TOLD HIM TO GET OF [*sic*] HIS VIETNAM KICK. INDIAN MATTERS WERE NOT EVEN MENTIONED."³³ Flynn remained bitter about the press release, which he viewed as an opportunistic stunt by McGovern to improve his image among South Dakota's Native Americans.

The Washington meeting marked the beginning of Pat Flynn's meteoric political career. Convinced that McGovern had lost touch with his constituents, Flynn set his sights on defeating him — an attainable objective, he reasoned, if he developed the media profile and political ties to challenge the well-financed Democrat. Flynn regarded election to the South Dakota Senate as a logical step toward the U.S. Senate race in 1974. In the capitol building in Pierre, he could sponsor one or two high-profile bills that might springboard him into a race with McGovern. Though committed to statewide issues, he would maintain pressure on McGovern, branding his anti-war rhetoric as unrepresentative of South Dakota sensibilities and detrimental to America's war effort in Vietnam.

Although his military record had elevated his public image, Pat Flynn viewed his limited higher education as a political liability, for he had attended Haskell Institute during the brief period in 1941-1942 and had only completed geology courses at Chapman College in Orange, California, in 1967. He considered a run for the South Dakota Senate in 1968, but instead chose to enroll at the University of South Dakota in Vermillion, where he studied English, history, and political science. While at the university, he volunteered his time to the Army ROTC department, lecturing on the Code of Conduct and POW issues.[34] He offered his opinion on the USS *Pueblo* incident in an editorial for the *Vermillion Plain Talk*, citing the debasement of "serious and far-reaching moral principles" when an American negotiator signed a false confession in exchange for the release of 82 *Pueblo* crewmen held for 11 months by the North Koreans. "A small Communist country," he wrote, "pulled off a major propaganda 'coup' on us to be exploited in the state controlled presses of Communist bloc and some neutral countries." He warned readers that the incident would tempt "[o]ther minor powers . . . to pull-off similar adventures."[35]

In 1970, Flynn joined the Republican Party, a switch that demonstrated his exasperation with the McGovern wing of the Democratic Party. The decision pleased Gregory and Tripp County Republican officials, who had lobbied the retired Marine to run for the Senate seat from District 25 — comprised of Gregory, Tripp, and Todd counties. Flynn announced his candidacy in the spring, though not without second thoughts, courtesy of an offer to fly covert missions in Southeast Asia for the CIA-funded Air America airlines.

During the 1960s and early 1970s, Air America (AA), whose motto was "We fly anywhere, anyplace, anytime — professionally," operated in obscurity while providing clandestine military and intelligence support to U.S. forces and their Southeast Asian allies. From their bases in South Vietnam, Laos, and Thailand, Air America pilots flew "black missions" along the Ho Chi Minh Trail and transported Hmong tribal fighters in their operations against Communist Pathet Lao and North Vietnamese forces in Laos. Whoever solicited Flynn about the AA assignment (he discussed the offer in a letter written to a "Tom") did so as a result of an intensification of secret operations in Laos in 1970. By the summer of that year, in response to increased North Vietnamese Army activities, Air America was operating over 48 fixed-wing aircraft and 30 helicopters in Laos. As the Communists drove the Hmong from their mountain homes, AA airlifted

46 million pounds of foodstuffs to the fleeing refugees. AA crews transported troops and refugees, flew medevac missions, and rescued downed airmen. Many missions in 1970 focused on the Ho Chi Minh Trail, where AA pilots dropped and extracted road watch teams, conducted night airdrops, night-monitored enemy infiltration routes, photographed northern Laos, and engaged in an array of clandestine missions that required night-vision glasses and other advanced technologies.[36]

The prospect of flying "black ops" intrigued Flynn, whose night-flying record and intelligence background made him a natural candidate for an Air America assignment. But his family commitments ultimately outweighed his lust for further adventures. "Would enjoy the work, though, confidentially," he wrote, "don't thrill to working in S.E. Asia with my family back here."[37]

So in the late summer of 1970, Flynn focused his attention on campaigning against the Democratic incumbent, Senator Randy Stenson of Colome in Tripp County. Candidate Flynn touted his long military career and his fearlessness, promising voters that if elected he would be "unafraid to give this area full representation." He self-financed most of his campaign, though contributions and paid advertising from the Gregory and Tripp Republicans bolstered his cause. Some individual contributions came from outside the district, including a $50 gift from a Sioux Falls admirer who saw it as her "privilege and duty to 'back the bullet'; . . . How fortunate we are," she wrote, "to have Pat devoting his time, talents, and energies toward good government."[38]

Campaigning in Stenson's home county proved challenging, but Flynn received strong support from the voters in Gregory County and in Todd County, the home of the Rosebud Sioux Indian Reservation. The possibility of one of their own becoming the first Lakota to serve in the South Dakota Senate excited Todd County's Indian voters, some of them distant relatives of the Republican candidate. Flynn enjoyed traveling through Mission, St. Francis, Rosebud, and other Todd County communities, though the reservation's grinding poverty served as a constant reminder of the economic gap separating the state's Indian and non-Indian populations.

Flynn took time during the campaign to address national issues. In a radio talk, he discussed "this campus thing that hit Berkeley about 8 years ago," adding that it had "finally arrived in our state." Flynn voiced his agreement with China's Mao Zedong, who had discovered:

that students can be a second army for an established single party regime, because the party controls the input into their young minds. And in that sense, I believe it's about time that both of our parties get together and see to it that our rational and proven constitutional principles receive equal time on our state supported campuses. Because, in the final analysis, as relates to individual views or international affairs, it is the united politics of the . . . United States that will keep the single party nations honest. And to this end I will so represent you the first of next year.[39]

Flynn's references to national affairs did no harm to his campaign. On November 3, he defeated Stenson and became the first South Dakotan of Native American descent to serve in the state Senate.

Senator Flynn was assigned to the Local Government, Natural Resources, and Taxation committees. He focused his agenda on wildlife conservation and the hot-button issue that defined his short political career — legalized gambling. Flynn's early bills called for restrictions on the hunting and destruction of predators such as foxes, rabbits, and coyotes — animals that in the early 1970s could be hunted from airplanes and snowmobiles. Flynn's Senate Bill (SB) 89 would have banned the shooting of wild animals from those vehicles, a practice that, in Flynn's words, failed to "dignify those natural resources." Flynn considered aerial hunting a barbaric act and described coyotes and foxes as "necessary to the balance of nature in South Dakota." As a means of pre-empting increasing federal regulations on predator control, Flynn pushed for a package of bills "designed to put predators in their proper place in [the] . . . environment and to assure their continuing life."[40]

A central feature of Flynn's conservation package was SB 250, a measure to prohibit the sale and application of predator poisons such as Compound 1080, a particularly virulent chemical that killed not only predators but any animals that fed on them. As a licensed crop sprayer, Flynn was not opposed to the use of all toxic chemicals. He rejected "environmentalist" arguments and clarified his position on insecticides and herbicides. "People in their hysterical concern over pollution could hurt the pesticide programs," he emphasized. "If they do, they shouldn't be too disturbed if they eventually have to pay $2 for a loaf of bread."[41]

Floor debate on SB 250 pitted Flynn and Charles Donnelly, a Democrat from Rapid City, against the state's sheep ranchers and Senator Alfred Burke, a Republican from Newell. Donnelly and Flynn adroitly defended the bill, and in the process, Flynn provided his Senate colleagues with a chuckle. When asked about the effects of Compound 1080 on humans, Donnelly responded that "no people have been killed. The problem isn't people, its eagles. Many eagles have been killed by eating the flesh of a coyote killed by the poison." Burke dismissed Donnelly's argument. "I've lived on the prairie all my life, and I think I know more about the prairie than you do," he stated. "I've yet to see any dead eagles." To which Flynn quipped, "I've got twelve of them; three of them have already been made into a war bonnet at the university, but you're welcome to look at the rest of them."[42]

Flynn's conservation measures grabbed the attention of voters, but it was his introduction of a legalized gambling bill that placed him at the center of a firestorm that dominated South Dakota politics in late 1971 and early 1972. In the opening stages of the debate, Flynn predicted that his gambling stance could cost him his political future. His prediction proved accurate.

The debate opened on November 30, 1971, when, during a discussion about tax revenues at an interim meeting of the Senate Taxation Committee, Flynn startled the committee members by announcing his intention to introduce a gambling bill. "You're going to hear a lot from me next session when I bring in a bill for legalized gambling, which I am going to do," he stated. Sounding a message oft-repeated in the coming months, Flynn derided the prevalence of "illegal back room games" that "condone violations of the law" while robbing South Dakota of potential revenues. "What is more immoral," Flynn asked, "illegal gambling, which we now have, or gambling in the open?" Though he recognized that his proposal could result in "political suicide," Flynn trumpeted the prospects for tax relief and additional state revenues generated by a government-regulated gambling industry.[43]

Flynn wanted voters, through a statewide referendum election, to approve or reject legalized gambling. His measure, introduced to the 47th Legislature on January 4, 1972, as Senate Joint Resolution No. 3 (SJR 3) and forwarded to the State Affairs Committee, called for voters during the next general election to amend Article III, Section 25 of the South Dakota Constitution. If approved, Flynn's one-sentence amendment would have empowered the Legislature, with the consent of the voters, to "provide for

Pat Flynn, on the floor of the South Dakota Senate, January 1971.

the operation, taxation, and regulation of games of chance in the state of South Dakota," a change that would pave the way for an expanded, but state-regulated, gaming industry.[44]

In a press release concerning the measure, Flynn predicted that gambling would generate a "major source of badly needed revenue" for the state. The construction of gambling venues along Nevada gaming lines would create a South Dakota industry capable of attracting "patronage by neighboring states and tourists" whose spending would ease citizens' tax burdens. An equally important motive "was to bring existing illegal gambling conditions in line with the law." "With our prevalent illegal violation of law by backroom establishments and for that matter the state itself ignoring the constitutionality of the race track," he wrote, "we still expect our young people to be law-abiding citizens?" Arguing that neither the Legislative, Judicial, or Executive branches should determine the future of South Dakota gaming, Flynn asked that the people be given "their constitutional right to vote on a major, though controversial, issue."

Reaction to the gambling bill was immediate, broad, and passionate. Some voters pleaded with Flynn to retract his proposal. "Legalize gambling, and in time the control of state government into the hands of ruthless gangsters run by a syndicate would be assured," argued one citizen in a letter to Flynn, adding that anyone supporting "such a scheme should be compared to a Judas selling out for a few pieces of silver." Other constituents wrote to warn of permanent damages caused by legal gaming. "The three damning D's of gambling are Debt, Degradation and death!" wrote an opponent, while another, asking Flynn to love his state "and the people in it more than this," feared the impact Flynn's proposal would have on "[b]ingo or small local carnival ways of raising a few dollars." Flynn received complaints from people who opposed the bill on religious grounds, including a scathing letter from a woman who charged that there was "altogether too much of the tax payers money spent for salaries on people such as you."

Yet for every opponent there was a supporter. Both the *Rapid City Journal* and *Huron Daily Plainsman* championed the idea of a gambling referendum, the *Plainsman* editors declaring that the "Flynn Plan Deserves Fair Hearing," especially in light of the Taxation Committee's draft proposal to explore state income and corporate taxes. In a nod to Flynn, the *Plainsman* noted that too often tax reform measures were "not even discussed simply because no individual has the courage to bring them up for debate." Alternatives to income taxes "should not be shunted aside without careful consideration," and those offering alternatives should be "commended, not castigated."[45] In a personal letter to Flynn dated December 17, 1971, *Plainsman* Vice President and Associate Publisher L. J. "Bud" Maher told Flynn that the Senator was "not all alone" in his beliefs. "We find a great deal of favorable local sentiment for your idea of legalized gambling," Maher wrote. A Sioux Falls woman echoed Maher's assessment in a letter to Flynn, remarking that she had found opinions in her circle to be "highly favorable" of legalized gaming.

Flynn's greatest support base was in western South Dakota, where restaurant and tavern owners, real estate brokers, tourist shops, newspaper editors, and at least one Catholic priest viewed legalized gambling as a potential boon to the economy. A Rapid City supporter drew comparisons between Prohibition-era bootleggers and contemporary illegal gamblers, and warned that "the religious [sic] people . . . did not stop gambling, merely drove it underground." A Presho man was far more blunt. He urged Flynn to "Fight like HELL!" against his opponents, including South Dakota's Governor, Richard F. Kneip, who, on January 17, voiced his opposition to SJR 3, promising to veto the bill if it came to his desk. The Presho voter — whose reaction to Kneip's stance was strikingly similar to Flynn's — resented the Governor's interference with the debate. "Kneip said: 'HE did not think the people of South Dakota are ready for gambling.' Since when does HE do the thinking for all the people??? LET THE PEOPLE DO THEIR OWN THINKING & DECIDE FOR THEMSELVES."[46]

For Flynn, no correspondence was more appreciated than a package from Charles V. Sederstrom, a Deadwood restaurant-owner and caterer. Sederstrom lauded Flynn for his "courage to take the lead on this controversial issue," and in a show of "moral support," enclosed a 39-page petition signed by nearly 600 Deadwood and Lead-area voters supporting Senator Flynn in his efforts to allow "the voters of South Dakota the opportunity of changing their constitution."[47]

Flynn needed all the support he could get, for on January 15, 1972, he was rushed to the Pierre hospital, the victim of a mild heart attack — the first of three he would suffer in the next seven years. Flynn spent two days in the hospital undergoing tests and resting with his wife, his mother, and his oldest sister, Rose Marie, of Pierre. He rested at his Pierre residence for a third day, but on January 18, in defiance of doctor's orders, addressed a widely publicized open hearing on SJR 3 in the State Affairs committee room.[48]

Flynn reminded the committee that state-regulated gambling could provide relief for "the over-burdened tax payer" of South Dakota. "Tourists are heading west with fat billfolds and coming back from Nevada with thin billfolds," he noted. Pointing out that "existing 'back-room' gambling" generated nothing for the state, Flynn tried to quell the concerns of those who in principle opposed all forms of gambling. "Passage of my resolution through both Houses and past [the] governor's veto power would place the question on the November ballot," he explained, adding that "a 'yes' vote by any legislator on this resolution should not be implied that he or she endorses some form of legalized gambling." On the contrary, SJR 3 would allow "the voters of South Dakota . . . the opportunity to be heard," a constitutional step that would "take the issue out of controversy, one way or the other."[49]

As the debate over SJR 3 reached a crescendo, Flynn met with stiff resistance — and threats — from out-of-state sources. At his Gregory home, Flynn began receiving mysterious phone calls from men claiming to represent "Las Vegas interests." Frances Flynn recalls answering the phone late in the evenings and hearing "strange voices" asking to speak to her husband. The messages Pat received were, in Frances's words, "straight to the point: 'Lay-off the gambling bill,' they'd say." The voices listed Flynn's Gregory and Pierre residences, detailed his daily routine in Pierre, and, in what was particularly troubling to Flynn, traced the routes his children walked to school. "They threatened to wipe him out if he pushed too hard for gambling," Frances remembers.[50] Flynn took the threats seriously, and, for the first time in his life, kept a loaded handgun in his Gregory home and in his motel room in Pierre.

Back in Pierre, the State Affairs Committee tried to kill SJR 3 by tabling it. Flynn responded with a strong public statement, criticizing the "double standard" that existed in a state where illegal gambling prospered. He encouraged legislators to give the voters a choice. "If the people vote it down, then we will have strict enforcement of the present laws. If they approve it, then it will add state revenues."[51]

Under the Legislature's Joint Rule 7-7 (which, pending the approval of one-third or more of the Senate, forces a committee to deliver a bill to the full chamber) Flynn "smoked out" SJR 3 from committee and forced it to a floor vote.[52] On January 28, Flynn took to the Senate floor to defend his measure. He had the support of Senator Donnelly, who, quoting Attorney General Gordon J. Mydland, outlined the "questionable" constitutionality of parimutuel racing under Article 3, Section 25. Donnelly challenged the opponents of Flynn's referendum bill, particularly those who claimed that the electorate was not ready for legalized gambling when, in principle and in practice, the electorate was ready for parimutuel betting.[53]

Following Donnelly's remarks, Flynn moved to amend a few words in the bill, a motion that prevailed. He then prepared himself for what he expected to be a rousing floor debate on the bill. No debate materialized. "To my astonishment," he wrote six weeks later, "not a single Senator rose to debate or even ask a question." SJR 3 was called to a vote, and by a 22 to 12 margin was rejected by the Senate.[54]

Flynn had suffered a humiliating defeat, made more difficult by his health problems. But he went down fighting, firing off a venomous four-and-a-half-page press release. Flynn accused the Governor of denying the voters' voice on legalized gambling, suggesting that Kneip was "apparently . . . satisfied with present non-enforcement" of illegal gambling. "The timing of the governor's opposition statement, in my opinion,"

Flynn wrote, "was an expression of total disregard of the dignity and ethics of his high office." Flynn chided his fellow Republicans, many of whom "would feel uncomfortable" with their names "on the same ballot as my resolution." In criticizing the "political maneuver" that killed his resolution, Flynn accused his opponents of "a masterful display of . . . political deceit by a majority of senators and a governor who chose to maintain the illegal status quo. . . ."

Recognizing that his incendiary remarks probably spelled the end of his career in state politics, Flynn concluded his press release with an announcement that he would not seek reelection for the South Dakota Senate. But he left the door open for a return to the political arena — possibly as a Democrat — "to take appropriate action to determine that George McGovern will not get past a primary in his bid for re-election to the U.S. Senate in two years."[55]

Flynn, who demonstrated little patience for capitol intrigues, lacked the subtleties of a successful politician. In Pierre, he learned that legislative success did not stem from independent initiatives or visionary reforms. Success depended on loyalty to a speaker, a majority leader, a committee chair, or the Governor. Political savvy was defined as a legislator's skill at compromising and "logrolling," an arrangement wherein two legislators traded votes to guarantee support on bills of interest to one another. Such an environment, wherein principles were sacrificed to party demands, debates and votes were predetermined by backroom agreements, and referendums were feared by elected officials, proved frustrating to the ex-Marine from Dog Ear Lake. Fittingly, one of Flynn's final acts in the Senate was his co-sponsoring of a resolution to honor the achievements of Billy Mills, a Lakota, an ex-Marine, and a gold medal winner in the 10,000 meter race at the 1964 Olympic Games in Tokyo.[56]

Political scientists argue that incumbents must practice "damage control" if they expect to retain their seats. Alan Rosenthal warns state legislators "to be careful not to annoy too many people." Freshmen legislators should recognize their weak position and avoid taking risks so as "not to expose themselves. . . ." If there are ways "to straddle a fence, vote on both sides, or not have to choose sides at all," Rosenthal writes, successful politicians "will jump at the opportunity."[57] In his gamble to pass SJR 3, freshman Senator Flynn disregarded these fundamental lessons in political survival. As Flynn had predicted in late 1971, his pursuit of legalized gambling spelled his political suicide.

Though he lacked the resources and party funding to stage a serious race for the U.S. Senate in 1974, Flynn continued to challenge George McGovern's anti-Vietnam crusade — which, during the 1972 presidential campaign, was a staple of the evening news. Even in the midst of the gambling debate, Flynn had taken time to strike at McGovern. In a response to a citizen's letter to the *Huron Daily Plainsman* calling for McGovern to turn himself over to Hanoi as a POW, Flynn reminded the readers that America's POWs would "defend the principles of this great nation." On the other hand, he continued:

> there are certain radical elements within our country, political and otherwise, in high positions whose "no-win" statements are read by our prisoners of war as a part of their Maoist orientation; elements who take issue with our chief executive on matters of foreign affairs involving our national security and American lives. Unfortunately, these people are without adequate backgrounds or executive responsibility.[58]

Flynn concluded his letter with a stinging rebuke of McGovern's anti-war rhetoric, and, returning to his introductory comments, insisted "that our Senator McGovern is not qualified to be a prisoner of war."

Flynn became increasingly incensed at McGovern's efforts to force a unilateral withdrawal of U.S. troops from South Vietnam — efforts that, in Henry Kissinger's words, eroded the Nixon administration's negotiating position with the North Vietnamese, effectively "reducing the North's incentive for serious negotiation."[59]

McGovern's televised address of October 10, in which the candidate spoke for the United States on behalf of POWs and their families, galled Flynn. McGovern stated that the POWs "sit and think of us — of their homes, their families, of children who are growing up without fathers, of a country they may never see again." McGovern ridiculed what he called Nixon's "promise to end the war," insisting that the promise meant little "to the families of the brave men who waste away in the cells of Hanoi." He argued that an end to the bombings and fighting was necessary if "we are ever to see these prisoners again."[60]

From firsthand experiences with Communist interrogators, Flynn knew that the North Vietnamese would use McGovern's remarks to erode prisoner morale and self-respect. In fact, McGovern did nothing to alleviate the suffering of American POWs; on the contrary, his and other activists' anti-war statements intensified the captives' humiliation. POW James "Nick" Rowe described Hanoi Radio broadcasts of quotations from Senators McGovern, Fulbright, and Mansfield's speeches as "the most devastating blows" to prisoners' morale. "We got every one of those just as soon as they came out."[61] The anti-war rhetoric pumped through compound radio speakers left POWs frustrated, uneasy, and in some cases, fearful of abandonment by their government. When North Vietnamese radio described planks from the platform of candidate McGovern along with interviews with Jane Fonda and Ramsey Clark, some POWs feared a Democratic victory. Several prisoners, recalls ex-POW George Day, threatened to emigrate to Australia, England, or Canada. "The POW consensus was that we wanted to go home, but not at that price."[62]

Despite his desire to unseat McGovern, Flynn lacked the financial resources, party support, and physical health to defeat the incumbent. For these reasons, Flynn's wife opposed her husband's bid for the U.S. Senate. Frances recalled:

> He did not have the support of the state Republicans anymore. He had fought many of them over his gambling bill, and I think he felt ostracized by them. He'd made too many enemies among Republicans. It's safe to say that he did not have my entire support. I knew he was going to get hurt in that campaign, and I didn't want to see that.[63]

Charles Donnelly, Flynn's old political ally, echoes Frances's assessment. Donnelly, who remembered Flynn as "a very exciting and energetic man," noted that when it came to the Legislature, "Pat was his own person, and not the greatest team player," a trait that cost him dearly in 1972. "Both Democrats and Republicans wondered why the hell he was a Republican," laughs Donnelly. "He was a populist, all the way down to his toes."[64]

Flynn made no bid for the U.S. Senate, but he tried to regain his state Senate seat in November of 1974. He ran a lackluster, single-issue campaign, again asking South Dakotans to reconsider his gambling resolution. His campaign lacked the energy of his 1970 bid. "His heart wasn't in it," Frances recalls. "He wanted it, but he didn't have the energy to fight for it."[65] Flynn was defeated soundly and walked away from politics for the last time.

Though Flynn buried the banner of legalized gambling in November 1974, the issue proved remarkably resilient. Illegal gaming proliferated in the mid-1970s, as the issue of state-regulated gambling smoldered beneath the surface of South Dakota politics. In the fall of 1979, just eight months after Flynn's death, the issue exploded on the front pages of South Dakota newspapers. On November 19, South Dakota Attorney General Mark Meierhenry and State Treasurer David Volk were surprised by reporters from the Associated Press and KSFY-TV (Sioux Falls) while playing blackjack in the backroom of the Peacock Bar in Winner, a town that Flynn represented in the early 1970s. A comedy of errors followed. Meierhenry denied collecting table winnings, even though reporters witnessed the dealer pushing chips toward him after a winning hand. The Attorney General responded that he played blackjack to prove the prevalence of illegal gaming in South Dakota. Within hours, Meierhenry closed the doors on the Peacock. But two days later, with he and Volk facing difficult questions from both the press and Governor William Janklow, Meierhenry revised his story and pled guilty to misdemeanor gambling charges.[66]

The Peacock Bar episode sparked an intense statewide debate that Flynn would have thoroughly relished. By a three-to-one margin, citizens polled by the Associated Press voiced their approval of legal gaming. Only 25 percent of those surveyed believed Meierhenry and Volk "had the right to break the law" by participating in an illegal blackjack game.[67] The twin pillars of Flynn's SJR 3 — participatory democracy and law enforcement — proved overwhelmingly popular with the South Dakota electorate.

In the 1980s, many South Dakota politicians, employing language and logic strikingly similar to that used by Flynn in 1972, defended legal gaming. In 1986, voters authorized a state lottery, and in 1989, Governor George Mickelson called for expanding the state's "scratch and match" lottery to include video lottery. "With proper safeguards," Mickelson argued, "a video lottery could provide the state treasury several million extra dollars."[68] In 1992, Representative Joyce Hodges of Lake Preston sponsored a "populist bill" to refer video lottery, already authorized by the state, to the voters in the upcoming election. Her colleague Scott Heidepriem argued, "There's nothing wrong with allowing the public to give the Legislature guidance. That's what we did when the question of expanding gambling in the state was put to the people."⁶⁹ The editors of the *Sioux Falls Argus-Leader*, the state's largest newspaper, backed the Hodges plan. "Legislators should let South Dakotans vote," they opined.⁷⁰

On November 3, 1992, South Dakota voters, by a margin of 64 percent to 34 percent, expressed their desire to keep video lottery. "People were saying 'It's the people's business what form of entertainment they want to play and let them make the decision,'" commented one gambling supporter.⁷¹ To this day, gambling remains legal in the state of South Dakota.

Several weeks after the 1992 election, an admirer of Pat Flynn placed a telephone call to his widow. It appears, said the caller, that "Pat Flynn was just ahead of his time."

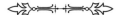

Chapter 9

Always Faithful

I have fought the good fight, I have
finished the race, I have kept the faith.
                                II Timothy 4:7

*P*AT FLYNN spent his retirement years pursuing his hobbies, following his children's careers and school activities, and chronicling his Lakota heritage. A self-taught artist, Flynn had, by the time of his retirement from the Marines, produced several impressive oil paintings and charcoal drawings. The construction of new Catholic churches in Gregory and Platte, South Dakota, in the late 1960s provided the retiree with an opportunity to share his creativity and religious vision with hundreds. He designed and constructed the Stations of the Cross and two window-sized steel sculptures for St. Joseph's in Gregory. Working with his mother, Lucille, he utilized shards from the old church's stained-glass windows to create windows for the new church.

Stations of the Cross designed and produced by Pat Flynn for St. Peter's Church, Platte, South Dakota.

Impressed by Flynn's volunteer work for St. Joseph's, Father R. J. Ortmeier of St. Peter's in Platte asked Flynn if he would design the Stations for his new church, dedicated in September 1969. Flynn accepted, and the completed product — a mixture of traditional and modern painting and metal work — is stunning. Each Station is a poster-size acrylic painting encased in a black steel frame and overlaid with steel symbols of the Passion: Pilate's water basin, a soldier's spear, a halo, a mallet and nail, the Virgin's silhouette, crosses. Prominent in the first and 15th Stations are crowns of thorns constructed from barbed wire to represent Flynn's own "total sense of rejection" as a POW. To penetrate the softening effects of the Stations' translucent Plexiglas facings, Flynn applied bold, sharp colors that capture the violence of the Crucifixion, the power of a thunderstorm, the liberation of the Resurrection. Above each painting are Roman numerals of rectangular steel key stock that, in the words of Ortmeier, "have a strong Indian influence." The entire effect, noted Ortmeier, is a "sense . . . of Our Savior's suffering long ago for sins of all men of all time as depicted by someone who has also known tremendous hardship." Valued at $3,000 in 1971, Flynn refused any payment from St. Peter's, contending that "as a pretty good sinner, I figure I'll need a lot going for me."[1]

When not practicing his art or designing and building homemade control-line and radio-control airplane models, Flynn worked on his fly-casting as he fished for large-mouth bass and bluegill on area lakes. Itching for some excitement, he accepted the position of Gregory Chief of Police after attending the three-week Law Enforcement Training Program at the Criminal Justice Training Center in Pierre in the fall of 1974. He enjoyed the community-building opportunities inherent in police work, but a another heart attack in August 1975 cut short a second career in law enforcement. Complicating Flynn's painful physical recovery were intense, recurring nightmares of solitary confinement, interrogation, and torture. His sleeping pattern disrupted, Flynn began rising each morning at 3:00 or 4:00 a.m. to work on a historical manuscript entitled *Courier from Spotted Tail*. Flynn traced his family's French-Canadian roots from the 17th century, when the first Boucher arrived in New France. The courier in Flynn's story is his great-grandfather, Francis Cashmere Xavier Boucher, the half-Sioux hunter-trader who married Spotted Tail's daughter and passed on to Flynn's grandparents many stories of the last days of the buffalo culture. Flynn's genealogy of his Canadian ancestors, his discussion of Spotted Tail's life and relationship with Crazy Horse, his original insights into Great Plains history, and his analysis of two centuries of Indian-white relations make for stimulating reading. Serious scholars of the fur trade, the Métis people,

One of the last photographs of Pat Flynn, on a fishing trip in Canada, August 1978.

the history of Dakota Territory, and early reservation life would find much of value in the few chapters that Flynn completed by the winter of 1978-1979.

In 1978, Pat and Frances became grandparents. Determined to conduct a naming ceremony for his grandson Michael, Flynn drove with his sister Grace to Mark Flynn's home in Prince George, British Columbia. Along the way, he visited sites and memorials central to the history of the Plains Indians, met with friends and relatives on several Indian reservations, and attended the giant Crow Fair Powwow in Montana. In Canada, Flynn fly-fished and played his trumpet in the mountains of British Columbia. He gave his grandson the name Long Elk, passing on the name given to him by his grandfather in 1934.

In February 1979, Pat Flynn's health suddenly deteriorated. On March 14, he was admitted to the Gregory Hospital, suffering from chest pains. The following day, he suffered a heart attack and Gregory physicians decided to immediately transport him to Sioux Falls. Flynn was allowed one final flight, this time aboard an emergency helicopter that would helilift him to Joe Foss Field in Sioux Falls, where he would be transported by ambulance to the Veterans Hospital. As his stretcher was loaded on the helicopter, Flynn smiled broadly and thanked the crew for the ride. He lost consciousness in the air between Gregory and Sioux Falls and never regained it.

Frances stayed by her husband's side for all of the next day. Occasionally, she heard Pat mumbling. One of his last words was "Popeye," a reference to the one-eyed bull snake that Flynn played with during his childhood days at Dog Ear Lake.

John Patrick Flynn, Jr., died peacefully in the early morning hours of St. Patrick's Day, 1979. His body was returned to Gregory, where Frances selected a gloss blue casket identical in color to the F4U Corsairs that Flynn flew in the 1940s and 1950s. Flynn was laid to rest in his Marine Corps dress-blue uniform, and on March 21, was carried into the funeral mass at St. Joseph's by U.S. Marines from a Reserve unit in Omaha. For music, Frances selected "The Impossible Dream," one of her husband's favorite songs. The memorial cards bore the words of "High Flight" by John Gillespie Magee, Jr.:

> Oh, I have slipped the surly bonds of Earth
> And danced the skies on laughter-silvered wings;
> Sunward I've climbed, and joined the tumbling mirth
> Of sun-split clouds — and done a hundred things
> You have not dreamed of — wheeled and soared and swung
> High in the sunlit silence. Hov'ring there,
> I've chased the shouting wind along, and flung
> My eager craft through footless halls of air. . . .
>
> Up, up the long, delirious burning blue
> I've topped the windswept heights with easy grace
> Where never lark, or ever eagle flew —
> And, while with silent, lifting mind I've trod
> The high untrespassed sanctity of space,
> Put out my hand, and touched the face of God.

Pat Flynn's body was borne from the church to the strains of "America the Beautiful" and "The Marine Corps Hymn." A cold north wind and sleet swept across the high ground of St. Joseph Catholic Cemetery, where a final prayer, taps, and the presentation of the colors to Frances Flynn marked the passing of a Marine, a son of South Dakota, a grandson of Lakota warriors.

Frances received dozens of sympathy cards and letters from Marine Corps friends and acquaintances, many of them extolling the virtues of her legendary husband. The words of Jack Vernon, who had served with Flynn at NAS Alameda in the mid-1960s, were particularly moving:

> My memories of your husband are associated with his tour of duty at Alameda, but I can recite stories of courage, integrity and humor about him which occurred when I was still in grammar school. Many people who never had the privilege of meeting your husband stand in awe of him. I still enjoy telling the story of him committing arson on an old H-34 Marine Reserve helicopter in the Sierras in order to save himself and the crew from death in the snow. Any Marine who ever knew him would have followed Chief to hell and back. The nickname "Chief" carried no negative connotation among his Marine friends — he simply was a Chief among us.
>
> The Marine Corps was diminished when he retired — officers of his character are too rare.[2]

In April 1979, Frances planted a small spruce tree at the head of her husband's gravesite. Today, that tree stands 15 feet tall and serves as a nesting place for mourning doves. If you visit the gravesite early on a spring morning, it is best to walk slowly and tread lightly. The tree's occupants stay close by, and those who startle them are greeted with a burst of wings as the doves slip the bonds of earth, in high flight, toward the rising sun.

Notes

Chapter 1 — Pages 1-21

1. Luther Standing Bear, *Land of the Spotted Eagle* (Lincoln: University of Nebraska Press, 1978), 68.
2. Virginia Driving Hawk Sneve, ed., *South Dakota Geographic Names* (Sioux Falls, SD: Brevet Press, 1973), 310, 423.
3. *Ibid.*, 423.
4. Jan Ashley, "James J. Flynn Family History," copy in the possession of the author; Gregory-Dixon Historical Society, comp. and ed., *Yesterday and Today in the Gregory Area* (Gregory, SD: Plains Printing Company, 1990), 38-39.
5. Gregory-Dixon Historical Society, *Yesterday and Today in the Gregory Area*, 38-39.
6. John P. "Pat" Flynn, Jr., untitled family history, 1979 (hereafter cited as Flynn History), in the personal papers of John P. "Pat" Flynn, Jr., in the possession of the author, Dakota Wesleyan University, Mitchell, SD (hereafter cited as Flynn Papers); Rose Marie (Flynn) Ashley, "John P. Flynn Family History," copy in the possession of the author.
7. Herbert S. Schell, *History of South Dakota*, 3rd rev. ed. (Lincoln: University of Nebraska Press, 1975), 277-283.
8. John P. Flynn to Lucille Flynn, April 30, 1963, letter in the Flynn Papers.
9. Grace (Flynn) Scott, interview with the author, Brighton, CO, November 16, 2000.
10. Paul Higbee, "Homestake's Last Ounce," *South Dakota Magazine*, Vol. 16, No. 6 (March/April 2001): 34-35.
11. Schell, *History of South Dakota*, 295.
12. Clipping from the *The Daily Pilot* (Newport and Costa Mesa, CA), n.d., in the Flynn Papers.
13. Remi Nadeau, *Fort Laramie and the Sioux Indians* (Englewood Cliffs, NJ: Prentice-Hall, 1967), 241-242; Don C. Clowser, *Dakota Indian Treaties: The Dakota Indians from Nomad to Reservation* (Deadwood, SD: Don C. Clowser, 1974), 110-111.
14. Flynn History.
15. Charles E. Hanson, Jr., "The Post-War Indian Gun Trade," *The Museum of the Fur Trade Quarterly*, Vol. 4 (Fall 1968): 1-3.
16. U.S. Senate, "A Bill for the Relief of F. C. X. Boucher," 64th Cong., 1st sess., December 12, 1915, S 2200, copy in the Flynn Papers.
17. George E. Hyde, *Spotted Tail's Folk: A History of the Brulé Sioux* (Norman: University of Oklahoma Press, 1961), 281, 298-300.
18. Gregory High School, "The Gorilla," 1941, in the Flynn Papers; clipping from the *Gregory Times-Advocate*, n.d., in the Flynn Papers.
19. Margaret Connell Szasz, *Education and the American Indian: The Road*

to Self-Determination Since 1928, 3rd rev. ed. (1974; Albuquerque: University of New Mexico Press, 1999), 64, 134-136.
20. Kenneth William Townsend, *World War II and the American Indian* (Albuquerque: University of New Mexico Press, 2000), 22.
21. Flynn's admission application, Haskell Institute, May 9, 1941, from the student file of John P. Flynn, Jr., Haskell Inventory, National Archives-Central Plains Branch, Kansas City, MO (hereafter cited as Haskell Student File).
22. *Ibid.*
23. Paul L. Fickinger to C. R. Whitlock, July 10, 1941, letter in Haskell Student File.
24. Review of a loan application by John P. Flynn, April 11, 1942, in Haskell Student File.
25. Townsend, *World War II and the American Indian,* 77-79.
26. John P. Flynn to Ruth M. Bronson, May 6, 1942, letter in Haskell Student File; Solon Ayers to John P. Flynn, June 24 and June 25, 1942, letters in Haskell Student File; Form DD 398, "Statement of Personal History" of John Patrick Flynn, Jr., 1962, in the Flynn Papers.

Chapter 2 — Pages 22-47

1. From "The Soldier's Faith," an address delivered to a meeting called by the graduating class of Harvard University, Memorial Day, May 30, 1895.
2. Civil Aeronautics Administration Civilian Pilot Rating Manual, issued to Flynn on December 9, 1942, in the Flynn Papers (hereafter cited as CPR Manual).
3. Newspaper clipping, source and date unknown, in the Flynn Papers; CPR Manual; John P. Flynn, Jr., to John P. Flynn, December 10, 1942, in the Flynn Papers.
4. Samuel Hynes, *Flights of Passage: Reflections of a World War II Aviator* (Annapolis, MD: Naval Institute Press, 1988), 29-31.
5. Matt Portz, "Memories of World War II Training," in Naval Aviation News Staff, *Naval Aviation Training, Vol. 1 of the Commemorative Collection Celebrating the 75th Year of Naval Aviation* (Washington, D.C.: Deputy Chief of Naval Operations and Commander, Naval Air Systems Command, n.d.), 10-12; Flight log of John P. Flynn, Jr., in the possession of Frances Flynn, Gregory, SD (hereafter cited as Flynn Flight Log); Hynes, *Flights of Passage,* 48.
6. John P. Flynn, Jr., to John P. Flynn, July 24, July 31, and August 10, 1943, letters in the Flynn Papers; War Department and Navy Department, Recognition Pictorial Manual (Washington, D.C.: Navy Department, 1943).
7. Hynes, *Flights of Passage,* 66-67.
8. John P. Flynn, Jr., to John P. Flynn, September 25, 1943, letter in the Flynn Papers; Flynn Flight Log; Tony Holmes, *Jane's Historic Military Aircraft* (London: HarperCollins, 1998), 102-103.
9. Barrett Tillman, *Vought F4U Corsair,* Vol. 4 of the *Warbird Tech Series* (North Branch, MN: Specialty Press, 1996), 5-10, 95; Holmes, *Jane's Historic Military*

Aircraft, 228; Boone T. Guyton, *Whistling Death: The Test Pilot's Story of the F4U Corsair* (New York: Orion Books, 1990), 164.
10. Tillman, *Vought F4U Corsair*, 30-33.
11. Ronald H. Spector, *Eagle Against the Sun: The American War with Japan* (New York: Free Press, 1985), 267-273.
12. Robert Sherrod, *History of Marine Corps Aviation in World War II* (Washington, D.C.: Combat Forces Press, 1952), 235.
13. *Ibid.*, 239; "History of VMF-111," VMF-111 File, Reference Section, Marine Corps Historical Center, Washington, D.C. (hereafter cited as VMF- 111 File); Robert D. Heinl, Jr., and John A. Crown, *The Marshalls: Increasing the Tempo*, Vol. 14 in *Operational History of the Marine Corps in World War II* (Washington, D.C.: Historical Branch, Headquarters USMC, 1954), 160.
14. Heinl and Crown, *The Marshalls*, 236, 246; VMF-111 File; Flynn Flight Log; John P. Flynn to Lucille Flynn, April 4, 1945, letter in the possession of Frances Flynn.
15. John P. Flynn to Lucille Flynn, April 4, 1945; VMF-111 Aircraft Action Report 234, Box 1633, Records of the Office of the Chief of Naval Operations, Record Group 38, National Archives, College Park, MD (hereafter cited as VMF-111 Action Report).
16. VMF-111 Action Report 250; Flynn Flight Log.
17. Sherrod, *History of Marine Corps Aviation*, 238, 246.
18. George Feifer, *Tennozan: The Battle of Okinawa and the Atomic Bomb* (New York: Ticknor & Fields, 1992), xi.
19. William J. Sambito, *A History of Marine Fighter Attack Squadron 312* (Washington, D.C.: History and Museums Division, Headquarters USMC, 1978), 1-6.
20. Hynes, *Flights of Passage*, 200-202, 210-211.
21. Charles S. Nichols, Jr., and Henry I. Shaw, Jr., *Okinawa: Victory in the Pacific*, Vol. 15 in *Operational History of the Marine Corps in World War II* (Washington, D.C.: Historical Branch, G-3 Division, Headquarters USMC, 1955), 258.
22. Gerald Astor, *Operation Iceberg: The Invasion and Conquest of Okinawa in World War II* (New York: Dell, 1995), 204-205.
23. Stanley Weintraub, *The Last Great Victory: The End of World War II, July-August 1945* (New York: Plume, 1996), 222-224; Benis Frank and Henry I. Shaw, *Victory and Occupation*, Vol. 5 of *History of U. S. Marine Corps Operations in World War II* (Washington, D.C.: Historical Branch, G-3 Division, Headquarters USMC, 1968), 429.
24. Frank and Shaw, *Victory and Occupation*, 430-431.
25. Hynes, *Flights of Passage*, 239-240.
26. Flynn Flight Log; VMF-312 War Diary, Box 51, USMC War Diaries, RG 127, National Archives, College Park, MD (hereafter cited as VMF-312 War Diary); copy of "Recommendations for Award-Strike/Flight System," in the Flynn Papers.
27. VMF-312 War Diary; "Statement of Second Lieutenant John Patrick Flynn (032419) USMCR," July 4, 1945, in *VMF-312 War Diary* (hereafter cited as Flynn Statement of July 4, 1945); "Lt. John Flynn in Thrilling Adventure," clipping from the *Winner Advocate*, n.d., in the Flynn Papers (hereafter cited as "Thrilling Adventure").
28. "Thrilling Adventure"; Flynn Statement of July 4, 1945; Air-Sea Rescue Report for

The Life of John P. "Pat" Flynn, Jr.   189

   Second Lieutenant John P. Flynn, in VMF-312 War Diary (hereafter cited as Rescue Report).
29. Rescue Report; Flynn Statement of July 4, 1945; "Thrilling Adventure."
30. Flynn Statement of July 4, 1945.
31. "Thrilling Adventure."
32. Weintraub, *The Last Great Victory*, 201.
33. *Ibid.*; Rescue Report; "Thrilling Adventure."
34. "Thrilling Adventure."
35. Copy of citation awarding the Purple Heart to Second Lieutenant John Patrick Flynn, Jr., August 30, 1945, in the Flynn Papers.
36. Summary of VMF-312 actions in World War II, n.d., in VMF-312 file, Box 368, Naval Aviation History Branch, Naval Historical Center, Washington D.C.; Sambito, *A History of Marine Fighter Attack Squadron 312*, 6.
37. Aircraft Action Report No. 5, Box 1619, MAG (Marine Air Group)-33 World War II Action and Operational Reports, Records of the Office of the Chief of Naval Operations, RG 38, National Archives, College Park, MD (hereafter cited as MAG-33 Reports); Flynn Flight Log.
38. John P. Flynn to Lucille Flynn, July 24, 1945, letter in the possession of Frances Flynn; Aircraft Action Report No. 7, MAG-33 Reports.
39. Flynn Flight Log; Hynes, *Flights of Passage*, 252.
40. Frank and Shaw, *Victory and Occupation*, 436; Flynn Flight Log.
41. MAG-33 Summary for the Month of September 1945, Box 20, USMC Aviation Unit War Diaries and Unit Histories (1941-1949), RG 127, National Archives, College Park, MD (hereafter cited as MAG-33 Summaries).
42. *Ibid.*
43. *Ibid.*; Hynes, *Flights of Passage*, 261-263.
44. Summary for the Month of October 1945, in MAG-33 Summaries.
45. Hynes, *Flights of Passage*, 263.
46. John P. Flynn to Lucille Flynn, September 22, 1945; Flynn Flight Log; Holmes, *Jane's Historic Military Aircraft*, 178-179.

Chapter 3 — Pages 48-70

1. John R. Bruning, *Crimson Sky: The Air Battle for Korea* (Dulles, VA: Brassey's, 2000), 113.
2. Charles A. Fleming, Robin L. Austin, and Charles A. Braley, III, *Quantico: Crossroads of the Marine Corps* (Washington, D.C.: History and Museums Division, Headquarters USMC, 1978), 78.
3. "Captain John P. Flynn, Jr., USMC, January 6, 1954," Reference Section, Marine Corps Historical Center, Washington, D.C.; newspaper clipping from an unidentified source, n.d., in the Flynn Papers.
4. Stanley Weintraub, *MacArthur's War: Korea and the Undoing of An American Hero* (New York: Free Press, 2000), 109; Robert R. Bowie and Richard Immerman,

Waging Peace: How Eisenhower Shaped an Enduring Cold War Strategy (New York: Oxford University Press, 1998), 14; James A. Winnefeld and Dana J. Johnson, *Joint Air Operations: Pursuit of Unity in Command and Control* (Annapolis, MD: Naval Institute Press, 1993), 39; Stanley Sandler, *The Korean War: No Victors, No Vanquished* (Lexington: University of Kentucky Press, 1999), 36.

5. Arthur Singer, *Arthur Godfrey: The Adventures of an American Broadcaster* (Jefferson, NC: McFarland & Co., 2000), 57, 133-134, 144-145; Flynn Flight Log.
6. Dozens of clippings of Flynn's weekly "Hunting and Fishing" column in *Gosport*, the base newspaper, are in the Flynn Papers; Frances Flynn, interviews with the author, 2001; Judith A. Bense, ed., *Archaeology of Colonial Pensacola* (Gainesville: University Press of Florida, 1999), 91, 97, 110.
7. Quoted in a *Gosport* clipping in the Flynn Papers, n.d.
8. "Statement in Security Council on Invasion of South Korea, Trygve Lie, 25 June 1950," in Spencer C. Tucker, ed., *Encyclopedia of the Korean War: A Political, Social, and Military History*, Vol. 3 (Santa Barbara, CA: ABC-Clio, 2000), 869-870; Wesley M. Bagby, *America's International Relations Since World War I* (New York: Oxford University Press, 1999), 169; Max Hastings, *The Korean War* (New York: Simon and Schuster, 1987); *The New York Times*, June 25, 1950, late city edition.
9. "Dean Acheson National Press Club Speech, 12 January 1950," in Tucker, *Encyclopedia of the Korean War*, Vol. 3, 828-830.
10. Sandler, *The Korean War*, 2-4; W. W. Rostow, *The United States in the World Arena: An Essay in Recent History* (New York: Harper & Row, 1960), 229-230; Bagby, *America's International Relations*, 169.
11. T. R. Fehrenbach, *This Kind of War: The Classic Korean War History* (Dulles, VA: Brassey's, 2000), 244-247; J. Robert Moskin, *The U.S. Marine Corps Story*, 3rd rev. ed. (New York: Little, Brown, and Co., 1992), 462-470; Hastings, *The Korean War*, 111-112; Sandler, *The Korean War*, xiii, 85-116.
12. Shu Guang Zhang, *Mao's Military Romanticism: China and the Korean War, 1950-1953* (Lawrence: University Press of Kansas, 1995), 112-116.
13. Xiaobing Li, Allan R. Millett, and Bin Yu, eds. and trans., *Mao's Generals Remember Korea* (Lawrence: University Press of Kansas, 2001), 17; Hastings, *The Korean War*, 147-164; Fehrenbach, *This Kind of War*, 237-250, 368; Sandler, *The Korean War*, 117-128.
14. Zhang, *Mao's Military Romanticism*, 118-119; Sandler, *The Korean War*, 129-134.
15. Sandler, *The Korean War*, 3, 135-147, 239-244.
16. Marine All-Weather Fighter Squadron 513, "Historical Diary of Marine All-Weather Squadron 513, October 1951" (CD-ROM version), 3, and Appendix E, Sec. 9-3, Archives Section, Marine Corps Historical Center, Washington, D.C. (hereafter cited as Historical Diary); Benjamin Houston Kristy, "The Flying Nightmares: An Operational History and Assessment of VMF(N)-513 at War in Korea, 1950-1953" (M.A. thesis, Kansas State University, 1995), 13; G. G. O'Rourke with E. T. Woolridge, *Night Fighters Over Korea* (Annapolis, MD: Naval Institute Press, 1998), 90-91; Fred G. Braitsch, "Night Intruders," *The Leatherneck*, Vol. 34 (December 1951): 25; Hastings, *The Korean War*, 264; Winnefeld and Johnson, *Joint Air Operations*, 45, 50.

17. Warren Thompson, "Wait Until Dark," *Wings*, Vol. 19 (October 1989): 15-18.
18. Historical Diary, October 1951, 2, and Appendix E, sec. 8; Conrad C. Crane, *American Airpower Strategy in Korea, 1950-1953* (Lawrence: University Press of Kansas, 2000), 137-139.
19. Li, *et.al.*, *Mao's Generals*, 23-24.
20. Historical Diary, October 1951, Appendix E, sec. 9, 1.
21. *Ibid.*, 27-28; Flynn Flight Log.
22. H. D. Bradshaw, "The Flying Nightmares: A History of VMFA-513, 1944-1966," 5, VMA-513 File (2/2), Reference Section, Marine Corps Historical Center, Washington, D.C.; Thompson, "Wait Until Dark," 15.
23. Thompson, "Wait Until Dark," 23.
24. Kristy, "The Flying Nightmares," 48, 101.
25. Norman Flinn, telephone interview with the author, October 7, 2000.
26. Historical Diary, October 1952, Appendix E, Sec. 9-2; Flynn Interview; Thompson, "Wait Until Dark," 22-24; Braitsch, "Night Intruders," 22; Tony Holmes, *Jane's Historic Military Aircraft* (London: HarperCollins, 1998), 140-141; Kristy, "The Flying Nightmares," 96, 100; Kalani O'Sullivan, "How It Was! Kunsan Airbase: VMF(N)-513: 'Flying Nightmares' (1951-1954)," available at www.geocities.com/yooni_99/howitwasa1a. html. (hereafter cited as Kunsan Airbase Web Site).
27. Kunsan Airbase Web Site; Flynn Interview; Historical Diary, October 1951, Appendix E, Sec. 9-2; Braitsch, "Night Intruders," 22; Kristy, "The Flying Nightmares," 50, 98.
28. Quoted in Thompson, "Wait Until Dark," 24.
29. Braitsch, "Night Intruders," 23.
30. Historical Diary, October 1951, Appendix E, Sec. 9, 1-3.
31. Flynn Interview; Kristy, "The Flying Nightmares," 36; Kunsan Airbase Web Site; Sandler, *The Korean War*, 179.
32. Flynn Interview; Kristy, "The Flying Nightmares," 102-104.
33. Quoted in Thompson, "Wait Until Dark," 22.
34. Kristy, "The Flying Nightmares," 102-104.
35. Quoted in Li, *et. al.*, *Mao's Generals*, 56.
36. 1st Marine Air Wing citation for Captain John P. Flynn, awarding him a Gold Star in lieu of his second Distinguished Flying Cross, 1952, in the Flynn Papers; Historical Diary, February 1952, 14.
37. Thompson, "Wait Until Dark," 23.
38. O'Rourke, *Night Fighters Over Korea*, 128.
39. Kunsan Airbase Web Site; Flynn Interview.
40. O'Rourke, *Night Fighters Over Korea*, 98.
41. *Ibid.*
42. "Korea 1950: War," *Columban Mission*, October 2000, 6.
43. The description of Father Maginn's death and Father Burke and Pat Flynn's discovery of Maginn's remains is taken from interviews with Frances Flynn and from a newspaper clipping from an unidentified source in the Flynn Papers.
44. Kristy, "The Flying Nightmares," 16-18; Holmes, *Jane's Historic Military Aircraft*, 178-179, 200.

45. Harlo Sterrett to the author, e-mail correspondence, December 13, 2000; Flinn Interview.
46. The description of Flynn's operational accident at K-8 on April 22, 1952, is taken from the following sources: Historical Diary, April 1952, Appendix F, Statement 14; Walter S. Andariese, "Seven Hundred Feet-Straight Down," an unpublished transcript found in the personal papers of John P. Flynn; Flinn Interview; John P. Flynn to Lucille Flynn, April 29, 1952, letter in the Flynn Papers; John P. Flynn to Jack and Grace Russell, excerpts of the letter reprinted in the *Winner Advocate*, May 22, 1952; Kunsan Airbase Web Site.

Chapter 4 — Pages 71-90

1. Marine All-Weather Fighter Squadron 513, "Historical Diary of Marine All-Weather Squadron 513, May 1952" (CD-ROM version), 1, Archives Section, Marine Corps Historical Center, Washington, D.C. (hereafter cited as Historical Diary); John P. Flynn, Jr., "A Red Rose for Valor," unpublished essay, 1968, Flynn Papers.
2. Historical Diary, May 1952, Appendix F, Statement 16; Russell Stoneman, telephone interview with the author, February 27, 2001.
3. Flynn Flight Log; Historical Diary, May 1952, Appendix F, Statement 16; H. H. Porter to "Jay," May 19, 1952, copy of letter provided to the author by Dr. Peter Perla, Center for Naval Analysis, Alexandria, VA (hereafter cited as Porter Letter).
4. *Boston Post*, December 4, 1953, and January 5, 1954; "Six More Killed in Korea," *The Unicorn* (published by Theta Xi Fraternity), January 1954, 5; press release, MIT News Service, August 27, 1954, copy courtesy of Dr. Peter Perla.
5. Porter Letter; Dr. Peter Perla, telephone interview with the author, November 19, 2000.
6. Porter Letter; Flynn, "A Red Rose for Valor," 7.
7. Historical Diary, May 1952, Appendix F, Statement 16.
8. Historical Diary, May 1952, Appendix F, Statement 16; "Statement of Captain John P. Flynn, Jr., 032419, USMC, Regarding the Fate of Dr. Irving Shaknov," copy in the Flynn Papers (hereafter cited as Statement of Captain Flynn); Flynn, "A Red Rose for Valor," 4.
9. Statement of Captain Flynn; Historical Diary, May 1952, Appendix F, Statement 16.
10. Flynn, "A Red Rose for Valor," 4; Statement of Captain Flynn; Admiral Robert B. Carney to Mr. and Mrs. William M. Shaknov, October 9, 1953, copy of letter in the Flynn Papers; Historical Diary, May 1952, Appendix F, Statement 16; Headquarters 1st Marine Air Wing, "Information concerning the disappearance of Captain John P. Flynn, Jr., 032419, USMC," n.d., copy in the Flynn Papers; COMNAVFE to CNO, "Investigation report on the disappearance of Dr. Irving Shaknov," May 28, 1952, copy in the Flynn Papers; "Statement by D. Y. Barrerra, OEG, on talk with Captain Flynn on Sunday, September 6, 1953," copy courtesy of Peter Perla.
11. Biography of Dr. Irving Shaknov, courtesy of Dr. Peter Perla; "Speedletter,

COMNAVFE to CNO, May 1952," copy courtesy of Dr. Peter Perla; Statement of Captain Flynn; map of the Flynn-Shaknov crash site, courtesy of Dr. Peter Perla.
12. Statement of Captain Flynn; John P. Flynn, Jr., to Commandant of the Marine Corps, "Report on Period of Captivity," January 27, 1954, copy in the Flynn Papers (hereafter cited as Flynn Captivity Report); *The Tidings* (a publication of the Catholic Diocese of Los Angeles), March 12, 1954; *Gregory Times-Advocate*, October 22, 1953; John P. Flynn, Jr., interview with Mrs. I. W. Haggard, *Mitchell Daily Republic*, October 1954 (hereafter cited as Haggard Interview); clipping from *The Daily Pilot*, n.d., in the Flynn Papers (hereafter cited as *Daily Pilot* Interview).
13. N. W. Flinn to John P. Flynn, May 3, 1965, letter in the Flynn Papers (hereafter cited as Flinn Letter); Norman Flinn, telephone interview with the author, October 7, 2000; Historical Diary, May 1952, Appendix F, Statement 16.
14. Haggard Interview; Flynn, "A Red Rose for Valor," 5.
15. Flynn, "A Red Rose for Valor," 5-6; *Oakland Tribune*, December 5, 1965; *Daily Pilot* Interview.
16. Stoneman Interview; *Daily Pilot* Interview; Flynn, "A Red Rose for Valor," 6.
17. Testimony of Captain John P. Flynn, Jr., in the Court of Inquiry concerning Colonel Frank H. Schwable, USMC, March 2, 1954, Office of the Judge Advocate General, Department of the Navy, Washington, D.C., 551 (hereafter cited as Court of Inquiry Testimony); *Daily Pilot* Interview; Flynn, "A Red Rose for Valor," 6.
18. Flynn, "A Red Rose For Valor," 6-7; *Daily Pilot* Interview.
19. *The Tidings* Interview; newspaper clipping from an unidentified source entitled "Ready for Martyrdom," 1954, in the Flynn Papers; *Daily Pilot* Interview.
20. Flynn Captivity Report; Court of Inquiry Testimony, 519.
21. Xiaobing Li, Allan R. Millett, and Bin Yu, eds. and trans., *Mao's Generals Remember Korea* (Lawrence: University Press of Kansas, 2001), 157-158; Shu Guang Zhang, *Mao's Military Romanticism: China and the Korean War, 1950-1953* (Lawrence: University Press of Kansas, 1995), 181-182.
22. Zhang, *Mao's Military Romanticism*, 186; Stanley Sandler, *The Korean War: No Victors, No Vanquished* (Lexington: University of Kentucky Press, 1999), 208; James Angus MacDonald, Jr., "The Problems of U.S. Marine Corps Prisoners of War in Korea" (M.A. thesis, University of Maryland, 1961), 220; T. R. Fehrenbach, *This Kind of War: The Classic Korean War History* (Dulles, VA: Brassey's, 2000), 414.
23. Zhang, *Mao's Military Romanticism*, 182-183.
24. Quoted in John R. Bruning, Jr., *Crimson Sky: The Air Battle for Korea* (Dulles, VA: Brassey's 2000), 114.
25. G. S. Moakley, "U.S. Army Code of Conduct Training: Let the POWs Tell Their Stories" (M.A. thesis, U.S. Army Command and Staff College, Fort Leavenworth, KS, 1976), 88.
26. MacDonald, "The Problems of U.S. Marine Corps Prisoners of War in Korea," 175.
27. Max Hastings, *The Korean War* (New York: Touchstone, 1987), 287-288.
28. Court of Inquiry Testimony, 519.
29. "Former POW of Chinese Recalls Red Torture," clipping from an unidentified newspaper, n.d., in the Flynn Papers. The clipping includes remarks made by Flynn

to the Santa Ana (CA) Exchange Club in 1954 (hereafter cited as Exchange Club Remarks); Flynn Captivity Report.
30. Exchange Club Remarks; *Oakland Tribune*, December 5, 1965; *Daily Pilot* Interview.
31. John McCain with Mark Salter, *Faith of My Fathers* (New York: Random House, 1999), 206.
32. Court of Inquiry Testimony, 530; *Oakland Tribune*, December 5, 1965.
33. *Oakland Tribune*, December 5, 1965.
34. *Washington Post*, February 20, 1954.
35. Walker M. Mahurin, *Honest John: The Autobiography of Walker M. Mahurin* (New York: G.P. Putnam's Sons, 1962), 189.
36. William Stueck, *The Korean War: An International History* (Princeton, NJ: Princeton University Press, 1995), 244.
37. William H. Funchess, telephone interview with the author, September 22, 2000.
38. MacDonald, "The Problem of Marine Corps Prisoners of War in Korea," 60-61.
39. Exchange Club Remarks; *Oakland Tribune*, December 5, 1965; Court of Inquiry Testimony, 521-522.
40. Mahurin, *Honest John*, 205.
41. *Oakland Tribune*, December 5, 1965.
42. Anthony Farrar-Hockley, *The Edge of the Sword* (London: Buchan & Enright, 1985), 234.
43. *Oakland Tribune*, December 5, 1965; Court of Inquiry Testimony, 522.
44. *Washington Post*, March 10, 1954.
45. *Oakland Tribune*, December 5, 1965.
46. Court of Inquiry Testimony, 523-524.
47. *Oakland Tribune*, December 5, 1965.
48. Court of Inquiry Testimony, 523.
49. *Ibid.*, 524.
50. Statement of D. Y. Barrer, OEG, on talk with Captain Flynn on Sunday, September 6, 1953, copy courtesy of Dr. Peter Perla; *Oakland Tribune*, December 5, 1965.
51. Court of Inquiry Testimony, 525.
52. *Daily Pilot* Interview.
53. Pat Meid and James M. Yingling, *Operations in West Korea*, Vol. 5 of *U.S. Marine Operations in Korea, 1950-1953* (Washington, D.C.: Headquarters U.S. Marine Corps, 1972), 433; Flynn Captivity Report.

Chapter 5 — Pages 91-112

1. Robert C. Doyle, *Voices from Captivity: Interpreting the American POW Narrative* (Lawrence: University Press of Kansas, 1994), 3.
2. *The Tidings* (a publication of the Catholic Diocese of Los Angeles), March 12, 1954; Frances Flynn's description of the events of May 16, 1952, was added as a

"Postscript" to John P. Flynn's unpublished essay, "A Red Rose for Valor" (1968), in 2001.
3. C. C. Hall to Mrs. John P. Flynn, Jr., May 20, 1952, letter in the Flynn Papers; John R. Burnett to Frances Flynn, May 19, 1952, letter in the Flynn Papers.
4. C. H. West, Jr. to Frances Flynn, November 25, 1952, letter in the Flynn Papers.
5. Duane Thorin, interview with the author, Chambers, NE, October 9, 2000; Chief Petty Officer Thorin, a Navy helicopter pilot, was captured in February 1952. Andrew Riker, telephone interview with the author, September 21, 2000; Ensign Riker, also assigned to Camp 2 Annex, was shot down while attached to VA 923. James Angus MacDonald, Jr., "The Problems of U.S. Marine Corps Prisoners of War in Korea" (M.A. thesis, University of Maryland, 1961), 60, 134, 162-163, 185; Pat Meid and James M. Yingling, *Operations in West Korea*, Vol. 5 of *U.S. Marine Operations in Korea, 1950-1953* (Washington, D.C.: Headquarters U.S. Marine Corps, 1972), 416, 422-423. Norman Duquette to the author, e-mail letter, September 19, 2000; Duquette spent 20 months as a POW.
6. John P. Flynn, Jr., to Commandant of the Marine Corps, "Report on Period of Captivity," January 27, 1954, copy in the Flynn Papers (hereafter cited as Flynn Captivity Report).
7. Andrew Riker, letter to the author, November 13, 2000; John P. Flynn, Jr., list of prisoners held in Camp 2 Annex, in the Flynn Papers.
8. William H. Funchess, telephone interview with the author, September 22, 2000; William H. Funchess, *Korea POW: A Thousand Days of Torment* (Clemson, SC: published privately, 1997), 110-111; Riker Interview; Mira Stout, *One Thousand Chestnut Trees: A Novel of Korea* (New York: Riverhead Books, 1998), 75-76.
9. Vernon Huber to the author, telephone interview, March 24, 2001; First Lieutenant Huber was shot down on his 44th mission with the U.S. Air Force's 49th Fighter-Bomber Wing. Walker M. Mahurin, *Honest John: The Autobiography of Walker M. Mahurin* (New York: G. P. Putnam's Sons, 1962), 193.
10. Harry Ettinger, telephone interview with the author, September 21, 2000; Ettinger was a Navy pilot confined in Camp 2. Huber Interview; Riker Interview; Thorin Interview; MacDonald, "The Problems of U.S. Marine Corps Prisoners of War in Korea," 65-66, 189.
11. *Gregory Times-Advocate*, October 22, 1953.
12. Funchess, *Korea POW*, 105.
13. Riker Interview; Thorin Interview; Huber Interview; MacDonald, "The Problems of U.S. Marine Corps Prisoners of War in Korea," 220.
14. MacDonald, "The Problems of U.S. Marine Corps Prisoners of War in Korea," 65; Raymond B. Lech, *Broken Soldiers* (Urbana: University of Illinois Press, 2000), 93-95; Meid and Yingling, *Operations in West Korea*, 426-428.
15. Albert D. Biderman, *March to Calumny: The Story of American POWs in the Korean War* (New York: Macmillan, 1963), 70.
16. Max Hastings, *The Korean War* (New York: Simon & Schuster, 1987), 294.
17. MacDonald, "The Problems of U.S. Marine Corps Prisoners of War in Korea," 70-73.
18. Riker Interview; William Lindsey White, *The Captives of Korea: An Unofficial*

White Paper on the Treatment of War Prisoners: Our Treatment of Theirs, Their Treatment of Ours (New York: Scribners, 1957), 109-110, 131.
19. *Los Angeles Times*, May 23, 1966.
20. Funchess Interview.
21. *Oakland Tribune*, December 5, 1965.
22. William G. Thrash, telephone interview with the author, September 22, 2000.
23. Riker Interview.
24. Harlo E. "Ed" Sterrett, letter and e-mail letter to the author, December 13, 2000. Sterrett mailed the author an object he had meant to present to Flynn, but never had the opportunity to do prior to Flynn's death in 1979 — the POW hat issued to Flynn by the Chinese at the Annex. Sterrett had obtained the hat in July 1953,when Flynn, his hut mate, was removed from the Annex and placed in a month-long solitary confinement.
25. Thorin Interview. Thorin, a Navy helicopter pilot captured in February 1952, was assigned to the Annex after a failed escape attempt in the summer of 1952.
26. Riker Letter.
27. Thorin Interview.
28. Riker Letter.
29. Joseph Kutys, telephone interview with the author, March 24, 2001.
30. *Los Angeles Times*, May 23, 1966.
31. *The Tidings*, March 12, 1954; *Rapid City Journal*, March 3, 1954; *Oakland Tribune*, December 5, 1965; Sterrett Letter; Duane Thorin, *A Ride to Panmunjom* (Chicago: Henry Regnery Company, 1956).
32. *Gregory Times-Advocate*, October 22, 1953; "Former POW of Chinese Recalls Red Torture," clipping from an unidentified newspaper, n.d., in the Flynn Papers. The clipping includes remarks made by Flynn to the Santa Ana (CA) Exchange Club in 1954 (hereafter cited as Exchange Club Remarks).
33. John P. Flynn, Jr., "MORALE: Pride and Compassion," 1960, in the Flynn Papers.
34. *Ibid.*
35. Exchange Club Remarks.
36. Thorin Interview.
37. Flynn Captivity Report; MacDonald, "The Problems of U.S. Marine Corps Prisoners of War in Korea," 220; Thorin Interview.
38. Flynn, "MORALE," 3.
39. Thorin Interview.
40. Flynn, "MORALE," 3; Thorin Interview.
41. Flynn Captivity Report; Sterrett Letter; Thorin Interview.
42. Testimony of Captain John P. Flynn, Jr., before the Court of Inquiry concerning Colonel Frank H. Schwable, USMC, March 2, 1954, Office of Judge Advocate General, Department of the Navy, Washington, D.C., 527 (hereafter cited as Court of Inquiry Testimony).
43. *Ibid.*, 527-528, 552.
44. Major Walter R. Harris to the Commandant of the Marine Corps, December 9, 1953, copy of letter in the Flynn Papers; Commandant of the Marine Corps to Secretary of the Navy, December 21, 1953, copy of letter in the Flynn Papers; Flynn Captivity Report.

45. Thorin, *A Ride to Panmunjom*, 237, 251-254.
46. *Ibid.*, 262.
47. *Gregory Times-Advocate*, October 22, 1953.
48. Court of Inquiry Testimony, 528-529.
49. Flynn Captivity Report.
50. Thorin Interview.
51. John Toland, *In Mortal Combat: Korea, 1950-1953* (New York: Quill, 1991), 581-582.
52. Flynn Captivity Report; Toland, *In Mortal Combat*, 581; Thorin Interview.
53. Commandant of the Marine Corps to Frances Flynn, Western Union telegram, September 5, 1953, in the Flynn Papers.
54. John P. Flynn, Jr., to Frances Flynn, September 6, 1953, Western Union telegram, in the Flynn Papers.
55. Sterrett Letter.

Chapter 6 — Pages 113-127

1. Testimony of Captain John P. Flynn, Jr., before the Court of Inquiry concerning Colonel Frank H. Schwable, USMC, March 2, 1954, Office of the Judge Advocate General, Department of the Navy, Washington, D.C., 525-526 (hereafter cited as Court of Inquiry Testimony).
2. Newspaper clipping (possibly from the *Orange County Register*), n.d., in the Flynn Papers.
3. James Angus MacDonald, Jr., "The Problems of U.S. Marine Corps Prisoners of War in Korea" (M.A. thesis, University of Maryland, 1961), 227-228.
4. "Statement of D. Y. Barrer, OEG, on talk with Capt. Flynn," September 6, 1953, copy courtesy of Dr. Peter Perla in the possession of the author; Admiral Robert B. Carney to Mr. and Mrs. William M. Shaknov, October 9, 1953, copy of the letter in the Flynn Papers; John J. McGrew to John P. Flynn, October 16, 1953, letter in the Flynn Papers; "Statement of Captain John P. Flynn, Jr., 032419, USMC, Regarding Fate of Dr. Irving Shaknov," September 23, 1953, copy in the Flynn Papers.
5. T. R. Fehrenbach, *This Kind of War: The Classic Korean War History* (Dulles, VA: Brassey's, 2000), 450.
6. Elizabeth L. Tierney, "MTG-10"(1953), in Marine Training Group-10 File, Reference Branch, Marine Corps Historical Center, Washington, D.C.
7. Tony Holmes, *Jane's Historic Military Aircraft* (London: HarperCollins, 1998), 112-113, 326-327; G. G. O'Rourke, with E. T. Woolridge, *Night Fighters Over Korea* (Annapolis, MD: Naval Institute Press, 1998), 91; Flynn Flight Log.
8. *Navy Times*, January 16, 1954.
9. Commandant of the Marine Corps General Lemuel C. Shepherd to Secretary of the Navy Robert B. Anderson, December 21, 1953, copy of the letter in the Flynn

Papers; Major Walter R. Harris to Shepherd, December 9, 1953, copy of the letter in the Flynn Papers.
10. Remarks of the Honorable Robert B. Anderson, Secretary of the Navy, at presentation ceremonies in the Pentagon, January 11, 1954, in the Flynn Papers.
11. John Barnett, telephone interview with the author, February 18, 2001.
12. Robert Sherrod, *History of Marine Corps Aviation in World War II* (Washington, D.C.: Combat Forces Press, 1952), 158-163, 167-168, 173; *Washington Post*, January 24 and February 19, 1954; Raymond Lech, *Broken Soldiers* (Urbana: University of Illinois Press, 2000), 165.
13. Lech, *Broken Soldiers*, 167-168.
14. *Ibid.*, 168-169.
15. *Ibid.*, 170-175.
16. John Toland, *In Mortal Combat: Korea, 1950-1953* (New York: Quill, 1991), 552-553.
17. "Transcript of Deposition by Colonel Frank H. Schwable," in Lech, *Broken Soldiers*, Appendix C, 299-302.
18. *Washington Post*, January 24 and 28, 1954.
19. Lech, *Broken Soldiers*, 240; J. Robert Moskin, *The U.S. Marine Corps Story*, 3rd rev. ed. (Boston: Little, Brown and Company, 1992), 167-168.
20. *Washington Post*, February 18, 1954; Court of Inquiry Testimony, 516.
21. *Washington Post*, February 19, 1954.
22. *Ibid.*, February 25, 1954; Lech, *Broken Soldiers*, 240.
23. Court of Inquiry Testimony, 522-523.
24. *Ibid.*, 524.
25. *Ibid.*, 525.
26. *Ibid.*, 525-526.
27. *Ibid.*, 529.
28. *Ibid.*, 540.
29. *Ibid.*, 551-552.
30. *Washington Post*, March 4 and 10, 1954.
31. Quoted in Lech, *Broken Soldiers*, 240-241.
32. *Huron Daily Plainsman*, March 5, 1954.
33. *Ibid.*, March 5, 1954, and February 7, 1971.

Chapter 7 — Pages 128-154

1. T. R. Fehrenbach, *This Kind of War: The Classic Korean War History* (Dulles, VA: Brassey's, 2000), 29.
2. Robert R. Bowie and Richard H. Immerman, *Waging Peace: How Eisenhower Shaped an Enduring Cold War Strategy* (New York: Oxford University Press, 1998), 174, 193-195; David Kaiser, *American Tragedy: Kennedy, Johnson, and the Origins of the Vietnam War* (Cambridge, MA: Belknap Press, 2000), 14-19.
3. Quoted in Bowie and Immerman, *Waging Peace*, 200-201.

4. Henry A. Kissinger, *Nuclear Weapons and Foreign Policy* (New York: Council on Foreign Relations, 1957), 30.
5. Quoted in Lawrence Freedman, *Kennedy's Wars: Berlin, Cuba, Laos, and Vietnam* (New York: Oxford University Press, 2000), 19; Neil Sheehan, *A Bright Shining Lie: John Paul Vann and America in Vietnam* (New York: Vintage Books, 1988), 59.
6. Sheehan, *A Bright Shining Lie*, 59.
7. Freedman, *Kennedy's Wars*, 287-290.
8. Flynn Flight Log; *The Flight Jacket* (base newspaper of MCAS El Toro, CA), September 10, 1954.
9. Details about the deaths of Bell, Beswick, Wagner, and Williams found in notes written by Flynn in 1978 or 1979, located in the Flynn Papers (hereafter cited as Notes on POW Trauma); Paul L. Martelli to the author, e-mail letter, January 4, 2001. Martelli, a Marine aviator and former POW, was stationed at El Toro following the Korean War.
10. James Angus MacDonald, Jr., "The Problems of U. S. Marine Corps Prisoners of War in Korea" (M.A. thesis, University of Maryland, 1961), 105-107.
11. Flynn, Notes on POW Trauma.
12. U.S. Veterans Administration, Office of Planning and Program Evaluation, Studies and Analysis Service, *Study of Former Prisoners of War* (Washington, D.C.: Government Printing Office, 1980), 4-5, 91, 148-154.
13. Jerry Miller, *Nuclear Weapons and Aircraft Carriers: How the Bomb Saved Naval Aviation* (Washington, D.C.: Smithsonian Institution Press, 2001), 57. The description of Flynn's duties with VMF-314 is taken from various military records in the Flynn Papers.
14. "History/Chronology of VMF(AW)-314," VMF-314 Folder 2/2, Reference Section, Marine Corps Historical Center, Washington, D.C.; Flynn Flight Log; *The Flight Jacket*, August 5, 1955; Commander, Air Force Special Weapons Center, Air Research and Development Command to Major John P. Flynn, Jr., June 7, 1955, copy in the Flynn Papers.
15. James A. Winnefeld and Dana J. Johnson, *Joint Air Operations: Pursuit of Unity in Command and Control, 1942-1991* (Annapolis, MD: Naval Institute Press, 1993), 46, 50, 57.
16. *Ibid.*
17. John P. Condon, *U.S. Marine Corps Aviation*, Vol. 5 of the *Commemorative Collection Celebrating the 75th Year of Naval Aviation* (Washington, D.C.: Deputy Chief of Naval Operations and Commander, Naval Air Systems Command, n.d.), 25, 31; Conrad C. Crane, *American Airpower Strategy in Korea, 1950-1953* (Lawrence: University Press of Kansas, 2000), 28-29.
18. Crane, *American Airpower Strategy*, 135, 182; William Green and Gordon Swanborough, *The Great Book of Fighters* (Osceola, WI: MBI Publishing, 2001), 496-498; Miller, *Nuclear Weapons and Aircraft Carriers*, 73; Flynn Flight Log.
19. Quoted in a clipping from an unidentified newspaper (almost certainly the Chanute Air Force Base newspaper), n.d., in the Flynn Papers.
20. Dwight D. Eisenhower, Executive Order 10631, "Code of Conduct for Members of the Armed Forces of the United States," August 17, 1955, in Albert D. Biderman,

March to Calumny: The Story of American POWs in the Korean War (New York: Macmillan, 1963), Appendix B, 278.
21. "History of VMA(AW)-225," VMA-225 Folder 2/2, Reference Section, Marine Corps Historical Center, Washington, D.C.
22. Tony Holmes, *Jane's Historic Military Aircraft* (London: HarperCollins, 1998), 292-293; Miller, *Nuclear Weapons and Aircraft Carriers*, 134-135; Nicholas A. Veronico and Marga B. Fritze, *Blue Angels: 50 Years of Precision Flight* (Osceola, WI: MBI Publishing, 1996), 78-93.
23. Miller, *Nuclear Weapons and Aircraft Carriers*, 134-135.
24. Holmes, *Jane's Historic Military Aircraft*, 292.
25. Miller, *Nuclear Weapons and Aircraft Carriers*, 73-74.
26. Nels A. Parson, Jr., *Missiles and the Revolution in Warfare* (Cambridge, MA: Harvard University Press, 1962), 37-44.
27. Miller, *Nuclear Weapons and Aircraft Carriers*, 158-161; Richard "Dick" Hoffman, telephone interview with the author, October 7, 2000; Clifford Warfield, telephone interview with the author, October 8, 2000. Hoffman and Warfield flew with Flynn in VMA-225.
28. *Navy Times*, April 26, 1967.
29. Hoffman Interview.
30. Warfield Interview.
31. *Ibid.*; Hoffman Interview.
32. John W. R. Taylor, comp. and ed., *Jane's All the World's Aircraft, 1960-1961* (New York: McGraw-Hill, 1960), 299; Warfield Interview; Hoffman Interview.
33. Hoffman Interview.
34. Miller, *Nuclear Weapons and Aircraft Carriers*, 108-109.
35. John P. Flynn to Lucille Flynn, September 6 and 14, and October 28, 1959, postcards in the Flynn Papers; E. T. Miller, ed., *USS Essex-CVA 9 Cruise Book* (U.S. Navy, 1960), 24-91 (hereafter cited as *Essex Cruise Book*).
36. Quoted in a clipping from an unidentified military newspaper, n.d., in the Flynn Papers.
37. *Ibid.*
38. Flynn Flight Log; *Essex Cruise Book*, 82-83; *The Denver Post*, January 27, 1960.
39. John P. Flynn to Frances Flynn, November 14, 1959, letter in the possession of Frances Flynn; *Essex Cruise Book*, 258; Warfield Interview; Flynn Flight Log.
40. Warfield Interview.
41. Hoffman Interview; "None on the 22nd — All on the 23rd," a press release from an unidentified source (probably the USS *Essex*), January 23, 1960, in the Flynn Papers.
42. "None on the 22nd" press release; *Essex Cruise Book*, 174-175.
43. Command and Staff College, *Air University, Maxwell AFB, Comstaff 1961* (yearbook of the CSC), 5, 48, 56, 78-79, 100-102, 124-125, 138-139, 170.
44. John P. Flynn, untitled thesis paper for the Command and Staff College, 1961, in the Flynn Papers, 1-30.
45. Quoted in a newspaper clipping from an unidentified source, n.d., in the Flynn Papers; Neal A. Byrd to John P. Flynn, December 8, 1961, letter in the Flynn Papers.

46. Larry Willis, telephone interview the author, February 19, 2001.
47. J. F. Carey to Commanding General, Aircraft, Fleet Marine Force, Pacific, November 1961, copy of letter in the Flynn Papers.
48. Willis Interview.
49. George C. Herring, *America's Longest War: The United States and Vietnam, 1950-1975* (New York: Alfred A. Knopf, 1986), 75, 81, 85-87.
50. Robert H. Whitlow, *U.S. Marines in Vietnam: The Advisory and Combat Assistance Era, 1954-1964* (Washington, D.C.: History and Museums Division, Headquarters USMC, 1977), 60.
51. John P. Flynn to Frances Flynn, October 26, 1962, letter in the Flynn Papers.
52. Frank Petersen, telephone interview with the author, October 10, 2000.
53. Flynn to Flynn, October 26, 1962; Frank E. Petersen with J. Alfred Phelps, *Into the Tiger's Jaw: America's First Black Marine Aviator — The Autobiography of Lt. Gen. Frank E. Petersen* (Novato, CA: Presidio Press, 1998), 124-125.
54. Petersen, *Into the Tiger's Jaw*, 124-125; Petersen Interview; Flynn to Flynn, October 26 and October 31, 1962, letters in the Flynn Papers.
55. Petersen, *Into the Tiger's Jaw*, 125.
56. Flynn to Flynn, October 26, 1962.
57. Petersen Interview.
58. Richard Tregaskis, *Vietnam Diary* (New York: Holt, Rinehart and Winston, 1963), 18, 113; Flynn to Flynn, October 31, 1962; Whitlow, *U.S. Marines in Vietnam*, 75.
59. Whitlow, *U.S. Marines in Vietnam*, 75.
60. Sheehan, *A Bright Shining Lie*, 74.
61. Tregaskis, *Vietnam Diary*, 18, 26, 34, 71, 91-96; Sheehan, *A Bright Shining Lie*, 65; John Mecklin, *Mission in Torment: An Intimate Account of the U.S. Role in Vietnam* (New York: Doubleday & Company, 1965), 59; Reinhardt Leu, telephone interview with the author, October 7, 2000.
62. Leu Interview; Whitlow, *U.S. Marine Operations in Vietnam*, 113-115.
63. John P. Flynn to Frances Flynn, April 8, 1963, letter in the Flynn Papers; "Wing and Division Stage CPX," *Torii Teller* (base newspaper of MCAS Iwakuni), n.d., 5-6.
64. *Torii Teller*, August 23, 1963, 4.

Chapter 8 — Pages 155-179

1. Quoted in P. J. O'Rourke, *Parliament of Whores: A Lone Humorist Attempts to Explain the Entire U.S. Government* (New York: Atlantic Monthly Press, 1991), 47.
2. Flynn Flight Log; clipping from an unidentified newspaper, n.d., in the Flynn Papers.
3. *The Sacramento Bee*, May 13, 1965; Bertrand E. Clemens to John P. Flynn, November 18, 1964, letter in the Flynn Papers; Walnut Creek Lions Club to John P. Flynn, April 15, 1964, certificate of appreciation in the Flynn Papers; Robert Nunes to John P. Flynn, n.d., letter in the Flynn Papers.

4. *Oakland Tribune*, May 28, 1965.
5. *Oakland Tribune*, March 24, 1965.
6. *Ibid.*, March 23, 1965.
7. *Ibid.*, March 24, 1965.
8. *Ibid.*, March 23, 1965.
9. *Oakland Tribune*, March 23 and March 24, 1965.
10. Frances Flynn, telephone interview with the author, November 29, 2001.
11. *The Catholic Voice* (Alameda, CA), April 8, 1965.
12. Frances Flynn Interview.
13. *The Catholic Voice*, April 8, 1965; *Oakland Tribune*, May 23, 1965.
14. Quoted in a clipping from an unidentified newspaper in the Flynn Papers.
15. W. C. Lemke to R. L. Bryson, August 15, 1965, copy of letter in the Flynn Papers.
16. "Unit History, Marine Air Control Squadron-4," in MACS-4 File, Reference Branch, Marine Corps Historical Center, Washington, D.C.
17. Commanding General, 3rd Marine Air Wing to Lieutenant Colonel John P. Flynn, copy of memorandum in the Flynn Papers. The description of Flynn's MACS-4 duties is found in his post-retirement resume, probably written in 1966 or 1967, in the Flynn Papers.
18. *Los Angeles Times*, May 23, 1966.
19. Clipping from the *Sioux Falls Argus-Leader*, September 1966 (n.d.), in the Flynn Papers; *Winner Advocate*, November 24, 1966.
20. John McCain with Mark Salter, *Faith of My Fathers* (New York: Random House, 1999), 241.
21. John P. Flynn to Veterans Administration, Sioux Falls, SD, July 22, 1970, copy of letter in the Flynn Papers.
22. Flynn to George McGovern, April 5, 1967, copy of letter in the Flynn Papers.
23. *The New York Times*, April 26, 1967.
24. Congressional Record, 90th Cong., 1st sess., 1967, 113, pt. 63, 1-10, copy in "Vietnam File," Box 15, George S. McGovern Papers, Dakota Wesleyan University, Mitchell, SD.
25. John P. Flynn, "Under Our Flag," 1968 or 1969, in the Flynn Papers.
26. John P. Flynn, untitled essay, 1967 or 1968, in the Flynn Papers.
27. *Huron Daily Plainsman*, n.d., 1971, clipping in the Flynn Papers.
28. Dennis Flynn, telephone interview with the author, February 11, 2001. Frances Flynn also provided valuable information on the McGovern meeting, noting that her husband returned from Washington "thoroughly disgusted" at Senator McGovern and unforgiving about the "rough tone" in which he addressed him. Frances Flynn, telephone interview with the author, March 10, 2001.
29. *Huron Daily Plainsman*, February 1971 (n.d.).
30. In 1970 and 1971, Flynn shared his recollections of the May 1967 meeting with McGovern in both public forums and private correspondence. Flynn's description of the meeting can be found in the *Huron Daily Plainsman*, February 1971 (n.d.), and in a letter from John P. Flynn to "Tom," August 22, 1970, copy in the Flynn Papers. A letter from Duane Thorin to John P. Flynn, April 19, 1970, in the Flynn Papers, includes references to Flynn's meeting with McGovern.
31. John P. Flynn to "Tom," August 22, 1970.

32. George McGovern to Pat Flynn, May 17, 1967, letter in the Flynn Papers.
33. *Mitchell Daily Republic*, May 27, 1967. Dennis Flynn echoes his brother's sentiments, noting that Pat Flynn and McGovern "discussed Vietnam and politics" but did not discuss Indian affairs.
34. John P. Flynn to Robert W. Obermeier, March 11, 1970, copy of letter in the Flynn Papers.
35. John P. Flynn, "The Ship and the Principle," *Vermillion Plain Talk*, January 16, 1969; *Sioux City Journal*, December 26, 1968.
36. Spencer C. Tucker, ed., *Encyclopedia of the Vietnam War: A Political, Social, and Military History*, Vol. 1, 9-10; John S. Bowman, ed., *The Vietnam War Almanac* (New York: World Almanac Press, 1985), 451-452; John P. Flynn to "Tom," August 22, 1970, copy of letter in the Flynn Papers.
37. Flynn to "Tom," August 22, 1970.
38. Jan Blackstone to a "Mr. Johnson," October 26, 1970, letter in a collection of campaign materials from Flynn's 1970 Senate race, in the Flynn Papers.
39. Transcript of Flynn radio address, n.d., probably aired on KWYR Radio, Winner, SD, in October 1970, in the Flynn Papers.
40. *Huron Daily Plainsman*, February 7, 1971; South Dakota Legislative Assembly, 46th Session, 1971, Senate Bill No. 89, copy in the Flynn Papers; South Dakota Legislature, Proceedings of the Senate, 46th Legislative Session (1971), 182 (hereafter cited as *Senate Journal*).
41. *Huron Daily Plainsman*, February 7, 1971; *Rapid City Journal*, December 29, 1971; *Senate Journal* (1971), 577-579; South Dakota Legislature, Proceedings of the House of Representatives, 46th Legislative Session (1971), 631, 643.
42. *Mitchell Daily Republic*, March 1971 (n.d.).
43. *Rapid City Journal*, December 1, 1971.
44. State of South Dakota, Senate, Senate Joint Resolution No. 3, introduced by Mr. Flynn, 47th Legislative Assembly, 1972, copy in the Flynn Papers.
45. *Huron Daily Plainsman*, December 3, 1971.
46. Bill Capp to John P. Flynn, January 17, 1972, in the Flynn Papers. Capp's is one of many letters of support received by Flynn in the winter of 1971-1972, all in the Flynn Papers.
47. Charles V. Sederstrom to John P. Flynn, January 16, 1972, letter and Sederstrom's petition in the Flynn Papers.
48. Diary of Lucille Flynn, 1972, in the possession of Grace (Flynn) Scott, Brighton, CO.
49. Statement by John P. Flynn to the Senate State Affairs Committee, January 18, 1972, text in the Flynn Papers; Paul Cross, "Capitol Crossroads," *Rapid City Journal*, n.d., in the Flynn Papers.
50. Frances Flynn, telephone interview with the author, April 29, 2001.
51. Clipping from an unidentified newspaper, n.d., in the Flynn Papers.
52. *Senate Journal* (1972), 382.
53. Press release from the office of Senator Pat Flynn, 1972.
54. *Ibid.*; *Senate Journal* (1972), 480-481.
55. Flynn press release, 1972; *Rapid City Journal*, March 16, 1972.
56. *Senate Journal* (1972), 748-749.

57. Alan Rosenthal, *The Decline of Representative Democracy: Process, Participation, and Power in State Legislatures* (Washington, D.C.: Congressional Quarterly Press, 1998), 26.
58. John P. Flynn to the editor of the *Huron Daily Plainsman*, January 11, 1972.
59. Quoted in Richard Sobel, *The Impact of Public Opinion on U.S. Foreign Policy Since Vietnam* (New York: Oxford University Press, 2001), 90.
60. George S. McGovern, *An American Journey: The Presidential Campaign Speeches of George McGovern* (New York: Random House, 1974), 110-111.
61. Quoted in Stuart I. Rochester and Frederick Kiley, *Honor Bound: American Prisoners of War in Southeast Asia, 1961-1973* (Annapolis, MD: Naval Institute Press, 1999), 181.
62. *Ibid.*, 566.
63. Frances Flynn, telephone interview with the author, May 1, 2001.
64. Charles Donnelly, telephone interview with the author, May 7, 2001.
65. Frances Flynn interview, May 1, 2001.
66. *Sioux Falls Argus-Leader*, November 21, 1979; *Rapid City Journal*, November 20, 23, and 25, 1979.
67. *Ibid.*, November 24, 1979.
68. Quoted in the *Sioux Falls Argus-Leader*, January 11, 1989.
69. Quoted in *ibid.*
70. Quoted in *ibid.*, February 9, 1992.
71. Quoted in *ibid.*, November 4, 1992.

Chapter 9 — Pages 180-185

1. *The Bishop's Bulletin* (Diocese of Sioux Falls), January 1972. St. Peter's recently removed Flynn's stations and replaced them with a new set.
2. Jack Vernon to Frances Flynn, March 19, 1979, letter in the Flynn Papers.

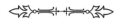

Bibliography

Manuscript Sources

Dakota Wesleyan University, Mitchell, SD
  George S. McGovern Papers
Frances Flynn, unpublished memoir, 2001 —
John P. "Pat" Flynn, Jr., Papers, in the possession of Sean J. Flynn, Dakota Wesleyan University, Mitchell, SD
Lucille Flynn, Diary, in the possession of Grace (Flynn) Scott, Brighton, CO
Marine Corps Historical Center, Archives Section, Washington, D.C.
  Historical Diary of Marine All-Weather Fighter Squadron 513 (CD-ROM version), October 1951-May 1952
Marine Corps Historical Center, Reference Section, Washington, D.C.
  MACS-4 File
  MTG-10 File
  VMA-225 File
  VMA-513 File
  VMF-111 File
  VMF-314 File
National Archives-Central Plains Branch, Kansas City, MO
  Haskell Institute Inventory, student file of John P. Flynn, Jr.
National Archives, College Park, MD
  Record Group 38, Office of the Chief of Naval Operations
  Record Group 127, USMC War Diaries
Naval Historical Center, Naval Aviation History Branch, Washington, D.C.
  VMF-312 File
Office of the Judge Advocate General, Department of the Navy, Washington, D.C.
  Transcript of the testimony of Captain John P. Flynn, Jr., in the Court of Inquiry concerning Colonel Frank H. Schwable, March 2, 1954

Author Interviews and Correspondence

Barnett, John. Former Marine Corps aviator. Telephone interview, February 18, 2001.
Donnelly, Charles. Former South Dakota state Senator. Telephone interview, May 7, 2001.
Duquette, Norman. Korea POW in Camp 2. E-mail correspondence, September 19, 2000.

Ettinger, Harry. Korea POW in Camp 2. Telephone interview, September 21, 2000.
Flinn, Norman. Marine Corps aviator with VMF(N)-513 in the Korean War. Telephone interview, October 7, 2000.
Flynn, Dennis. Brother of John P. "Pat" Flynn, Jr. Telephone interview, February 11, 2001.
Flynn, Frances E. Widow of John P. "Pat" Flynn, Jr. Interviews and correspondence, 2000-2001.
(Flynn) Scott, Grace. Sister of John P. "Pat" Flynn, Jr. Interview, Brighton, CO, November 16, 2000.
Funchess, William H. Korea POW in Camp 2. Telephone interview, September 22, 2000.
Hoffman, Richard. Marine Corps aviator with VMA-225 on USS *Essex*, 1959-1960. Telephone interview, October 7, 2000.
Huber, Vernon. Korea POW in Camp 2 Annex. Telephone interview, March 24, 2001.
Kutys, Joseph. Korea POW in Camp 2 Annex. Telephone interview, March 24, 2001.
Leu, Reinhardt. Marine Corps helicopter pilot and Commanding Officer of HMM-162 in South Vietnam, 1962-63. Telephone interview, October 7, 2000.
Martelli, Paul L. Former Marine Corps aviator and Korea POW. E-mail correspondence, January 4, 2001.
Perla, Peter. Member of Center for Naval Analysis. Telephone interview, November 19, 2000.
Petersen, Frank E. Former Marine Corps Lieutenant General and author of *Into the Tiger's Jaw*. Telephone interview, October 10, 2000.
Riker, Andrew. Korea POW in Camp 2 Annex. Telephone interview, September 21, 2000, and correspondence, November 13, 2000.
Sterrett, Harlo E. Korea POW in Camp 2 Annex. Correspondence, December 13, 2000.
Stoneman, Russell. Marine Corps aviator with VMF(N)-513 in the Korean War. Telephone interview, February 27, 2001.
Thorin, Duane. Korea POW in Camp 2 Annex and author of *A Ride to Panmunjom*. Interview, Chambers, NE, October 9, 2000.
Thrash, William G. Marine Corps aviator and Korea POW held temporarily in Camp 2 Annex. Telephone interview, September 22, 2000.
Warfield, Clifford. Former VMA-225 aviator and aviation record-setter. Telephone interview, October 8, 2000.
Willis, Larry. Former Marine Corps aviator. Telephone interview, February 19, 2001.

Newspapers

Boston Post, 1953, 1954
The Catholic Voice (Alameda, CA), 1965
The Daily Pilot (Newport and Costa Mesa, CA), n.d.
The Denver Post, 1960
The Flight Jacket (MCAS El Toro, CA), 1954-1955

Gosport (NAS Pensacola, FL), 1950-1951
Gregory (SD) *Times-Advocate*, 1953
Huron (SD) *Daily Plainsman*, 1954, 1960, 1971-1972
Los Angeles Times, 1966
Mitchell (SD) *Daily Republic*, 1954, 1967, 1971
Monterey Peninsula Herald, 1943
Navy Times, 1967
The New York Times, 1950-1954
Oakland (CA) *Tribune*, 1965
Orange (CA) *County Resister*, n.d.
Rapid City (SD) *Journal*, 1954, 1970-1974, 1979
The Sacramento (CA) *Bee*, 1965
Sioux City (SD) *Journal*, 1968
Sioux Falls (SD) *Argus-Leader*, 1966, 1970-1974, 1979, 1989, 1992
The Tidings (Catholic Diocese of Los Angeles), 1954
Torii Teller (MCAS Iwakuni, Japan), 1963
Vermillion (SD) *Plain Talk*, 1969
Washington Post, 1953-1954
Winner (SD) *Advocate*, 1952, 1966

Books

Astor, Gerald. *Operation Iceberg: The Invasion and Conquest of Okinawa in World War II*. New York: Dell, 1995.
Bagby, Wesley M. *America's International Relations Since World War I*. New York: Oxford University Press, 1999.
Bense, Judith A., ed. *Archaeology of Colonial Pensacola*. Gainesville: University Press of Florida, 1999.
Biderman, Albert D. *March to Calumny: The Story of American POWs in the Korean War*. New York: Macmillan, 1963.
Bowie, Robert R., and Richard H. Immerman. *Waging Peace: How Eisenhower Shaped an Enduring Cold War Strategy*. New York: Oxford University Press, 1998.
Bowman, John S., ed. *The Vietnam War Almanac*. New York: World Almanac Press, 1985.
Bruning, John R., Jr. *Crimson Sky: The Air Battle for Korea*. Dulles, VA: Brassey's, 2000.
Clowser, Don C. *Dakota Indian Treaties: The Dakota Indians from Nomad to Reservation*. Deadwood, SD: Don C. Clowser, 1974.
Condon, John P. *U.S. Marine Corps Aviation*. Vol. 5 of *Commemorative Collection Celebrating the 75th Year of Naval Aviation*. Washington, D.C.: Naval Air Systems Command, n.d.
Crane, Conrad C. *American Airpower Strategy in Korea, 1950-1953*. Lawrence: University Press of Kansas, 2000.

Doyle, Robert C. *Voices from Captivity: Interpreting the American POW Narrative.* Lawrence: University Press of Kansas, 1994.
Driving Hawk Sneve, Virginia, ed. *South Dakota Geographic Names.* Sioux Falls, SD: Brevet Press, 1973.
Farrar-Hockley, Anthony. *The Edge of the Sword.* London: Buchan & Enright, 1985.
Fehrenbach, T. R. *This Kind of War: The Classic Korean War History.* Dulles, VA: Brassey's, 2000.
Feifer, George. *Tennozan: The Battle of Okinawa and the Atomic Bomb.* New York: Ticknor and Fields, 1992.
Fleming, Charles A., Robin L. Austin, and Charles Braley III. *Quantico: Crossroads of the Marine Corps.* Washington, D.C.: History and Museums Division, Headquarters U.S. Marine Corps, 1978.
Frank, Benis, and Henry I. Shaw. *Victory and Occupation.* Vol. 5 of *History of U.S. Marine Corps Operations in World War II.* Washington, D.C.: Historical Branch, G-3 Division, Headquarters U.S. Marine Corps, 1968.
Freedman, Lawrence. *Kennedy's Wars: Berlin, Cuba, Laos, and Vietnam.* New York: Oxford University Press, 2000.
Funchess, William H. *Korea POW: A Thousand Days of Torment.* Clemson, SC: published privately, 1997.
Green, William, and Gordon Swanborough. *The Great Book of Fighters.* Osceola, WI: MBI Publishing, 2001.
Gregory-Dixon Historical Society, comp. and ed. *Yesterday and Today in the Gregory Area.* Gregory, SD: Plains Printing Company, 1990.
Guyton, Boone T. *Whistling Death: The Test Pilot's Story of the F4U Corsair.* New York: Orion Books, 1990.
Hastings, Max. *The Korean War.* New York: Simon and Schuster, 1987.
Heinl, Robert D., Jr., and John A. Crown. *The Marshalls: Increasing the Tempo.* Vol. 14 of *Operational History of the Marine Corps in World War II.* Washington, D.C.: Historical Branch, Headquarters U.S. Marine Corps, 1954.
Herring, George C. *America's Longest War: The United States and Vietnam, 1950-1975.* New York: Alfred A. Knopf, 1986.
Holmes, Tony. *Jane's Historic Military Aircraft.* London: HarperCollins, 1998.
Hyde, George E. *Spotted Tail's Folk: A History of the Brulé Sioux.* Norman: University of Oklahoma Press, 1961.
Hynes, Samuel. *Flights of Passage: Reflections of a World War II Aviator.* Annapolis, MD: Naval Institute Press, 1988.
Kaiser, David. *American Tragedy: Kennedy, Johnson, and the Origins of the Vietnam War.* Cambridge, MA: Belknap Press, 2000.
Kissinger, Henry. *Nuclear Weapons and Foreign Policy.* New York: Council on Foreign Relations, 1957.
Lech, Raymond. *Broken Soldiers.* Urbana: University of Illinois Press, 2000.
Li, Xiaobing, Allan R. Millett, and Bin Yu, eds. and trans. *Mao's Generals Remember Korea.* Lawrence: University Press of Kansas, 2001.
McCain, John, with Mark Salter. *Faith of My Fathers.* New York: Random House, 1999.
McGovern, George S. *An American Journey: The Presidential Campaign Speeches of George McGovern.* New York: Random House, 1974.

Mahurin, Walker M. *Honest John: The Autobiography of Walker M. Mahurin.* New York: G. P. Putnam's Sons, 1962.

Mecklin, John. *Mission in Torment: An Intimate Account of the U.S. Role in Vietnam.* New York: Doubleday & Company, 1965.

Meid, Pat, and James M. Yingling. *Operations in West Korea.* Vol. 5 of *U.S. Marine Operations in Korea, 1950-1953.* Washington, D.C.: Headquarters U.S. Marine Corps. 1972.

Miller, E. T., ed. *USS Essex-CVA-9 Cruise Book.* U.S. Navy, 1960.

Miller, Jerry. *Nuclear Weapons and Aircraft Carriers: How the Bomb Saved Naval Aviation.* Washington, D.C.: Smithsonian Institution Press, 2001.

Moskin, J. Robert. *The U.S. Marine Corps Story.* 3rd rev. ed. New York: Little, Brown, and Company, 1992.

Nadeau, Remi. *Fort Laramie and the Sioux Indians.* Englewood Cliffs, NJ: Prentice-Hall, 1967.

Nichols, Charles S., Jr., and Henry I. Shaw, Jr. *Okinawa: Victory in the Pacific.* Vol. 15 of *Operational History of the Marine Corps in World War II.* Washington, D.C.: Historical Branch, G-3 Division, Headquarters U.S. Marine Corps, 1955.

O'Rourke, G. G., with E. T. Woolridge. *Night Fighters Over Korea.* Annapolis, MD: Naval Institute Press, 1998.

Parson, Nels A., Jr. *Missiles and the Revolution in Warfare.* Cambridge, MA: Harvard University Press, 1962.

Petersen, Frank E., with J. Alfred Phelps. *Into the Tiger's Jaw: America's First Black Marine Aviator — The Autobiography of Lt. Gen. Frank E. Petersen.* Novato, CA: Presidio Press, 1998.

Portz, Matt. "Memories of World War II Training." Naval Aviation News Staff. *Naval Aviation Training.* Vol.1 of *Commemorative Collection Celebrating the 75th Year of Naval Aviation.* Washington, D.C.: Deputy Chief of Naval Operations and Commander, Naval Air Systems Command, n.d.

Rochester, Stuart I., and Frederick Kiley. *Honor Bound: American Prisoners of War in Southeast Asia, 1961-1973.* Annapolis, MD: Naval Institute Press, 1999.

Rosenthal, Alan. *The Decline of Representative Democracy: Process, Participation, and Power in State Legislatures.* Washington, D.C.: Congressional Quarterly Press, 1998.

Rostow, W. W. *The United States in the World Arena: An Essay in Recent History.* New York: Harper & Row, 1960.

Sambito, William J. *A History of Marine Fighter Attack Squadron 312.* Washington, D.C.: History and Museums Division, Headquarters U.S. Marine Corps, 1978.

Sandler, Stanley. *The Korean War: No Victors, No Vanquished.* Lexington: University of Kentucky Press, 1999.

Schell, Herbert S. *History of South Dakota.* 3rd rev. ed. Lincoln: University of Nebraska Press, 1975.

Sheehan, Neil. *A Bright Shining Lie: John Paul Vann and America in Vietnam.* New York: Vintage Books, 1988.

Sherrod, Robert. *History of Marine Corps Aviation in World War II.* Washington, D.C.: Combat Forces Press, 1952.

Singer, Arthur. *Arthur Godfrey: The Adventures of an American Broadcaster.* Jefferson, NC: McFarland & Company, 2000.
Sobel, Richard. *The Impact of Public Opinion on U.S. Foreign Policy Since Vietnam.* New York: Oxford University Press, 2001.
Spector, Ronald H. *Eagle Against the Sun: The American War with Japan.* New York: Free Press, 1985.
Standing Bear, Luther. *Land of the Spotted Eagle.* Lincoln: University of Nebraska Press, 1978.
Stout, Mira. *One Thousand Chestnut Trees: A Novel of Korea.* New York: Riverhead Books, 1998.
Stueck, William. *The Korean War: An International History.* Princeton, NJ: Princeton University Press, 1995.
Szasz, Margaret Connell. *Education and the American Indian: The Road to Self-Determination Since 1928.* 3rd rev. ed. Albuquerque: University of New Mexico Press, 1999.
Taylor, John W. R., comp. and ed., *Jane's All the World's Aircraft, 1960-61.* New York: McGraw-Hill, 1960.
Thorin, Duane, *A Ride to Panmunjom.* Chicago: Henry Regnery, 1956.
Tillman, Barrett. *Vought F4U Corsair.* Vol. 4 of *Warbird Tech Series.* North Branch, MN: Specialty Press, 1996.
Toland, John. *In Mortal Combat: Korea, 1950-1953.* New York: Quill, 1991.
Townsend, Kenneth William. *World War II and the American Indian.* Albuquerque: University of New Mexico Press, 2000.
Tregaskis, Richard. *Vietnam Diary.* New York: Holt, Rinehart and Winston, 1963.
Tucker, Spencer C., ed. *Encyclopedia of the Korean War: A Political, Social, and Military History.* 3 vols. Santa Barbara, CA: ABC-Clio, 2000.
_____, ed. *Encyclopedia of the Vietnam War: A Political, Social, and Military History.* 3 vols. Santa Barbara, CA: ABC-Clio, 1998.
U.S. Air Force. *Comstaff 1961.* Montgomery, AL: Air University, Maxwell Air Force Base, 1961.
U.S. Veterans Administration. *Study of Former Prisoners of War.* Washington, D.C.: U.S. GPO, 1980.
Veronico, Nicholas A., and Marga B. Fritze. *Blue Angels: 50 Years of Precision Flight.* Osceola, WI: MBI Publishing, 1996.
White, William Lindsey. *The Captives of Korea: An Unofficial White Paper on the Treatment of War Prisoners: Our Treatment of Theirs, Their Treatment of Ours.* New York: Scribners, 1957.
Whitlow, Robert H. *U.S. Marines in Vietnam: The Advisory and Combat Assistance Era, 1954-1964.* Washington, D.C.: History and Museums Division, Headquarters U.S. Marine Corps, 1977.
Weintraub, Stanley. *The Last Great Victory: The End of World War II, July-August 1945.* New York: Plume, 1996.
_____. *MacArthur's War: Korea and the Undoing of an American Hero.* New York: Free Press, 2000.
Winnefeld, James A., and Dana J. Johnson. *Joint Air Operations: Pursuit of Unity in Command and Control.* Annapolis, MD: Naval Institute Press, 1993.

Zhang, Shu Guang. *Mao's Military Romanticism: China and the Korean War, 1950-1953*. Lawrence: University Press of Kansas, 1995.

Electronic Documents

O'Sullivan, Kalani. "How it Was! Kunsan Airbase: VMF(N)-513: 'Flying Nightmares' (1951-1954)." Available from www.geocities.com/yooni_99/ howitwasa1a.html.

Theses

Kristy, Benjamin Houston. "The Flying Nightmares: An Operational History and Assessment of VMF(N)-513 at War in Korea, 1950-1953." M.A. thesis, Kansas State University, 1995.

MacDonald, James Angus, Jr. "The Problems of U.S. Marine Corps Prisoners of War In Korea." M.A. thesis, University of Maryland, 1961.

Moakley, G. S. "U.S. Army Code of Conduct Training: Let the POWs Tell Their Stories." M.A. thesis, U.S. Army Command and Staff College, Fort Leavenworth, KS, 1976.

Articles

Braitsch, Fred G. "Night Intruders." *The Leatherneck*, Vol. 34 (December 1951): 21-25.

Hanson, Charles E., Jr. "The Post-War Indian Gun Trade." *The Museum of the Fur Trade Quarterly*, Vol. 4 (Fall 1968): 1-10.

Higbee, Paul. "Homestake's Last Ounce." *South Dakota Magazine*, Vol. 16, No. 6 (March/April 2001): 34-35.

"Korea 1950: War." *Columban Mission* (monthly magazine published by Columban Fathers) (October 2000): 3-8.

Thompson, Warren. "Wait Until Dark." *Wings*, Vol. 19 (October 1989): 14-35.

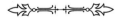

Index

by Lori L. Daniel

— A —

Acheson, Dean, 55
African, 129
African American, 99, 149
Air America (AA), 167-168
Alabama
  Montgomery, 146-147
    Maxwell Air Force Base, 146
      Air University, 146-147
        Command and Staff College (CSC), 146-147
          Wing III, Seminar 29, 146
Allies, 33-35, 45, 55
Almond, Edward (Major General), 56
America, 2, 17, 19, 27, 99, 129, 148, 166, 176
  Great Plains, 7, 10, 12-13, 182
American, xiv, 7, 16, 19, 21, 34, 37-38, 40, 43, 45, 47, 49, 53, 55-56, 63, 72, 78-81, 87-88, 93, 96, 98-100, 102, 104-109, 112, 115, 122, 126, 134, 136, 141, 146, 148, 151, 166-167, 176
  military, 165
  military history, 114
  plane, 27, 34-35, 79
Anderson, Robert B., 118-119
APS radar system
  see radar
"A Red Rose for Valor," 74-75, 79-80
Argentina, 137
Arizona
  Yuma
    Marine Corps Air Station (MCAS), 156
Armed Forces Week, 156
A Ride to Panmunjom, 103, 108
Asia, 55, 87, 121, 127, 129, 148, 150, 154, 156
  Southeast, 129, 148, 165, 167-168
Associated Press, 119, 178
  Wirephoto, 93
Atomic era, 49
Australia, 56, 96, 137, 177

— AIRCRAFT —

A-4 Skyhawk "Heinemann's Hot Rod," xiii, 137, 139, 146, 154, 161
A-4B Skyhawk, 155
A-26 Invader, 137
AD-5N Skyraider, 136-137
B-24 bomber, 34
B-25 Mitchell bomber, 67
B-26, 73
B-29 Superfortress, 40, 122
Beechcraft SNB-5 Expeditor, 118, 120, 132
C-47 Skytrain, 61
Curtiss Robin, 10
Douglas A4D-2 (A-4) Skyhawk, 136
Douglas F3D-2 Skyknight, 118, 130
F3D Skyknight, 131
F6F Hellcat, 154
F7F Tigercat, xv
F7F-3N Tigercat, 58, 67-68, 72-73, 75-76, 122
F9F-2 Panther, 130
F9F-5 Panther, 133
F-84E Thunderjet, 134
F-84F Thunderstreak, 134-136
F-86 Sabre, 134
FG-1 Corsair, 29, 32
Grumman F7F-3 Tigercat, 47
Grumman F9F-8B Cougar, 136
Grumman TBF Avenger, 27
H-34 Marine Reserve helicopter, 185
Link Trainer, 28
Lockheed TV-2 Sea Star trainer, 130
Mercury space capsule, 156
Mig-15 (Soviet), 134
Mitsubishi Jack (Japanese), 39
Mitsubishi Zero (Japanese), 39
N2S biplane, 26
Nakajima Frank (Japanese), 39
PB4Y-2 Dumbo seaplane, 35, 42-44
PB4Y-2 Privateer, 61, 64, 73-74
  "Fat Face," 61-62, 64, 74-75
  "Flytrain," 61
  "Lightning Bug X-Ray," 74
Piper Cub J-3, 23
PV-1 Vega Ventura, 120
SH-34 helicopter, 157
Skylab (SL-2), 144-145
SNJ Trainer, 28-29, 49
Spitfire (British), 29
UH-34D Choctaw helicopter, 150-151
Vought
  F4U Corsair "Whistling Death," xv, 29-30, 34-36, 40, 42, 44-45, 47-48, 136, 153-154, 184
  F4U-4 Corsair, 57
  F4U-5N Corsair, 57, 59-60, 64-65, 76-77, 118
Vultee Trainer, 28

— B —

Bare, Robert (Major General), 123
Barker, Jodie, xii
Barnett, John, 119
Batchelor, Claude J. (Corporal), 122
Battle of
  Bloody Ridge, 56
  Chongchon, 56
  Heartbreak Ridge, 56
  Imjin River, 88
  the Bulge, 72
  the Little Bighorn, 12
Bauman, G. F. (Executive Officer Major), 139, 142-145
Before the Battle, 162-163
Beirut, 140
Belgium, 56
  St. Vith, 72
Bell, Richard "Ding," 130, 132
Berry, E. Y. (Congressman), 120
Beswick, Byron H. "Buzz," 130, 132
Biderman, Albert D., 98
Biological warfare, 80-82, 88, 107, 114, 121, 126
"Black mission," 167-168
Bley, Roy H. (Major), 120-121, 123, 125
Boag, A. R. (Lieutenant Colonel), 139-140, 143-145
Bolivia, 147
Bolt, John F. (Major), 134
Boucher, Francis Cashmere Xavier, 12-13, 182
Bourgholtzer, Ray, 68
British, 51
  Commonwealth, 104
  Gloucestershire Battalion, 88
  plane, 27, 29
  Royal Air Force, 120
British Columbia, 183
Bruning, John R., 48
Burke
  Alfred (Senator), 170
  Patrick Joseph "Paddy" (Father), 66
Burnett, John R. (Lieutenant Colonel), 92

— C —

Cain, John T. (Master Sergeant), 89, 96, 119
California, xiii, 8, 53, 93, 117, 119, 127, 156, 164
  Alameda, 154, 157
    Falcons Model Builders Club, 156
    Naval Air Station (NAS), 154-156, 159-160, 185
    St. Joseph High School, 159
    Western Associated Modelers, 156
  Baja California, 108
  Berkeley, 168

California *(continued)*
  Bridgeport, 156, 159
  Camp Pendleton, 32, 161, 163
    Aviation Combat Conditioning Program, 32
  China Lake, 139
    Naval Ordnance Test Station, 139
  Dana Point, xiii
  Del Monte, 25-27
    Navy Pre-Flight School, 25-26
      4th Battalion, 25
        Company G, Platoon 1, 25
  El Toro, xiii, 57, 117-118, 130, 133, 139, 147, 162
    Marine Corps Air Station, xiii, 57, 130-131
      Marine Corps Survival School, 130
      Marine Training Group (MTG)-10, 117, 130
  Hamilton AFB, 159
  Livermore, 26-27
    Naval Air Station (NAS), 26
      Ground School, 27
        Aircraft Recognition, 27
      Primary Flight School, 26
  Miramar Air Station, 48
  Mojave Desert, 130, 133
  Orange, 91, 112, 115, 167
    Chapman College, 167
  Pickel Meadows, 156-157
    Marine Corps Cold Weather Training Center (CWTC), 156, 159
  Sacramento Valley, 155
    Lions Club, 156
    Navy League, 156
    Rotary Club, 156
  San Diego, 32, 47, 147
    Naval Air Station (NAS) North Island, 147
  San Francisco, 115, 164
    Bay Area, 155-156, 161
    Golden Gate Bridge, 115
  Sonora Pass, 157
  Stead AFB, 159
  Stockton, 157, 159
Cambodia, 148
Canada, 56, 177, 183
  Quebec, 12
Canadian, 12, 133, 182
  French, 12, 182
Capitalism, 97
Capone, Al, 5
Caroline Islands, 32-34
  Langar Island, 33
  Ponape Island, 34-35
Catholic, 3, 5, 69, 103, 124, 156, 172, 180

Catholic *(continued)*
  Irish, 11
  Roman, xiv, 89, 103, 119
  Catholicism, 83
Cato, Mr., 19-20
"Centurion," 143, 144-146
China, 80-81, 126, 168
  Fushun, 81
  Nationalist, 55
  Peking, 81
  People's Republic of (PRC), 56, 79, 80-81, 98
China Monthly Review, 97
China Sea
  East, 42-43
Chinese, xiv-xv, 11, 56-57, 61-63, 71, 75-83, 86-89, 93, 96-100, 102, 104-110, 112-113, 115, 120-127, 136
  air force, 80
  army, 56
  communist, 79
  interrogator, 86
    Laughing Boy, 86, 88-89
    Little Boy, 86-87
    Quasimodo, 86
Chinese Civil War, 104
Chinese People's Volunteer Forces (CPVF), 56, 59, 64-65, 80-81
  9th Army Group, 56
Christian, 44, 124
Churchill, Winston, 98
CIA, 167
Clark, Ramsey, 177
Code of Conduct for Members of the Armed Forces of the United States, xiv, 99, 130, 136, 147, 154, 162-163, 167
  Lectures, 147-148
Cold War, 146, 154
Cole, J. Frank (Major), 37
Colombia, 147
Columbia University, 72
Communism, 83, 97, 99, 117, 127, 165
  Asian, 164
Communist, xiv, 55, 59-60, 63-64, 72, 74, 78, 80-82, 86, 98-99, 103, 106, 109-110, 112, 114, 117, 121-123, 125-129, 136, 148, 151, 153, 155-156, 162, 167
  American, 113
  torture, 88
    menticide, 88
Compound 1080, 169-170
Connolly, R. P. (First Lieutenant), 144-145
Cooper, Thomas (Rear Admiral), 123
Courier from Spotted Tail, 182
Cousteau, Jacques-Yves, 51

Crimson Sky: The Air Battle for Korea, 48
Crook, George (General), 12
Cuban, 138
Czechoslovakian, 5

— D —
Daily Worker, 97
Dakota Territory, 183
  Whetstone Indian Agency, 12
Dakota Wesleyan University (SD), xii
Dalton, H. G. (Colonel), 162
Davis
  Jay (Captain), 161
  Robert R. (Lieutenant Colonel), 60
Day
  George, 177
  Richard M. (Major), 37
D-Day, 40
Dean, William (Major General), 123
Democrat Party, 164, 166-169, 175, 177
Dickenson, Edward S. (Corporal), 122
Dillberg, Bud, 68
Donnelly, Charles, 169, 174, 177
Douglas Aircraft Corp., 136
Doyle, Robert C., 91
Drought, 8, 10
Dulles, John Foster, 98, 128-129
Dust storm, 8
  "black blizzard," 10
Dutch, 126
Dvořák, Antonin, 19

— E —
Eisenhower, Dwight D. (President), 98, 118, 128, 136, 141
Engine
  Pratt & Whitney XR-2800 Double Wasp, 29, 67
England, 72, 120, 177
  Stanmore, 120
English, 12, 82, 86-87, 97, 100, 167
Enlai, Zhou (Premier), 81
Enoch, Kenneth (Lieutenant), 81-82
Enos, J. (Captain), 144-145
Ermatinger, Paul J. (Captain), 141
Euro-American, 12
Europe, 16, 23, 141
  Eastern, 55
  Western, 55, 129
European, 7, 140-141, 150
  Theater, 72
Ezell, Dee E. (Major), 123

— F —
Far East, 129

Far East *(continued)*
  Air Force, 133
Farrar-Hockley, Anthony, 88
Fehrenbach, T. R., 128
Feightner, E. L. (Commander), 143
Fink, Jerry, xiii-xiv
Flight
  flat-hatting, 27
  in-flight blackout, 26
  instrument flying, 28
  rat race, 28
Flinn, Norman (Captain), 60, 67, 76-77
Florida, 49
  Caucus Shoal, 51
  Gulf Beach, 51
  Jacksonville, 29, 33, 146
    Mayport Naval Air Station (NAS), 146
    Naval Air Station, 29-30, 33
    Marine Barracks, 29
  Key West, 68
  McGree Jetties, 51
  Pensacola, 51, 53
    Pensacola Naval Air Station, 48-49, 52-54, 76
    Corry Field, 49
    Naval Air Training Command (NATC), 48
    Pensacola Goslings, 49
    Pensacola Officers Club, 49
    Pensacola Enlisted Men's Club, 49
  Pensacola Bay, 51
  Pensacola Beach, 51
  Pickens Jetty, 51
  Pickens Docks, 51
  Santa Rosa Island, 51
Flynn, 7
  Colleen, xii, 116, 159
  Deborah, xi
  Dennis, 5-6, 164-166
  Erminnie Grace "Minnie" (Ingalls), 2-4
  Frances, xi, 15, 17, 48-49, 51-52, 91-93, 112, 115-117, 159, 164, 174, 177, 183-185
    see also Gassen, Frances
  Grace (Scott), 5, 8, 11, 183
  James, 2-3
  James "Jim," 5
  John Patrick, Sr., 2-6, 8, 10
  John P. "Pat," Jr. (Lieutenant Colonel), xiii-xv, 2-11, 13-27, 29-30, 32-36, 38, 41-42, 44, 47, 50-54, 57 58, 60-62, 64-71, 74-76, 78-84, 86-91, 93-94, 99-117, 121, 123, 125-126, 129, 131, 134-148, 150, 152, 154-155, 157, 159-161, 163-164, 166-169, 171-184

Flynn *(continued)*
  John P. "Pat," Jr. *(continued)*
    All-Navy football, xiv, 49
    "Chief," xv, 67, 92, 100-101, 119, 141, 149-150, 185
    crop duster, 164, 169
    "Killer," 25
    "Long Elk," 11, 183
    music, 7, 13, 16-20
    spear gun, 83
    thresher operator, 21
  Lucille, 2-8, 10, 15, 180
    see also Gordon, Lucille
  Mark, xii, 48-49, 93, 116, 159, 164, 183
  Michael, 183
  Pets
    Coyote (pet coyote), 6, 9
    Mutt (dog), 6
    Popeye (snake), 6, 184
    Punky, 116
  Rose Marie, 5, 13, 16, 173
  Sean J., xv, 140
  Teresa, xii, 136
  Timothy "Tim," xii, 147
Flynn, Tom, 156-157, 160
Fonda, Jane, 177
Foreign Affairs, 129
Fort Laramie Treaty, 12
Foss, Joe (Captain), 25-26
Foster, William Z., 97
Fountain, M. T. (First Lieutenant), 144-145
France, 56
  Cannes, 140
  Paris, 141
Frank, Norva H. (Master Sergeant), 72-73
French, 12, 150
  Revolution, 101
Fulbright, William, 177
Funchess, William H. (First Lieutenant), 86, 96-97, 99

— G —
Gambling industry, 170-179
Gassen
  Dad, 15
  Frances, 13, 15-16, 30, 32, 47
    see also Flynn, Frances
  Mom, 15
Geneva Convention, 86, 97
George, Prince, 183
Germ warfare, xiv, 80, 82, 109, 113, 115
German, 5, 72
  plane, 27
German-Russian, 5
Germany
  Berlin, 141
Glenn, John (Major), 134
Godfrey, Arthur, 49, 52
Gone With The Wind, 16

Goodyear Aircraft Company, 29
Gordon
  Joseph "Joe," 2-4, 7-8, 10-11, 13, 74, 77
  Lucille, 3
    see also Flynn, Lucille
  Rosalie Boucher, 2-4, 10, 12-13
Gosport (FL), 53-54
Grasshopper infestation, 8, 10
Great Britain, 56, 96
Great Depression, 7-8, 10
Greece, 56, 147
  Athens, 140
    Acropolis, 140
    Parthenon, 141
  Thessaloniki, 140
Greek, 141
Gregory Times-Advocate (SD), 7, 117
Ground Controlled Approach (GCA), 65
Guatemala, 146
Gulf of Mexico, 51, 65

— H —
Halmgremson, "Slim," 4, 10
Hanes, John Vernon "J.V." (Lieutenant), 51, 142, 144-145
Harcher, Roger (Crew Chief Lance Corporal), 157, 159-161
Harmon, Millard F. (Lieutenant General), 34
Harris, Walter R. (Major), 102, 105-106, 118-119
Haskell Indian Nations University "Haskell Institute" (KS), xi, 16-17, 20-22, 167
Haskell Band, 19-20
Haskell Institute Orchestra, 18-19
Haskell Radio Club, 19
Keokuk Hall, 17
Registrar, 20
Hastings, Max, 82
Hawaii, 147
  Pearl Harbor, 19, 47, 120
Headed for Eden (play), 20
Heidepriem, Scott, 178
Heinemann, Ed, 137
Herring, George C., 148
Heylinger, Howard H. (First Lieutenant), 42-44
"High Flight," 184
Hill, Harry W. (Vice Admiral), 38
History of Marine Corps Aviation in World War II, 34
Hmong, 167
Ho Chi Minh Trail, 151, 165, 167-168
Hodges, Joyce (Representative), 178-179

Hoffman, Richard L. "Dick" (First Lieutenant), 139-140, 143-145
Holland, J. E. (Captain), 144-145
Holmes, Oliver Wendell, 22
Holt, H. N. (Colonel), 147
Hubbard, Kin, 155
Hungarian revolt, 141
Huron Daily Plainsman (SD), 172, 176
Hynes, Samuel, 25, 37-38, 40, 46

— I —

Illinois
 Chanute, 136
  Chanute Air Force Base, 136
   Officer Staff Commanders Course, 136
 Chicago, 2-5, 21
  Mt. Greenwood, 2
 Elgin, 2
Indian, xv, 10-12, 16, 20, 23, 89, 99, 102, 166, 168, 182
 American, 141
 Brulé Sioux, 12
 Chief Spotted Tail, xv, 11-13, 182
 Crazy Horse, xv, 11-13, 182
 Lakota, xv, 1-3, 11-13, 141, 168, 175, 180
 Lakota Sioux, 1, 103
 Luther Standing Bear, 1
 Métis, 12, 182
 Native American, xv, 11, 15, 20, 88, 99, 141, 166, 169
 Plains Indian, xv, 12, 183
 Rosebud Sioux Tribe, 16
 Sioux, xv, 2, 11-12, 23, 182
 Sitting Bull, 12
Indian Affairs, 166
Indian Reservation, 183
 Red Cloud Agency, 12
 Rosebud Sioux Indian Reservation (SD), 2, 17, 168
 Spotted Tail Agency, 12
 Whetstone Indian Agency (Dakota Territory), 12
Indonesia, 137, 148
Into the Tiger's Jaw, 149
Iowa
 Allison, 2
Ireland
 County Kerry, 2
  Tralee, 2
Irish, 5, 11, 21
Israel, 137
Italian plane, 27
Italy, 28
 Florence, 140
 Genoa, 140
 Naples, 140

Italy *(continued)*
 Rome, 140
  Coliseum, 141
  St. Peter's, 140
 Venice, 140
Iwo Jima, 32

— J —

Jane's All the World's Aircraft, 140
Janklow, William (Governor), 178
Japan, xv, 35, 40, 44-47, 66-67, 147
 Hiroshima, 45
 Imperial, 153
 Iwakuni, 149-150, 153
  Iwakuni Officers Club, 149, 153
  Marine Corps Air Station (MCAS), 148
  T. Harry's, 149
 Nagasaki, 45
 Tokyo, 44, 175
  Camp Omori, 44
Japanese, 10, 19, 26, 29, 32-35, 37-40, 42-45, 47, 78, 120, 153
 antiaircraft (AA), 34
 plane, 27
  Japanese Kate, 120
  kamikaze fighter, 37-39, 42
  "Floating Chrysanthemums," 37
 sepaku, 40
 sword, 39
Japanese island
 Honshu, 40
 Ishigaki, 40, 42
 Kikai Shima, 40, 42
 Kyushu Island, 33, 35, 40, 42-43, 45, 153
 Kawashi, 45
 Kushira Airfield, 45
 Mage Island, 43
 Mayako, 40
 Shikoku, 40
 Takana Shima, 44
 Tanega Shima, 43-44
Jerome, Clayton C. (Brigadier General), 120
Jerusalem, 140
Jewish, 72
Johnson
 Dana J., 133
 Lyndon (President), 164-166
Joint Air Command, 62
JP-5 jet fuel, 139-140

— K —

Kansas, 19
 Edwardsville, 23
 Fort Riley, 19
 Lawrence, xi, 16, 19, 21
 Topeka, 19

Kansas City Junior College (MO), 22
 Naval Aviation Cadet Training (NACT) Program, 22, 24, 57
Kansas City Times (MO), 119
Kansas University (KS), 19
Kennedy, John F. (President), 128-129, 148
Kerwin, Joseph P. (Lieutenant), 144-145
Kissinger, Henry (Dr.), 129, 176
Kittler, S. J. (Captain), 145
Kneip, Richard F. (Governor), 172-173
Korea, xiv, 39, 53, 55-57, 59-61, 66-68, 71, 81-82, 87-88, 98, 110, 112, 118, 120-121, 130, 132-134, 164-165
 Changsong, 106, 108
 Chosin (Changjin) Reservoir, 56
 Chunchon, 66
  St. Columban Mission Cathedral, 66
 Haeju, 76
 Hungnam, 56
 Inchon, 55, 57, 112, 115
 Kaedong, 60
 Kaesong, 109-110
 Kangnung, 64
  K-18 Airfield, 64, 68
 Kimpo, 57
 Koje-do Island, 110
 Koksan, 60, 62
 Korea Bay, 106
 Kunsan, 65, 72
  K-8 Airbase, 65, 68-69, 72
  K-13 Airbase, 68
  K-16 Air base, 68
 Manpojin, 109
 North (Democratic People's Republic of Korea [DPRK]), xiv, 47, 53, 55-57, 61, 64, 72-73, 78, 81, 88-89, 91, 93, 103-104, 106, 115, 121-122
 Obane Valley (No Name Valley), 93, 96
 Obul, 89, 96, 103
 Panmunjom, 81, 109-110
  Freedom Village, 109, 111-112
 Pike's Peak Interrogation Center, 80, 82, 84, 86-87, 89, 103, 108, 121, 123-124
 P'ohang, 120
 POW Camp 2, 86, 96-97
  Camp 2 Annex, 93-97, 99, 101-102, 104-108, 115, 118, 123
 POW Camp 3, 84-85, 106
 Pusan, 55, 57
  K-1 Airfield, 57

Korea *(continued)*
  Pusan Perimeter, 55
  Pyong Taek, 72, 120
    K-6 Airbase, 72-73, 76-77
  Pyoktong, 89
  P'Yongsan, 76
  Pyongyang, 55, 80
    Pyongyang radio, 53, 81
    Red 18, 72
    Red 19, 72
    Red 20, 72
  Sariwon, 60, 72-74, 76
  Seoul, 55-57, 60, 62, 72
  Sepori, 64
  Sinauyangri, 64
  Singosan, 60, 62, 64-65
  Sinmak, 60, 72-77, 79
  Sohung, 60
  South (Republic of Korea [ROK]), 53, 55-58, 66, 73, 82, 110, 112, 147
Korean, 55, 57, 60, 63, 66, 69, 77, 79-81, 89, 92, 96, 101, 106, 167
Korean War, xiv, 11, 82, 86, 103, 106, 132-133, 147
Kutys, Joseph (Captain), 102
Kuwait, 137

— L —
Land of the Spotted Eagle, 1
Laos, 147-148, 151-152, 167-168
La Rosa, Julius, 49
Latin America, 129
Lawrence, R. T. (First Lieutenant), 144-145
L-Day, 35
Lebanon intervention (1958), 141
Legionnaire, 127
Lehi, Judy, xii
Lemke, W. C. (Colonel), 161
Leu, Reinhardt (Lieutenant Colonel), 151, 153
Lie, Trygve (Secretary General), 55
Linscott, Henry (Major General), 122
Little, Alan M. G. (Dr.), 126
Logan, F. M. (First Lieutenant), 144-145
Lopez, Antonio (Sergeant), 156
Los Angeles Times (CA), 93, 103
Love, Peter, 104-105

— M —
MacArthur, Douglas (General), 55-56
MacDonald, James Angus, 82, 86
"Mae West" inflatable life jacket, 42
Magee, Jr., John Gillespie, 184

Maginn, James (Father), 66
Maher, L. J. "Bud," 172
Mahurin, Walker (Colonel), 87
Malaysia, 137
Manchuria, 55, 89, 106
Mansfield, Mike, 177
Maoism, 129, 176
March to Calumny: The Story of American POWs in the Korean War, 98
Mariana Islands, 40
Marshall Islands, 32-35
  Eniwetok Atoll, 33
    Eniwetok Island, 33-35, 45
  Ensetto Island, 33, 35
  Garu Island, 33, 35
  Joluit Atoll, 34
  Kwajalein Atoll, 33
    Roi Island, 33-34
  Kwajalein Island, 33-34
  Majuro Island, 35
  Maloelap Atoll, 34
  Mille Atoll, 34-35
  Namur, 33-34
  Wotje Atoll, 34
Marxism, 98
Marxist-Leninist, 82, 98
Massachusetts
  Boston, 2, 72, 118
Massachusetts Institute of Technology (MIT), 72-73, 115
  Division of Defense Laboratories, 73
  ROTC program, 72
McAvoy, John Francis (Master Sergeant), 68-69
McCain, John (Senator), 83, 162
McCarthy, Joseph (Senator), 113
McGee, Vernon (Lieutenant General), 111-112
McGovern, George S. (Senator), 164-167, 175-177
McKay Family, 13
McLaughlin, John N. (Lieutenant Colonel), 119
McMaster, William H. (Governor), 13
Medal
  Air Medal, 42, 120
  Bronze Star, 72
  Distinguished Flying Cross, 42, 64, 120
  Gold Star, 64
  Legion of Merit, 119
  Legion of Merit with a Gold Star, 120
  Letter of Commendation, 119
  Medal of Honor, 123
  Miraculous Medal, 79
  Purple Heart, 44
  U.S. Navy and Marine Corps Medal, 118
Mediterranean Sea, 129, 138, 140-141, 146

Meerlo, Joost K. M. (Dr.), 88, 126
Meierhenry, Mark (Attorney General), 178
MIA (missing in action), 92
Mickelson, George (Governor), 178
Midway Island, 47
Miller, Jerry (Commander), 138, 140
Mills, Billy, 175
Minnesota
  St. Paul, 7
Missouri
  Kansas City, 21, 24-25
Mitchell Daily Republic (SD), 166
Montana, 12
  Crow Fair Powwow, 183
Monterey Peninsula Herald (CA), 25-26
Morris, Philip (Lieutenant), 156
Murphy, Kenneth E. (Lieutenant Colonel), 123-125
Music, 5-7, 19-20
  "America the Beautiful," 184
  "Blue Berry Hill," 17
  "Carnival of Venice," 7, 19
  "Flight of the Bumble Bee," 17
  "From the New World," 19-20
  "God Bless America," 115
  "Humoreske," 20
  "September Song," 153
  "Taps," 17
  "The Impossible Dream," 184
  "The Marine Corps Hymn," 184
  "When the Saints Go Marching In," 153
Mydland, Gordon J. (Attorney General), 174

— **Military Regiments** —
1st Marine Air Wing (MAW), 57, 61, 87, 120-121, 134, 153
1st Marine Division, 55-56, 133, 161
1st Regiment, 55
5th Regiment, 55
3rd Marine Air Wing (MAW), 133, 162
3rd Marine Division, 153
7th Infantry Division, 56
9th Armored Division, 72
12th Naval District Band, 156
12th Strategic Fighter Wing, 133-135
24th Infantry Division, 123
140th Tank Battalion, 72
559th Strategic Fighter Squadron, 134
561st Strategic Fighter Squadron, 134-136

— **Military Regiments** —
(continued)
III Marine Expeditionary Force (MEF), 153
X Corps, 56
Carrier Air Group 10, 143
Eighth Army, 55-56
Essex Task Force, 141
Far East Air Force (FEAF), 57, 59, 73
Fifth Air Force, 59, 134
HMM-162, 150-151
Marine Air Control Squadron-4 (MACS-4), 161-162
Marine Air Group (MAG)
  MAG-12, 73, 77, 120
    Intelligence, 62
    Operations, 62
  MAG-16, 148
  MAG-33, 45-46
Marine Air Reserve Squadron-133, 155
Marine Air Reserve Training Detachment (MARTD), 155-156, 161
Task Force 58, 38
U.S. Sixth Fleet, 138, 140-141
VF-653, 57
VMA-312, 35
VMA-225, 136-141, 143-146
VMF-111 "The Devil Dogs Squadron," 32, 34-35
VMF-235, 57
VMF-312 "Checker Board Squadron," 36-37, 40, 42, 44-46
  Members of, 36
VMF-314, 133
VMF(N)-513 "The Flying Nightmares," 57-62, 64-67, 72-73, 76-77, 82, 87, 92, 107, 122, 125
  "Flytrain 05," 74
  Mission 1206 "Flytrain 06," 72, 76
VMF(N)-531, 120
VMF(N)-542, 130, 133

— **N** —
NASA, 138, 144-145
NATO, 55, 141, 146
Nazi SS, 126
Nebraska, 2-3, 5, 7, 101
  Fort Robinson, 12
  Keya Paha, 4
  Millboro, 4
  Omaha, 184
  Nelson, T. W. (Captain), 144-145
Netherlands, 56
Nevada, 171, 173
  Las Vegas, 174
  Naval Air Station (NAS) Fallon, 155

Nevada *(continued)*
  Naval Air Station (NAS) *(cont.)*
    Navy Bombing Target Areas, 155
Nevada Nuclear Test Site, 133
New France, 182
New Mexico
  Albuquerque, 147
    Defense Atomic Support Agency, 147
New York
  New York City, 55, 121
    Wall Street, 87, 98
New Zealand, 56, 137
Nicaraguan, 123
Night close air support (NCAS), 59
Night combat air patrol (NCAP), 57, 60, 62, 65
Nimitz, Chester W. (Admiral), 34
Nixon, Richard (President), 176
"No-gap" policy, 64
Normandy, 40, 72
North Africa, 23
North Carolina
  Cherry Point, 30, 48, 50-51, 136, 138-140, 146
    Marine Corps Air Station (MCAS), 30, 50-51, 130, 136
  Edenton, 136
    Marine Corps Air Station (MCAS), 136
      Headquarters & Maintenance Squadron-14, 136
  Greensboro, 32
  Parris Island, 32
North Korean People's Army (NKPA), 53, 55, 66, 80
Nunes, Robert "Bob" (Brother), 159

— **O** —
Oakland Tribune (CA), 99, 156-157, 160
Okinawa, xiv, 35-42, 44-46, 48, 67, 122, 147, 153-154, 165
  Awase Airfield, 45-46
  Dakeshi Ridge, 37
  Gunto, 40
  Kadena Airfield, 35, 37
  Kakazu Ridge, 37
  Kunishi Ridge, 37
  Sugar Loaf Hill, 37
  Wana Ridge, 37
Olympic Games (1964), 175
Omaha World Herald (NE), 119
Ondol (floor-heating system), 96, 103
Operation
  Big Switch, 109, 114
  ICEBERG, 35

Operation *(continued)*
  OLYMPIC, 40
  SHUFLY, 148, 150
  TEAM MATE, 153-154
  TEAPOT, 133
  Nuclear Weapons Test, 133
Ortmeier, R. J. (Father), 181-182

— **P** —
Pacific Ocean, xv, 23, 32, 34-35, 40, 45, 47, 55, 57, 110, 120, 130
  Theater, 25-26, 30, 37
  War, 30
Pacific Training Exercise (PACTRAEX), 133
Pathet Lao, 167
People's China, 81
Perla, Peter, xii
Petersen, Frank, 149-150
Phelan, Father, 32
Philippines, 47, 56, 147-148
Phillips, L. W. (Captain), 74
Pike, B. P. (First Lieutenant), 144-145
Plamondon, R. A. (Captain), 144-145
Polish, 5
  revolt, 141
Populist, 177
Porter, H. H., 73
Portz, Matt, 26
POW, 35, 82-83, 86-87, 89-90, 93, 96-101, 103-107, 109-110, 112, 114-115, 118, 123, 125-127, 130, 132-133, 136, 147, 155-156, 162, 167, 176, 182
  Allied, 43
  American, 114, 122, 177
  British, 88
  camp, 57, 80, 84-86
  germ-warfare confession, 123
  Korea, xiii-xiv, 118
  Marine Corps, 86, 99, 114
  "Progressive," 98, 119
  Senior Officer Present (SOP), 102, 105, 109, 118
  U.N. Command (UNC), 93, 96
    1st Platoon, C Company, 96
Pratt, John H., 123
Preacher, D. J. (Brigadier General), 156
Prohibition, 172
Pullman car, 27

— **Q** —
Quinn, John (Lieutenant), 81-82
Quonset hut, 46, 66

— **R** —
R&R (rest and recuperation), 66-67
Racism, 150

Radar
　APS radar system, 59
　APS-6, 59
　APS-19, 59
　British Mark IV aircraft intercept radar system, 120
　F7F-3(N) radar system, 125
　MPQ-14 ground-controlled radar bombing system, 59, 65
　SCR-720 radar, 67
Radio show
　"Fibber McGee and Molly," 53
　"One Man's Family," 53
　"The Green Hornet," 53
　"The Lone Ranger," 53
　"The Shadow," 53
Rapid City Journal (SD), 172
Red Cross, 37, 115
Reese, Clifford E. (Captain), 157, 159
Republican Party, 167-168, 170, 175, 177
Rickenbacker, Eddie, 26
Ridgway, Robin, xii
Riker, Andrew (Lieutenant), 98-102, 123
River
　Missouri, 12, 164
　Powder, 12
　Yalu, 55-57, 89, 93, 97, 100, 104-106
Roland, H. E., 62-63
Rongzhen, Nie (General), 64
Rosenthal, Alan, 175
Rowe, James "Nick," 177
Russian, 126
Ryukyu Islands, 35, 40, 44

— S —

Saudi Arabia, 146
Schilt, Christian (Major General), 122-123
Schwable, Frank H. (Colonel), 107, 113-114, 120-123, 125-126
Sea of Japan, 106
Sederstrom, Charles V., 173
Sells, J. D. (First Lieutenant), 144-145
Shaknov, Irving "Spike" (Dr.), 72-76, 115, 118
Shanghai News, 97
Shepherd, Lemuel C. (Commandant General), 113-114
Sherman, Paul D. (Colonel), 123, 125
Sherrod, Robert, 34-35
Ship
　Radar picket, 38, 42
　USS *Altamaha*, 47
　USS *Bollinger*, 32
　USS *Bon Homme Richard*, 138

Ship *(continued)*
　USS *Constellation*, 138
　USS *Essex*, 140-145
　　Carrier Air Traffic Control Center, 143
　USS *Forrestal*, 140
　USS *General Howze*, 115
　USS *Intrepid*, 140
　USS *Kitty Hawk*, 140
　USS *Missouri*, 46
　USS *Pueblo*, 167
　USS *Wright*, 49
Sierra Nevada Mountains, xv, 154, 156, 158-159, 161, 185
　Disaster Peak, 157-160
Singapore, 137
Sioux Falls Argus-Leader (SD), 179
Sixth Annual Topeka State Journal Golden Gloves State Championship, 19
Smith, Samuel S. (First Lieutenant), 44
Soper, Don (Mayor), 117
South Africa, 56
South Carolina
　Beaufort, 140
　　Marine Corps Air Station (MCAS), 140
South Dakota, xiv-xv, 1-3, 5-8, 10, 13, 21, 23, 25, 32, 39, 57, 74, 117, 120, 139, 154, 164-166, 169-173, 177-180, 185
　Black Hills, 10
　Bonesteel, 3
　Colome, 4, 13, 15, 117, 168
　　Colome High School, 13
　　Colome Cowboy Football, 13
　Dallas, 5
　Deadwood, 7, 10, 173
　　St. Ambrose Catholic School, 7
　Dog Ear, 5-6, 8, 15
　Dog Ear Buttes (Dog Ears Buttes), 1-2
　　Grandfather, 2
　　Grandmother, 2
　Dog Ear Lake, 1-7, 9-10, 19, 21, 30, 175, 184
　　Big Bowery Dance, 4
　　Dog Ear Pavilion, 4
　　Flynns' Community Picnic, 3, 8
　　Old Time Dance, 4
　　Trading Post and Entertainment Center, 4
　Gregory, 2-3, 5, 7, 13, 15, 117, 154, 164, 166, 173-174, 180, 182, 184
　　Flynn Brothers Farm, 3
　　Gregory High School, 13-15, 117
　　Gregory Gorillas Football, 13, 15

South Dakota *(continued)*
　Gregory *(continued)*
　　Gregory Hospital, 183
　　Gregory Rotary Club, 117
　　Gregory School Board, 3
　　J. J. Flynn and Company, 3
　　St. Joseph Catholic Cemetery, 184
　　St. Joseph Church, 3, 180, 184
　　St. Joseph Convent, 7
　Gregory County, 2-3, 5, 8, 13, 167-168
　Homestake Gold Mine, 10
　Lake Preston, 178
　Lead, 173
　Mission, 168
　Mitchell, xii, xv, 21
　　Naval Aviation Selection Board, 21
　Newell, 170
　Paxton Catholic Church, 3
　Pierre, 166, 173-175
　　Criminal Justice Training Center, 182
　　Law Enforcement Training Program, 182
　　Pierre Indian School, 5
　Platte, 164, 180-181
　　St. Peter's Church, 181-182
　　Stations of the Cross, 180-182
　Platte-Winner bridge, 164
　Presho, 172-173
　Rapid City, 170, 172
　Rosebud, 168
　Sioux Falls, 172, 178, 183-184
　　Joe Foss Field, 183
　　KSFY-TV, 178
　　Veterans Hospital, 184
　St. Francis, 168
　　St. Francis Mission School, 5
　Todd County, 167-168
　Tripp County, 3, 8, 39, 164, 167-168
　　Sherrif's Department, 39
　Vermillion, 167
　　University of South Dakota, 167
　Winner, 1, 4, 6, 164
　　Peacock Bar, 178
　Witten, 4
South Dakota Constitution, 170
　Article III, Section 25, 170
South Dakota Legion Convention, 126
South Dakota Legislature, 170, 178-179
　Senate, 167-171, 174-175
　　Legislature's Joint Rule 7-7, 174
　　Local Government Committee, 169

South Dakota Legislature *(cont.)*
  Senate *(continued)*
    Natural Resources Committee, 169
    Senate Bill (SB) 89, 169
    Senate Bill (SB) 250, 169
    Senate Joint Resolution No. 3 (SJR 3), 170, 173-175, 178
    State Affairs Committee, 170, 173-174
    Taxation Committee, 169-170, 172
Soviet, 55, 63, 81, 98, 129, 134, 140
  Kremlin, 55
  Red Army, 55
  Soviet Union, 55, 141
  see also USSR
Spain
  Barcelona, 140
  Palma, 140
Spanish, 51, 97
Spaulding, G. Warren, 20
Stalin, Josef, 98
Stalinism, 55
Standiford's Melody Brothers, 4
Stavisky, Stan, 123
Steinhardt, Jacinto, 118
Stenson, Randy (Senator), 168-169
Sterrett, Harlo E. "Ed" (Ensign), xii, 57, 67, 100, 112
Stewart, Ray, 64
Stoneman, Russell "Russ" (Captain), 72-73, 78
"Strategy of Flexible Response," 129
Study of Former Prisoners of War (1980), 97, 132
Suez Crisis (1956), 141
Sung, Kim Il, 55
Sylvester, L. W., 4

— T —

T-34 tank, 55
Taiwan, 147
Taylor, Maxwell D. (General), 129
Tennessee
  Memphis, 140
  Naval Air Station (NAS), 140
Texas
  Austin, 133, 136
  Bergstrom Air Force Base (AFB), 133-135
  Corpus Christi, 26-28, 48
    Naval Air Training Center (NATC), 26-29, 31
  Kingsville, 29
Thailand, 56, 147, 167
The Communist Manifesto, 97
The Decline and Fall of American Capitalism, 97

The New York Times, 119, 121
"The Sphinx" (enemy soldier), 106
The Twilight of Capitalism, 97
The Winner Band, 4
38th Parallel, 55-56, 64
This Kind of War: The Classic Korean War History, 128
Thomas, G. C. (Lieutenant General), 92
Thompson, Warren, 60
Thorin, Duane (Chief Petty Officer), xii, 101-106, 108, 110
Thrash, William G. (Lieutenant Colonel), 99, 119, 123
Toland, John, 121
Torokina Island, 120
Townsend, Kenneth William, 16, 20
Trappist monk, 88
Tregaskis, Richard, 151
Truman, Harry S. (President), 45, 49, 55-56, 98
Tsai (interpreter), 104-106
Turk, 141
Turkey, 56

— U —

Ugaki, Matome (Admiral), 37
Union of South Africa, 96
United Nations, 59, 81-82, 86, 93, 98, 103, 106, 110, 121
  Charter, 55
  Forces, 56
  General Assembly, 121
  Security Council, 55
  U.N. Command (UNC), 55-56, 109
United States, 28, 37, 46-47, 55-56, 63, 73, 78, 80-82, 87-88, 98-99, 104, 107, 110, 114, 117, 121-123, 129, 134, 141, 149, 151, 165, 169, 176
  Agriculture and Forestry Committee, 166
  Air Force, xiv, 49, 55-56, 73, 78, 81, 87, 89, 96, 108, 115, 119, 122, 129, 133-138, 146-147, 159, 161
    Air Force Command and Staff College, 129
    Cold War Strategy, 129
    Strategic Air Command (SAC), 129, 133-136, 141
  Army, 12, 34, 37, 49, 72, 86, 96, 102, 119, 122-123
    ROTC, 167
  Army Air Corps, 27
  Bureau of Indian Affairs (BIA), 16-17, 20
  Civil Aeronautics Administration, 23
  Civil Service, 30

United States *(continued)*
  Civil Service *(continued)*
    Government Girl Band, 32
    "Government Girls," 32
  Congress, 165
    House of Representatives, 164
    Senate, 164-167, 175-177
  Council on Foreign Relations, 129
  Department of Defense, 114, 119
  Department of the Navy, xii, 32
    Bureau of Supplies and Accounts, 32
    Office of the Judge Advocate General, xii
  Executive Order, xiv
  Forces, 164, 167
  Government, 12, 98
  Information Office, 141
  Joint Chiefs of Staff, 40, 121, 129
  Marine Corps, xiii-xv, 25, 28-29, 31-32, 34, 37-40, 43, 45, 47-49, 53, 55-56, 58, 64, 66-69, 73-74, 77-78, 86, 89, 92-93, 96, 101-102, 105-107, 110-113, 118-120, 122, 126, 129-130, 133-141, 143, 146-151, 153, 155-157, 159, 161-162, 167, 175, 180, 184-185
    Air, 28, 45, 56, 59, 130, 133, 155-156
    Barrier patrol, 42
    Combat air patrol (CAP), 38, 42
    Court of Inquiry, 113-114, 122
    Esprit de corps, xiv
    G-2 (Intelligence), 115, 147-148
    G-3, 161
    Headquarters, Aircraft Fleet Marine Force, Pacific, 147-148
    Infantry, 39, 41, 56
    Marine Corps Heritage Foundation, xi
    Marine Corps Historical Center, xi
    Marine Corps University Library, xi
    R.O. (radar operator), 66
    Record NAVMC 545A-DP, 32
    Reserve, 29, 155, 184
  Military, 166
  Navy, 25-28, 35, 49, 55-56, 67, 92, 112, 118-119, 122-123, 132-133, 137-139, 143, 145-146, 149-150, 153, 159

United States *(continued)*
  Navy *(continued)*
    Blue Angels, 137
    Bureau of Medicine and Surgery, 123
    Center for Naval Analysis (CNA), 72, 76
    Department of Medicine, 132
    Naval Air Corps Reserve, 20-21, 32
    Naval Air Training Command, 21
    Office of the Chief of Naval Operations, 73
    Operations Evaluation Group (OEG), 72-73, 76, 115, 118
    Reserve, 49
  Selective Service, 16
  State Department, 55, 126
United States Naval Academy, 120
University of
  Maryland, 82
  Missouri, 19
Ushijima, Mitsuru (Lieutenant General), 37, 40
USSR, 106, 128
  see also Soviet Union

— V —

Vermillion Plain Talk (SD), 167
Vernon, Jack, 185
Versailles Peace Conference, 33
Veterans Administration, 97, 132
Viet Cong, 148, 153, 165
Vietnam, 39, 83, 137, 148, 151, 156, 164-166, 176
  Hanoi, 165, 176
  Hanoi Radio, 177
  Mekong Delta, 148
  North, 165-166
  South, 129-130, 147-152, 165, 167, 176
  Da Nang, 150-151
  Quang Tri, 151
  Thua Thien, 151

Vietnamese, 148, 151, 153, 165
  North, 148, 162, 164-165, 167, 176-177
  Army, 167
  South Army (ARVN), 148, 150-151
Vietnam Diary, 151
Vietnam War, xiv, 162
Virginia
  Alexandria, 76
  Arlington, 123
    Henderson Hall Barracks, Building Four, 123
  Quantico, 48, 123
    Marine Air-Infantry School, 48
    Marine Corps Development Center, 123
Voices from Captivity: Interpreting the American POW Narrative, 91
Volk, David, 178

— W —

Wagner, Arthur, 130, 132
Wake Island, 34
Walker, Walton (Lieutenant General), 55
Ward, Jim, 17
Warfield, Clifford D. (Captain), 139-140, 143-145
Warner, John, xii
Warren, Gene, 4
Washington, 8
Washington Post, 113-114, 119, 122-123
Washington, D.C., xi, 30, 32, 55, 112, 114, 118, 147, 164-166
  Library of Congress, xi
  National Archives College Park Branch, xi
  Naval Historical Center, xi
  Pentagon, xiv, 99, 118, 123
  St. Ann's Catholic Church, 32
  Union Station, 32
  White House, 148
Weapon
  Atomic bomb, 45, 129, 134, 137
    Mark VII, 134

Weapon *(continued)*
  Atomic bomb *(continued)*
    Mark 28, 137
  Browning-Colt M2 machine gun, 30
  Germ bomb, 125
  High velocity aerial rocket (HVAR), 30
  Incendiary cluster, 35
  Missile
    Atlas ballistic, 138
    Jupiter C, 138
    Thor ballistic, 138
  MK 149 rocket, 45
  Nambu Type 96, 6.5-mm light machine gun, 39
  Napalm tank, 30, 35, 39, 56, 60-62, 73, 75, 78
  Nuclear weapon, 128-129, 133-134, 137-138, 140, 147
  Thompson sub-machine gun, 5
  Winchester carbine, 12
Weintraub, Stanley, 43
West Coast Sound Productions in California, 162
Western Union, 91
Westmoreland, William C. (General), 164
Whitehouse, M. L. (First Lieutenant), 144-145
Whitlow, Robert H., 150
Williams, Duke, Jr., 130, 132
Willis, Larry, 147-148
Wilson, William (Major), 96
Winnefeld, James A., 133
World War I, 7, 33
World War II, xiv, 20, 28, 35, 37, 39, 42, 45, 55, 67, 72, 78, 98, 120, 126, 140, 153
Wyoming, 12

— Y —

Yellow Sea, 65
Yellowstone National Park, 57

— Z —

Zedong, Mao (Chairman), 81, 98, 168